Meaningful Tone

Meaningful Tone

A Study of Tonal Morphology in Compounds,
Form Classes, and Expressive Phrases
in White Hmong

Martha Ratliff

Foreword by James Collins

NORTHERN

ILLINOIS

UNIVERSITY

PRESS

DeKalb

Library of Congress Cotaloging-in-Publication Data

Ratliff, Martha Susan, 1946-

Meaningful tone : a study of tonal morphology in compounds, form classes and expressive phrases in White Hmong / Martha Ratliff.

    p. c.m.

Includes bibliographical references and index.

ISBN: 978-087580-636-5 (alk. paper)

1. White Hmong dialect --Word formation. 2. White Hmong dialect --Phonetics. 3. White Hmong dialect --Grammar. I. Title.

This book is dedicated to
my parents

Rigdon K. Ratliff

and

Maureen M. Ratliff

TABLE OF CONTENTS

Chapter Three   TONALLY DEFINED FORM CLASSES

Chapter Four   TONAL MORPHOLOGY AND TONAL
ICONICITY IN TWO-WORD EXPRESSIVES

LIST OF TABLES

FOREWORD

In southwestern China and northern Southeast Asia, the scattered and diverse Hmong language communities compose a very large ethnic group of perhaps as many as 10,000,000 persons. Because of the historical impact of America's military involvement in Indo-China, beginning in 1975 Hmong groups and individuals from Southeast Asia have chosen to settle in the United States. Although these American Hmong do not constitute a large percentage of the total number of Hmong in the world, nonetheless today the number of Hmong residing in the United States exceeds 200,000. Some experts estimate that probably 50 percent of the Hmong population in this country lives in the upper Midwest region —Minnesota, Wisconsin, and Michigan—where they have become important members of their local communities and economies.

Long before diaspora studies became well-known, indeed for more than twenty-five years, Professor Martha Ratliff has worked with the Hmong speakers who live in the United States. Based on the data she collected before 1986 from her Hmong teachers, as well as available written sources, she completed her pioneering study of the interface of tone and morphology in the White Hmong dialect and earned her Ph.D. at the University of Chicago. Since then she has continued to study the language and the prehistory of the Hmong.

This innovative, one-of-its-kind morpho-phonological study— focused on linguistic tone and the role it plays in compounds, form classes, and expressives—is a scholarly and technical study that remains an important basic resource cited in contemporary books about language and society, both specialized essays about Southeast Asian languages as well as general studies about linguistics and human speech. Indeed, in Fall 2009 I was teaching a course on language endangerment and was pleased to see that, thanks to Martha Ratliff's work, Hmong's complex and creative expressive system had found its way into David Harrison's well-known book, *When Languages Die.* . The Hmong language is one of the few languages of Southeast Asia to make its way into contemporary studies of linguistics.

But even more importantly, with the dramatic rise in the number of America's Hmong people enrolled in universities and colleges, as well as the numerous and active Hmong community groups in this region, and the strong commitment of these students and community groups to Hmong language culture, the time has come to make Ratliff's landmark book more widely available to a growing readership. If in 1986 Professor Ratliff could write that she hoped that the Hmong in the United States and in other Western countries would "someday want to look at this study," we believe that the time, that "someday," has come now. We at NIU's Center for Southeast Asian Studies in association with NIU Press are pleased to present to the Hmong communities of America, their fellow Americans, and all the Hmong speakers and concerned language scholars of the world this important book, a record of the complexity of the Hmong language and the acumen of its speakers.

Co-Founder of the Southeast Asian Linguistics Society and former chair of the Linguistic Society of America's Committee on Endangered Languages and their Preservation, Professor Ratliff is professor of linguistics at Wayne State University in Detroit where she continues her research on the Hmong language and tone and other linguistic topics. This book is one of many of her contributions to the study of the Hmong language.

—*Dr. James Collins*

PREFACE

Since I began my research in the early 1980s, the Hmong (or Mong) in the United States have undergone a quiet change in status, from Southeast Asian refugees to Hmong Americans. In the 1970s and the 1980s, the Hmong were new to the United States and the frequent subjects of newspaper and magazine articles, all of which repeated the same set of dramatic facts about their involvement in the extension of the Vietnam War into Laos, their persecution, and their flight at the end of the war first to Thailand and then to the west. Most publicity about the Hmong at that time involved the use of the phrase "the plight of the Hmong".

Today Mee Moua, who was born in Laos, is a state senator in Minnesota, the Hmong are central characters in an award-winning movie by Clint Eastwood, and every other morning I wake up to radio news reports from NPR reporter Doualy Xaykaothao, who was also born in Laos and whose voice brings the nation news about the entire Asian world. Many formal institutions—social, academic, and educational—support the Hmong community. Most notable is Hmong National Development, which holds a large conference in a different U.S. city every year to discuss issues of mutual interest and to provide networking opportunities. Hmong informational, educational, and entertainment sites of varying quality are ubiquitous on the web. Individual Hmong men and women are earning the highest degrees in their fields and are serving their communities and other Americans as lawyers, doctors, teachers, politicians, and businesspeople. The Hmong ABC Bookstore in St. Paul is a vibrant business full of books about the Hmong and books written in Hmong. This is striking, given the fact that a generation ago in Laos only a small fraction of Hmong people were literate. This rapid change can be attributed in part to the way Hmong communities have actively supported education at every level and celebrated each individual's accomplishments in local ceremonies. Although many social and economic problems remain, the degree to which Hmong Americans have integrated themselves in such a short time into the wider society is remarkable.

The facts about the Hmong language do not change so quickly, however. While language has the flexibility to adapt to new technologies and changing situations, structural features of the language such as those presented here will be the same fifty years from now. Language change works through us slowly, and for the most part is not within our conscious control. Although the Hmong spoken in the United States is now filled with English loanwords, and some aspects of Hmong usage may now be subtly shifting to reflect English usage patterns, it would be quite surprising if any the facts about the morphological functions of tone presented in this book have changed since I began my research.

There is one large area of language proficiency loss that I would like to mention, however, apart from the expected decline of overall language proficiency among younger Hmong Americans, especially those who were born in this country. This is the loss of those verbal arts that flourish in a non-literate society, but slowly disappear as the written word gains dominance. There are three such arts that I find younger Hmong speakers do not practice, even if they are fluent in Hmong for conversational purposes: *kwv txhiaj*, a form of complex oral poetry; *lus rov*, disguised languages used for private speech; and disyllabic "expressives", the subject matter of chapter four of this book. These verbal arts require exposure, time, and practice to perfect, and on a busy American schedule, time is difficult to find. In order for these arts to be passed down through the generations, children need to be with their parents throughout the day, which is impossible when school and work take them in different directions. Despite the obvious benefits of formal education, there are trade-offs in cultural knowledge that must be acknowledged. We can only hope that these verbal arts are still alive and well in Southeast Asia and that, in the United States, it might be possible to find a way to gain the advantages of a western education without losing the benefits of a traditional education.

My own interest in the Hmong language was aroused when I met Hmong refugee students at Senn High School on the north side of Chicago, where I worked for a while in the early 1980s as an ESL teacher. Having completed class work for a PhD in Linguistics at the University of Chicago by that time, it did not take much research to discover that the language of my students was poorly described in comparison with other world languages. At that point, I gave up my first dissertation project on the exceedingly well-researched Germanic language family and turned my attention to Hmong-

Mien, a family about which little was known. I grew impatient with teaching English to the Hmong, as important as that work was, because I had become much more interested in what the Hmong could teach me. I left teaching in 1983 to complete the dissertation upon which this book is based.

A family of languages constitutes a large domain for research, especially when the family contains as many as thirty languages (Hmong is only one of these languages), and speakers of these languages may number as high as ten million. Since completing *Meaningful Tone*, I have continued to work on the Hmong-Mien language family because I enjoy working in a field where so much is yet to be learned. My book *Hmong-Mien Language History* (Pacific Linguistics, 2010) contains the results of my latest research on the history of the Hmong language and its relatives. The question I plan to address in the years to come has to do with ancient Hmong-Mien history, which, in the absence of written texts, can only be accessed through linguistic science, genetics, or archaeology. Hmong-Mien may provide a key with which we can unlock the mystery of Southeast Asian prehistory more generally, as these languages are spoken today where they have been spoken for the last two thousand years—primarily in southern China, squarely in the middle of an area of early rice cultivation that made possible the support of a large population. This population is now represented by five distinct language families: Sino-Tibetan, Austronesian, Tai-Kadai, Austroasiatic, and Hmong-Mien. How are they related, if at all?

I dedicate the second edition of this book with gratitude to the Hmong men and women who take pride in their language and culture, and who understand the value of studying their history.

—*Martha Ratliff*

ACKNOWLEDGEMENTS

Nyiaj-txiag nyob tsis kev;
Txiv ntoo nyob chaw siab.
"Riches are not found on the road;
The fruit grows high in the tree."
(Bertrais-Charrier *nyiaj*)

[Nothing worthwhile comes easily.]

I am deeply indebted to Gérard Diffloth, my primary faculty adviser and dissertation committee chair at the University of Chicago, for supervising the writing of this book, originally my doctoral dissertation. His help with countless questions of fact, technique, terminology, and style was invaluable. Moreover, I would like to thank him for serving as a model for me during my studies at Chicago. Always respectful of the people whose languages he studies, he is a master at collecting data, recognizing what is interesting about the data, and allowing the data to direct his generalizations about the language it represents. I hope to be able to do the same.

It was also my extraordinary good fortune to have had a private tutor and good friend of such expertise and generosity as David Strecker during the period in 1986 when I wrote my dissertation and the preceding two years of research. He was a constant source of help, advice, and support: both with respect to practically every page of this book and to my education in the fields of Hmong-Mien and Southeast Asian linguistics.

I would also like to thank Karen Landahl and Jim McCawley for their excellent suggestions and comments.

Although I have incorporated the majority of the comments and criticisms made by the four above-mentioned people, I have gone my own way in a number of instances; the errors of fact and argument which remain in this study are all, of course, mine alone.

This study would not have been possible without the help of my Hmong tutors. I would especially like to thank Xab Xyooj, my friend and primary language tutor, for his unfailing willingness to answer my endless questions. All of my tutors, Xab Xyooj, Kuam Yaj, Npis Yaj, and Lauj Pov Vaj, are people of integrity, intelligence, self-confidence, and good humor. It has been a pleasure working with them. I would also like to thank the following members of the Hmong community for their help in various aspects of this study: Yang Dao (Yaj Tsab), Xeev Nruag Xyooj, Txawj Tsab Xyooj, *niam* Xab Xyooj, and Cua Yaj.

For their expertise and helpful advice, I would like to thank Paul Benedict, Nerida Jarkey, Jacques Lemoine, and Wang Fushi.

For his excellent translations of important Chinese sources, I would like to thank Jiang Zixin.

For their work on the map in appendix D, I would like to thank Patricia Hernlund and Simon Yeh. I am also grateful to Joe Davy (Npliaj Siab) for his contribution of the cover photograph.

For their support in realizing the publication of this book, I would like to thank Lesley Brill, John Hartmann, Annie Jaisser, the Wayne State University Office of Research and Graduate Studies and College of Liberal Arts, and the Center for Southeast Asian Studies at Northern Illinois University. I am especially grateful to Grant A. Olson for his careful stewardship of the manuscript.

And finally, to my mother Maureen Ratliff, and to my husband Tony Eliassen, for their remarkable faith and support, my love and gratitude.

Meaningful Tone

CHAPTER ONE

INTRODUCTION

1   Purpose and Scope of this Study

It is my intention in this study to present and discuss three morphological functions of tone in White Hmong, which belongs to the West Hmongic subgroup of the Hmong-Mien (Miao-Yao) family of southern China and Southeast Asia. The primary function of tone in White Hmong, as in other Asian tone languages, is one of lexical discrimination. There are seven lexically contrastive tones:

tob (55)[1]	deep
toj (52)	hill
tov (24)	to add water
tos (22)	to wait
to (33)	to pierce
tog (42)	to sink
tom (21ʔ)	there

The morphological functions of tone herein discussed are: (1) compound formation by tone change (tone sandhi), (2) word class definition by tone, and (3) the use of tone to define morphology and convey certain meanings in expressive phrases. Two areas that are pertinent to this topic but which will not be discussed here are affective tone change (for example, the use of the breathy tone to convey negative judgment) and the interaction of tone and intonation.

---

[1] In this orthography, final consonants represent tones. The pitch of these tones is indicated by numbers on a five-point scale, where "5" is high and "1" is low.

Although the employment of tone to perform tasks other than the discrimination of one word from another is characteristic of a number of languages in the Southeast Asian area, no attempt will be made here to map out these tendencies by discussing neighboring languages in detail. The focus of this study is the dialect of one language and its properties, with appeal to comparative evidence from related dialects when the function of tone under discussion can best be understood from a historical perspective. Information about similar phenomena in unrelated (or very distantly related) neighboring languages will only be brought in tangentially.

2   Significance of a Study of the Morphological Functions of Tone in White Hmong

The study of the morphological functions of tone in Hmong is interesting and important historically. It requires the reconstruction and elucidation of earlier stages of the language (chapter two), and at the same time it reveals very recent language change that previews the future (chapter three). For example, a phonetically motivated tone sandhi system, in fossil form, has become a device for compound formation (chapter two), dependent sandhi forms have been promoted to independent status, with interesting semantic splits (chapter two, section 4.1); and two-word analytic constructions have collapsed into the first word, with resultant tone change and the formation of tonally defined form classes (chapter three, sections 3 and 5.1). In addition to the dynamic nature of my object of study, I find that there are four areas of endeavor to which it will make a contribution.

2.1   As a Contribution to Areal Studies

Countless studies on different issues related to tone in individual Southeast Asian languages exist, as well as a good number of articles on the similarities of tonal development from one of these languages to another. To my knowledge, however, there are only two groundbreaking articles on the morphological functions of tone in Southeast Asian languages taken as a geographically related group, neither of which has been developed by others in the more than twenty-five years since they were written: E. J. A. Henderson's 1965 "The Topography of Certain Phonetic and Morphological

2

Characteristics of South East Asian Languages" and her 1967 "Grammar and Tone in South East Asian Languages." In her 1967 paper, Henderson attempted to do broadly and briefly (with examples from Tiddim Chin, Bwe Karen, Vietnamese, Bangkok Thai, Southern Thai of Songkhla, and Chinese) what I have attempted to do here in depth for White Hmong: that is, to discuss all of the morphological functions of tone that are attested. This broad view of tone as an organizational tool is an important complement to studies of the development of lexically contrastive tone in the area. Since the ways in which tone is used to mark morphological classes are similar across language and family boundaries in Southeast Asia, a description of these "secondary" functions of tone will contribute to a definition of the linguistic area. More important, it should reveal that lexical tone is adaptable to new tasks in some languages more than in others. It may then be possible to set up a typology of Southeast Asian tone languages that will show how those languages in which tone has morphological functions share characteristics of phonology, syntax, and/or word structure as well.

Henderson (1965a: 432) claims that the White Hmong territory (which from her maps appears to be the western part of North Vietnam and northeastern Laos) constitutes a "concentration area" of phonological characteristics that she has identified as Southeast Asian. Such Southeast Asian characteristics that White Hmong exemplifies include lexically contrastive pitch and phonation type, and lexically contrastive aspiration, retroflexion, and prenasalization of initial stop consonants. White Hmong is shown in my study to be a good representative of the Southeast Asian area with regard to the morphological functions of tone as well, in that it demonstrates every one of the four types of interaction of "grammar and tone" discussed in Henderson's 1967 paper:

(1) Tonally defined grammatical classes (pp. 171-174): Yes. See discussion of White Hmong numerals, pronouns, denominal prepositions, and demonstrative nouns in chapter three.

(2) Tonal variation and compounding (p. 174): Yes. See chapter two on tone sandhi compounds.

(3) Tonal alternation in reduplicative expressions (p. 175): Yes, marginally. See chapter two, section 4.1.

(4) Tonal alternation to express anaphoric reference (p. 177): Yes. See chapter three on demonstrative nouns, section 5.

The information presented in this study and in the sources listed in section 3.3 will help insure that Hmong will be represented in such future areal studies (none of this material was known when Henderson wrote on "Grammar and Tone in South East Asian Languages"). It will also help insure that when it is represented, it will be represented correctly. In the "Topography" paper (Henderson 1965a), White Hmong was one of the fifty-nine languages included, but three mistakes were made due to lack of adequate data: (1) It is indicated (p. 416) that Hmong has lexically contrastive voicing of initials (it does not); (2) It is indicated (p. 423) that Hmong is characterized by lexically contrastive prenasalization but not by lexically contrastive preglottalization. Under most analyses (but not the one adopted here, see section 3.1.1) Hmong has both. It should be marked for both, with a note as to the current difference of opinion; (3) It is indicated (p. 425) that only Javanese has contrasting prenasalized dental and retroflex stops (Hmong does also).

2.2   As a Contribution to the Study of Tone Language Types

The Hmong-Mien family contains dialects that are characterized by a particularly high number of tones (anywhere from three to twelve) and which show interesting tone inventory pecularities: (1) phonation type is a correlate of tone in many Hmongic dialects, including the two spoken by refugees in the United States, White Hmong and Green Hmong; (2) as many as five level tones have been reported for SHIDONGKOU,[2] ZONGDI, and XISHANJIE; (3) as many as four falling tones have been reported for MEIZHU and ZONGDI; (4) as many as twelve lexically contrastive tones have been reported for LONGMO and ZONGDI. Hmongic tone systems have developed through tone splits conditioned by (1) aspiration in the initial in West Hmongic dialects (for example, ZONGDI); (2) prenasalization of the initial in North Hmongic dialects (for example, DONGTOUZHAI); (3) part of speech in one West Hmongic dialect (SHIMEN). The aforementioned tone splits are in addition to the original split conditioned by voicing in the initial consonant, which affected most, but not all,

---

[2] The sources of information about the Hmongic dialects mentioned in this study are contained in appendix D, "Sources and Map." Except for White Hmong and Green Hmong, all dialect names are place names and appear in capital letters to distinguish them from the locations they also represent.

4

Hmongic dialects. The tone systems of MEIZHU and LONGMO have also been enriched by new tones arising through tone sandhi.

White Hmong is fairly typical of the family in its tone inventory (see section 3.1.3 to follow): there are seven lexically contrastive tones, one of which has a syntactically conditioned variant; a phonation contrast characterizes one tone and another tone is checked by a glottal stop.

Languages with a high number of lexically contrastive tones are primarily monosyllabic-word languages. These languages are characterized by tone changes where one tone is substituted for another, that is, paradigmatic replacement, more often than by tone changes where the phonetic features of one tone influence the phonetic features of a neighboring tone. I claim that this is due to the heavy burden placed on tone to serve as an identifying mark for the word in "short-word" languages. In a White Hmong word, for example, there are only three variables: the initial consonant, the final or rhyme, and the tone. Each one of these components of the word has to retain its integrity if speakers are to discriminate successfully among all the aspects of the real world their language encodes. If a syntagmatic tone change rule such as "all words in a phrase following an initial high tone word will change to low tone" were to operate in White Hmong, the altered words would most likely lose all meaning.

My generalization about large tone inventory languages, such as White Hmong, underlies the account of tone sandhi presented in chapter two and the arguments for the idea of paradigmatic replacement presented there. It also explains why the tonally defined form classes described in chapter three are small: if large word classes, such as noun and verb, were defined by particular tones, the ability of tone to do its main job, the identification of individual words, would be seriously reduced. The language would become, in effect, a two-tone language, since the majority of words are either nouns or verbs.

Tone brings morphological organization only to the interesting outskirts of a language with many tones. I claim that this remains the case, unless the nature of the canonical word begins to change through compounding. As the word becomes longer, it takes on more components to share the burden of lexical discrimination, and tone is freed to take greater part in the morphological structure of the language.

2.3   As a Contribution to the Literature on Tonal Iconicity

A familiar concept to those who have seriously approached the subject of sound symbolism in either "prosaic" words or in special word classes ("expressives" or "ideophones") is that the smallest meaningful units in language are often as small as a single segment, or even as small as a single feature (see Diffloth 1976: 261).[3] Since consonants and vowels are common to all languages and lexical tone but to a subset thereof, it is not surprising that there has been less research on tonal iconicity.

In chapter four I present information on tonal icons (morphemes comprised of two tones) in White Hmong expressive words. In this study, "tone" is a phonological term and is understood to include a number of co-occuring source properties: (1) fundamental frequency ("pitch"), (2) fundamental frequency change ("contour"), (3) phonation type ("clear," "breathy," "creaky"), and (4) duration. The properties of tone that lend themselves to sound symbolic exploitation in White Hmong are primarily phonation contrast (the breathy tone plays a major role in expressive words), contour (especially level-level, fall-fall, rise-rise, and fall-rise), and, to a lesser extent, pitch. That the iconic value of phonation contrast and contour should be greater than that of the primary tone cue, pitch, is a finding that should have relevance to a study of tonal icons in other languages.

2.4   As a Contribution to the Field of Hmong-Mien Linguistics

Up until 1975, those working in the field of Hmong-Mien (Miao-Yao) linguistics were Chinese linguists (most notably, Wang Fushi and Chang Kun), European and American scholars with wide interests in Asian and Southeast Asian linguistics (André G. Haudricourt, Paul Benedict, G. B. Downer, and Thomas A. Lyman) or missionary linguists (Sam Pollard, Yves Bertrais-Charrier, Ernest Heimbach, Herbert Purnell, and Jean Mottin). Following the fall of Laos to the Pathet Lao in 1975, the first Hmong and Mien refugees came to the United States, and their presence here in increasing numbers (the Hmong population was estimated at 65,000 in 1983 [Olney 1986: 181]) provided many more American linguists

---

[3] See Bolinger (1950: 117-136); Rhodes and Lawler (1981: 318-342), for the analysis of such subsyllabic morphemes in English.

with an opportunity to work with the languages of these hitherto fairly inaccessible people.[4]

The study of the dialects of the Hmong-Mien languages spoken in the United States is just barely underway. At this point, any work done on White or Green Hmong is of significance because new features of these dialects are inevitably discovered by each new contributor. Until now, there has been no major study of White or Green Hmong morphotonemics. There have been, though, important smaller contributions: the introductory comments on tone sandhi and the tonally defined locative classes by the dictionary compilers Heimbach (1979: 443-454) and Lyman (1974: 39-40) and by Mottin (1978: 18-21), the author of the sole White Hmong grammar, and the insightful study by Downer (1967), "Tone-Change and Tone-Shift in White Miao." In addition to providing a much more detailed discussion of White Hmong tone sandhi (chapter two) and the tonally defined locative classes (chapter three, sections 4 and 5), topics that have been a matter of interest to the above-named investigators, this study covers new ground: the existence of three more tonally defined form classes (numerals, pronouns, sex classes; chapter three) and the existence of an expressive morphology in which tone plays a key role (chapter four).

---

[4] Within the last fifteen years, many Western scholars have made the study of the Hmong-Mien languages one of their primary interests: Paul Benedict (Proto-Hmong-Mien reconstruction), Marybeth Clark (White Hmong syntax), Christopher Court (Iu Mien syntax), Gordon Downer (Hmong-Mien comparative linguistics), Jerold Edmondson (Pa Hng), Judith Fuller (White Hmong syntax and discourse), Annie Jaisser (White Hmong syntax, discourse, and phonetics of tone), Nerida Jarkey (White Hmong phonetics and serial verb constructions), Brenda Johns (Hmong semantics and stylistics), Charles Li (Green Hmong syntax and discourse), Herbert Purnell (Proto-Hmong-Mien reconstruction, Iu Mien register and language/music relationship), Elizabeth Riddle (White Hmong syntax and discourse), David Solnit (Biao Min phonology), David Strecker (Mun phonology, Hmong phonology and stylistics, Proto-Hmong-Mien reconstruction), and Martha Ratliff (White Hmong phonology, tonology, syntax, expressive language, Shimen Hmong tone, and Hmong-Mien historical problems). There are undoubtedly omissions in this list, for which I apologize.

3   White Hmong

3.1   Phonology

In the charts that follow, the phonetic transcription of the consonant and vowel phonemes is the work of Nerida Jarkey (1985a, 1985b). Her analysis represents a refinement of the phonetic descriptions of the segmental phonemes offered by Smalley (1976: 89, 95) and Mottin (1978: 5-13) with regard to place of articulation, manner of release, and the characterization of such important details as lip rounding in the *ts*- series. The orthography used is the Romanized Popular Alphabet (RPA) developed by the missionaries Linwood Barney, William Smalley, and Yves Bertrais-Charrier in Laos in the early 1950s (for discussion of the choice of this orthography for this study, see section 3.2 below).

Consonant phonemes are shown in table 1 and vowel phonemes are shown in table 2.

Table 1: White Hmong Consonant Phonemes

	bilabial	lab/lat rel	lab/dent	[dental]	fric rel	palatalized]	[alveolar	lamino-	post-alv]	palatal	velar	uvular	glottal
V-LESS UNASP STOPS	*p* p	*pl* pl̥		*t* t	*tx* ts	*c* ƫ	*d* ɖ	*ts* tʃ	*r* ʈ		*k* k	*q* q	*ʔ* ʔ
V-LESS ASP STOPS	*ph* pʰ	*plh* pl̥		*th* tʰ	*txh* tsʰ	*ch* ƫʰ	*dh* ɖʰ	*tsh* tʃʰ	*rh* ʈʰ		*kh* kʰ	*qh* qʰ	*h* h
PRE-NASAL STOPS	*np* mb	*npl* mbl		*nt* nd	*ntx* ndz	*nc* ɲɟ		*nts* ndʒ	*nr* ɳɖ		*nk* ŋg	*nq* NG	
PRE-NASAL ASP STOPS	*nph* mbʰ	*nplh* mbl̥		*nth* ndʰ	*ntxh* ndzʰ	*nch* ɲɟʰ		*ntsh* ntʃʰ	*nrh* ɳʈʰ		*nkh* ŋkʰ	*nqh* nqʰ	
VOICED FRICS			*v* v					*z* ʒ					
V-LESS FRICS			*f* f	*x* s				*s* ʃ		*xy* ç	*g* ɢ		*h* ɦ
VOICED NASALS	*m* m	*ml* ml		*n* n						*ny* ɲ	*g* ŋ		
V-LESS NASALS	*hm* m̥	*hml* ml̥		*hn* n̥						*hny* ɲ̥			
VOICED LIQUID				*l* l									
V-LESS LIQUID				*hl* l̥									
GLIDE										*y* ɲ			

9

Table 2
White Hmong Vowel Phonemes

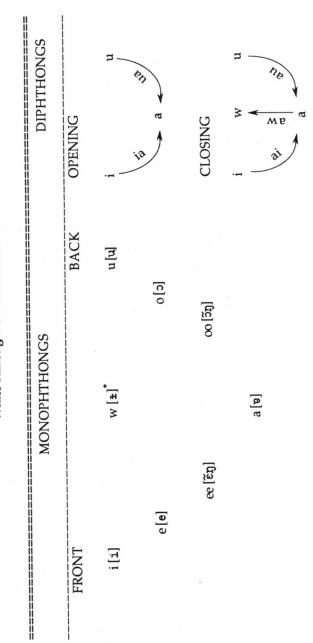

3.1.1 Tones

The representation of tone by two numbers on a five-point scale, where 5 represents the highest point and 1 the lowest, is used below to roughly indicate the values of the seven lexical tones of White Hmong:

-b	55
-j	52
-v	24
-s	22
-ø	33
-g	42
-m	21ʔ (with the syntactically determined variant -d 213)

Notes on problems with the representations of these tones follow:

(1) The difference between the -s tone (22) and the -ø tone (33) seems to involve something other than pitch. It may be duration: there is a certain "chanted" quality to the mid level tone, which has no perceivable fall at the end, while there is a more natural tapering at the end of the low level tone (the slight fall at the end of the low level tone was also observed by Huffman 1985: 5). It is interesting to note, though, that some speakers have been observed to substitute the -s tone for the -ø tone in certain words and the -ø for the -s tone in certain words. This tone confusion cannot be accounted for at this time by anything other than the similarity in pitch between the two.[5]

(2) The breathy (-g) tone has been the object of some interesting research by Marie Huffman (1985). She found that the phonation contrast between this tone and three clear-voiced tones (-j, -s, -m) was consistently displayed in two different kinds of measurements, one acoustic and one physiological. In her acoustic study, using an analysis of wideband spectograms, she found that the fundamental frequency of the -g tone was prominent with respect to the second harmonic, an indication of the "breathiness" that had been discovered by other phoneticians. Using the technique of inverse

---

[5] In tone sandhi, -ø > -s is one of the possible changes, but it cannot account for the tone confusion in the particular cases reported to me by Annie Jaisser, among others.

filtering to analyze recordings of airflow, she also found that the duration of the closed phase of the glottal pulse was shorter in the -g tone than in the other tones.

Both J. C. Catford and Gérard Diffloth, listening to tokens of this tone, noted that there is a whispered quality to the Hmong breathy tone, which distinguishes it from the more fully voiced "murmur" of a language like Gujarati. Catford (personal communication to Alexis Manaster-Ramer) confirmed my impression that it was of his "whispery" type (1977: 99).

Another complication involving the -g tone is that I have perceived differences between male and female speakers with regard to the placement of this "whispery fall" on their respective pitch ranges: for men, -g is a low breathy fall (31); for women, -g is a high breathy fall (53).[6] Although this needs to be confirmed by careful measurement, my perception of this difference leads me to believe that the phonation contrast is the primary phonetic cue, fundamental frequency change ("contour") the secondary phonetic cue, and fundamental frequency itself ("pitch") only the tertiary phonetic cue of this tone.

(3) The "checked" (-m) tone is noticeably shorter than the other tones and is terminated in a glottal stop (Huffman 1985: 10). Neither Smalley perceived (1976: 100) nor Huffman (1985: 5) measured any creaky phonation accompanying this tone. Lyman (1974: 38) describes the -m tone as one characterized by creaky voice in Green Hmong, however; and David Strecker (personal communication) reports that he and other linguists have perceived the White Hmong -m tone as creaky as well. My conclusion is that the -m tone can tolerate a fair amount of allophonic variation. Any one of the following can serve as the primary cue: a final glottal, creaky voice, or a combination of the two.

(4) The -d tone, a syntactically determined realization of words that usually bear the -m tone, is noticeably longer than the other tones. This is probably because this derivative tone arose when a following demonstrative adjective was absorbed into an -m tone word (see chapter three, section 5.1).

---

[6] The value of 42 for the -g tone is, hence, a compromise value between the 31 and 53 values I have perceived. Another interesting difference between men's and women's speech that others and I have noticed is the tendency for women to use prolonged, over-high sentence particles more often than men.

A number of possibilities exist for further research into the phonetics of White Hmong tones. They include: (1) the determination of the correct representation of the relative pitches of these tones (Huffman has measured the fundamental frequencies of tokens of only four); (2) experiments with whispered speech to determine the nonpitch cues of these tones; and (3) experiments with synthetic speech to determine the relative weighting of the three cues of the -g tone mentioned above.

3.2 On the Decision to Use the Romanized Popular Alphabet in this Study

Although the RPA orthography has annoyed a number of linguists who cannot or will not get used to final consonant letters as tone markers, I have decided to use it in this study for several reasons: (1) it is a good orthography in that it represents phonemic contrasts in a clear and consistent way; (2) it is simple to work with in that it requires no special typewriter keys or computer fonts; (3) it is similar to those orthographies developed in China for Hmong speakers, also on the basis of clarity and ease (for example, the Hmong-Shuad dictionary (1958), where -b is a tone marker corresponding to White Hmong -b and -d is a tone marker corresponding to White Hmong -v; and (4) it is the orthography accepted by the majority of Hmong in the United States and in other Western countries, a few of whom, I trust, will someday want to look at this study. Besides the use of final consonant letters as tone markers, there are two other minor complications: (1) Since the final slot has been preempted by tone markers, the one final consonant that does exist in the language, [ŋ], is indicated by a doubling of the vowel. Only [ɛ̃ŋ] ee and [ɔ̃ŋ] oo occur in White Hmong; [ɐ̃ŋ] aa occurs as well in Green Hmong; (2) After Vietnamese custom, x is used for [s] and s is used for [ʃ] (and z for [ʒ]).

White Hmong words are predominantly monosyllabic. There are, though, a few high frequency, bisyllabic words. I write these bisyllabic words as one word: pojniam 'wife' (literally 'woman-woman'), menyuam 'child' (literally 'little-little'). Compounds formed by tone sandhi are written with a hyphen: nqaij-nyug 'beef' (literally 'meat-cow'), pob-ntoos 'tree stump' (literally 'lump-tree').

13

3.3   Sources

In addition to the four native speakers of Hmong with whom I have worked over the past three years, I have used the standard sources for White Hmong and the closely related Green Hmong:[7]

Bertrais-Charrier, Yves, R. P.
1964   *Dictionnaire Hmong (Mèo Blanc)-Français.* Vientiane: Mission Catholique.

Heimbach, Ernest E.
1979   *White Hmong-English Dictionary.* Revised edition. (Linguistic Series IV, Data Paper no. 75, Southeast Asia Program, Cornell University). Ithaca: Southeast Asia Program.

Yang Dao
1980   *Dictionnaire Français-Hmong Blanc.* Paris: Comité National d'Entraide et Jacques Lemoine.

Mottin, Jean
1978   *Eléments de grammaire Hmong Blanc.* Bangkok: Don Bosco Press.

Lyman, Thomas Amis
1974   *Dictionary of Mong Njua: A Miao (Meo) Language of Southeast Asia.* The Hague: Mouton.

---

[7] These two mutually intelligible dialects are so close that the primary sources for one can serve as very good secondary sources for the other. In terms of tone inventories and the phonetics of tone, they are practically identical (with slightly different historical developments that account for cognate words occasionally having different tonal realizations in the two dialects: see chapter two, section 2.2.1). Their similarities and differences with regard to the members of the form classes discussed in chapter three are instructive. The fact that more Western linguists have focused on White Hmong up to this point is an accident of circumstance, and I am happy to report that more work on Green Hmong is now beginning to appear, including a functional grammar by Charles Li (in progress).

Xiong Lang, Xiong Joua, and Xiong Nao Leng

1983   *English-Mong-English Dictionary.* Milwaukee:
        published by the authors.

My four tutors were all young men in their 20s at the time of our collaboration. They are all speakers of White Hmong and come from the following provinces in Laos: Louang Prabang (Xab Xyooj, Kuam Yaj, Npis Yaj) and Sam Neua (Lauj Pov Vaj). There are no significant differences in their speech.

Each tutor contributed his own particular strength to the meetings we had. Xab Xyooj, my primary tutor, is intellectually curious, patient, and careful, and has great interest in and respect for his culture. Kuam Yaj, of the four, has the greatest interest in the mechanics of his own language and has talents proper to both a linguist and a teacher. Lauj Pov Vaj was the co-instructor in the intensive Hmong class at the Southeast Asian Studies Summer Institute in 1985 and was of the greatest help with conversational Hmong (the number of formal interviews we had on matters addressed in this study was small). I was fortunate to have had Npis Yaj as my first tutor, since his pronunciation of the fifty-eight initial consonant contrasts was the clearest of the four speakers. All four tutors were self-confident in their judgments and did not hesitate to correct me or tell me "no," for which reason I came to trust the information they provided.

The written sources were used as a starting point for chapters two and three (the study of tone sandhi and tonally defined form classes). My tutors were consulted when I needed to have more information about possible words and phrases, and semantic and pragmatic interpretations. Chapter four, on the role of tone in two-word expressives, was written almost solely on the basis of work with my tutors.

4   Hmong-Mien

4.1   On the Family Designation "Hmong-Mien"

The name I propose to use in reference to the family of which White Hmong is a member is "Hmong-Mien" rather than "Miao-Yao," the Chinese name that has been used by Chinese and Western scholars alike until recently. "Hmong-Mien" is the name that is being used increasingly by American linguists. The decision to change names is not capricious; it was made in order to designate a strictly linguistic, as opposed to ethnic, classification, and in order to refer these languages by (forms of) the names the people themselves use and prefer.

The first and most important argument in favor of this terminological change is that "Miao-Yao," as it is used in China, is not a purely linguistic designation. These are minority nationality names, and nationalities are determined by language, geography, socio-economics, and culture. Thus, the "Miao" people of Hainan Island actually speak a form of "Yao," the "Hei Yao" of Libo district, Guizhou province speak a form of "Miao" (the dialect referred to as YAOLU, after the village name, in this study), and the "Tahua Yao" of Xishanjie village, Guizhou province speak "Miao" of the Pa Hng branch (referred to as XISHANJIE in this study). Peoples of the "Yao nationality" speak languages belonging to four different groups: the Mienic division of Hmong-Mien, the Hmongic division of Hmong-Mien, the Kadai family, and Chinese (Mao, Meng, and Zheng 1982: 5-8). A change to the designation "Hmong-Mien" will eliminate the necessity of explaining in which sense the old names are being used.

Judging from the nine forms Wang Fushi records (1979: 27) for the root for "Hmong" in his comparative study of the initials and finals of dialects of the family, it may be that the Chinese term "Miao" ("Meo" in Thai and Lao) is a sinicization of the name the Hmongic people use to refer to themselves, as for example the following representative sampling of forms (see especially the SHIMEN and FUYUAN forms):[8]

$\underset{.}{m}hu^{33}$(A1)	YANGHAO
qo^{35}-$\underset{.}{\varsigma}o\eta^{35}$(A1)	JIWEI
$\underset{.}{m}o\eta^{43}$(A1)	XIANJIN
a^{55}-$\underset{.}{m}au^{55}$(A1)	SHIMEN
$\underset{.}{m}o\eta^{55}$(A1)	QINGYAN
$\underset{.}{m}ho\eta^{24}$(A1)	GAOPO

---

[8] I am grateful to David Strecker for pointing out that Benedict has proposed another hypothesis: that Archaic Chinese $*miog^A$ 'Miao' was a loan from Proto-Austro-Tai $*mlyau$, a variant of the form that means 'person/(we) the people'. "Hmong," according to him, is a backloan from Chinese.

maŋ²²(A1)   ZONGDI
a⁵⁵-m̯jo³¹(A)   FUYUAN
mhoŋ³³(A1)   FENGXIANG

"Hmong" is better than "Miao," though, in that it has wider geographical representation, and it retains the voiceless nasal initial and final nasal of the ancient Hmong name. More important, it does not have any of the derogatory associations connected with the Southeast Asian form of "Miao," "Meo." The name change we propose for the independent reason of clarity of reference is supported by the dislike Hmong speakers of Laos and Thailand feel for the term "Meo."[9]

A related problem has to do with our difficulty in translating the Chinese term for an intermediate linguistic grouping, fangyan (*fāngyán*). It is usually translated 'dialect' in English, whereas it actually represents a larger grouping than we understand dialect to represent. For example, if a fangyan is divided into sub-fangyan (*cìfāngyán*), the different sub-fangyan are mutually unintelligible. Hence, the decision was made to use the Chinese terms themselves in this study when using the Chinese names for particular groups, or, if the simpler geographical names are used ("West Hmongic," "East Hmongic," "North Hmongic"), to translate fangyan as 'branch', a term that is usefully adaptable. The classification of White Hmong is, then:

language family	Hmong-Mien
language group	Hmongic
fangyan	Sichuan-Guizhou-Yunnan
	(or West Hmongic branch)
sub-fangyan	Sichuan-Guizhou-Yunnan
dialect	White Hmong

---

[9] Schein (1986: 76-77) reports that there is no corresponding dislike of the term "Miao" by Hmong in China now, even though the term had been derogatory in the past. David Strecker (personal correspondence), though, has received reports that "Miao" is still resented in China though most are resigned to it.

The English term "language" would probably most closely correspond to the term sub-fangyan (or to the term fangyan in the case of a fangyan which is not divided into sub-fangyan).[10]

4.2   Internal Relationships

The family tree in table 3 was assembled by David Strecker, on the basis of Chinese research and analysis.[11] The only innovation attributable to Strecker is the placement of five "Bunu" languages within the West Hmongic branch. Chinese linguists have conceded that they belong there, but they have stopped short of placing them there because of the tradition of treating the people designated by the ethnic label "Bunu" separately. Benedict proposes that Na-e be established as a separate branch of Hmong-Mien because of certain unique features that he regards as extremely conservative (Benedict, 1986; Strecker, 1987). Since this analysis is controversial, Na-e is marked "unclassified" for the time being. The dialects referred to in this study fit into the diagram in table 3 in the manner specified in the sources list (appendix D).

---

[10] My understanding of these terms is due in large part to conversations with David Strecker and Gérard Diffloth.

[11] Unclassified: Na-e (possibly Pa Hng) and nine major groups within the Hmongic branch (Wang 1983: 1).

Table 3: The Hmong-Mien Family

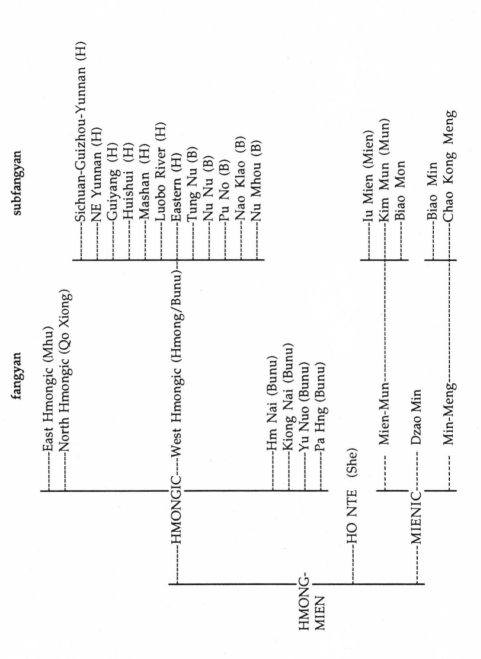

	fangyan	subfangyan
	East Hmongic (Mhu)	
	North Hmongic (Qo Xiong)	
	West Hmongic (Hmong/Bunu)	Sichuan-Guizhou-Yunnan (H)
		NE Yunnan (H)
		Guiyang (H)
		Huishui (H)
		Mashan (H)
		Luobo River (H)
HMONGIC		Eastern (H)
		Tung Nu (B)
		Nu Nu (B)
		Pu No (B)
		Nao Klao (B)
		Nu Mhou (B)
	Hm Nai (Bunu)	
	Kiong Nai (Bunu)	
	Yu Nuo (Bunu)	
	Pa Hng (Bunu)	

HMONG-MIEN

HO NTE (She)

	fangyan	subfangyan
	Mien-Mun	Iu Mien (Mien)
		Kim Mun (Mun)
		Biao Mon
MIENIC	Dzao Min	
	Min-Meng	Biao Min
		Chao Kong Meng

19

The Hmong-Mien family is not as diverse internally as Indo-European, but it is certainly more diverse than many believe. It is not simply a family with two languages, each of which has a collection of dialects. Strecker (personal communication) has likened Hmongic to Germanic in its internal complexity; Mienic is less complex.

Historically, the Mienic languages preserved the Proto-Hmong-Mien finals better than did the Hmongic languages. The corresponding generalization is often made that the Hmongic languages preserved more of the Proto-Hmong-Mien initials. In the Hmongic languages, there has been a split in the original D-tone words:[12] those words ending with *-? in Proto-Hmong-Mien merged with Proto-Hmongic tone C; they regularly correspond to D-tone words in Mienic. Finally, important vocabulary items have different roots in the two main divisions (Solnit 1985: 178):

	White Hmong	Iu Mien
pig	mbua C1	tuŋ B2
black	du A1	ciə? D1
white	daw A1	pɛ? D2

Within Hmongic there is still quite a bit of diversity. The Institute of Nationality Languages (1962) reports only thirty-two to forty per cent shared vocabulary between any two of the three main branches (East, North, and West Hmongic). East Hmongic is characterized by loss of contrastive prenasalization. North Hmongic has tone sandhi systems that are regressive like those of Mienic, whereas West Hmongic has progressive tone sandhi systems. Even within the West Hmongic branch, the phonological systems are diverse: for example, there are dialects with as few as three tones and with as many as twelve tones; SHIMEN has retained contrastive voicing in initial consonants while most other dialects have lost the voiced series; FUYUAN has retained contrastive preglottalization in initial consonants. An example of a Proto-Hmongic root taken from Wang's comparative study will give a feeling for the degree of difference evidenced within Hmongic (1979: 43):

---

[12] A discussion of the Proto-Hmong-Mien tone categories follows in section 4.3.1.

Nose *mbr- >

zɛ¹³(C2)	YANGHAO (East Hmongic)
mʐə⁴²(C2)	JIWEI (North Hmongic)
ɳtʂu¹³(C2)	XIANJIN (West Hmongic)
mbɣ⁵³(C2)	SHIMEN (West Hmongic)
mpjou²¹(C2)	QINGYAN (West Hmongic)
mplɯ²²(C2)	GAOPO (West Hmongic)
mpʐu¹³(C2)	ZONGDI (West Hmongic)
mpju²⁴(C)	FUYUAN (West Hmongic)
ntsi³¹(C2)	FENGXIANG (West Hmongic)

4.3   On the Status of the Reconstruction of Proto-Hmong-Mien

4.3.1   Tones

The first major work in Hmong-Mien comparative linguistics was done by Chang Kun in a series of articles on Proto-Hmong-Mien tones (1947, 1953, 1966, 1972). Tone is the great organizing principle in Hmong-Mien, as it is in Chinese and Tai: since so few contrasts are involved, it is on the basis of tone correspondences that cognates were chiefly determined. This work necessarily preceded work on the reconstruction of the initials and the finals. Apart from Chang's body of work, which details the reconstruction of the original tones and traces subsequent splits and mergers, there are three other articles that make contributions to the history of Proto-Hmong-Mien tones: Li, Ch'en, and Ch'en, "Some Problems Concerning Initials and Tones in the Miao Language" (1959), Haudricourt, "Bipartition et tripartition des systèmes de tons dans quelques langues d'Extrême-Orient" (1961), and Downer, "Tone-Change and Tone-Shift in White Miao" (1967) (where the important fact that words with Proto-Hmong-Mien *-ʔ merged with tone C in Proto-Hmongic is mentioned in a footnote). Purnell, "Toward a Reconstruction of Proto-Miao-Yao" (1970), includes tables of tonal correspondences that have proved very valuable.

In broad outline, Hmong-Mien tonal development is the same as the development of tone in Chinese or Tai. Leaving the question of the origin of the first tones aside, we may say that there were three tones in Proto-Hmong-Mien originally: A, B, and C. These tones were pronounced on unchecked syllables (those with either a vocalic or nasal final). These syllables contrasted with checked syllables (those with a stop consonant final), which were tonally undifferentiated. At some point, these checked syllables acquired distinctive pitch also, and became part of the basic tone system— tone D. These four tones split into eight in most dialects upon the neutralization of the voicing contrast in the initial consonants: the voiced series was lost, and it is theorized that a high-low split in each tone (corresponding to *voiceless-*voiced initial) resulted. Subsequent splits and mergers account for the variety of tone systems seen today in the different Hmongic dialects.

The White Hmong tones described above (section 3.1.3) correspond to the reconstructed Proto-Hmong-Mien tone categories as follows (note the merger between B2 and D1):

A	B	C	D
Series 1 (*C- voiceless)			
55(-b)	24(-v)	33(-ø)	22(-s)
Series 2 (*C- voiced)			
52(-j)	22(-s)	42(-g)	21ʔ(-m)

The breathiness in the -g tone (category C2) is related to the fact that the initial consonant was originally voiced. Breathiness (or voiced aspiration) characterizes many of the type 2 tones in the Hmongic dialects spoken in China: this is especially true of tone categories B2 and C2.

The four basic tones of Proto-Hmong-Mien have been referred to in different ways by different authors. In this study, I follow Chang's example and use A (A1, A2), B (B1, B2), C (C1, C2), and D (D1, D2). These historical categories are involved in my explanations of the development of the West Hmongic tone sandhi system (chapter two) and the development of the tonally defined form classes (chapter three).

The "A, B, C, D" form of reference to ancient tone categories corresponds to other forms of reference as follows:

	A1	A2	B1	B2	C1	C2	D1	D2
Chang	A1	A2	B1	B2	C1	C2	D1	D2
Downer	1a	1b	2a	2b	3a	3b	4a	4b
Wang	1	2	3	4	5	6	7	8

For ease of exposition, I will regularize the notation to A1, A2... in the quoted material from Downer and Wang in this study.

4.3.2 Initials

The first major study of Proto-Hmongic initials was Chang Kun "Proto-Miao Initials" (1976). In "The comparison of initials and finals of Miao fangyan" (1979), Wang Fushi established 121 initial consonant correspondences and assigned phonetic values to each on the basis of a comparison of almost 600 roots in each of nine representative dialects. In his preface (p. 17), Wang acknowledged the work of Chang and represented his own contribution as one of supplementation, revision, and rearrangement. Purnell's dissertation, "Toward a Reconstruction of Proto-Miao-Yao" (1970) has been largely superceded by the work of Wang, but it is still a useful compilation of the materials available to him at the time.

The Proto-Hmong-Mien consonant values have not been established, but they are not anticipated to differ greatly from the Proto-Hmongic consonants, since the languages of the Hmongic side of the family typically preserve the initials of Proto-Hmong-Mien (most of the dialects of Hmongic have large initial consonant inventories and only one final consonant, -ŋ, or -n/-ŋ as allophones),whereas the languages of the Mienic side of the family typically preserve more of the final contrasts (including vowel length and the final consonants -p,-t, [-ʔ], -m, -n, -ŋ), as was mentioned in section 4.2 above.

Proto-Hmong-Mien initial consonants involve contrastive voicing, aspiration, and prenasalization in labial, alveolar, retroflex, velar, and uvular stops. There are affricates. There are preglottalized, voiceless, and voiced nasals and liquids. There are clusters involving liquids in the labial, retroflex, and uvular series (for more details, see Wang 1979: 17-18).

4.3.3 Finals

Reconstruction of the finals of Proto-Hmong-Mien has been undertaken only very recently due to the need for good data from both sides of the family: as was noted above, more of the final contrasts were preserved on the Mienic side.

The finals of Proto-Hmongic have been reconstructed by Wang Fushi in his 1988 article on Miao-Yao reconstruction in Minzu

Yuwen. Wang had outlined thirty-two final correspondence sets for Proto-Hmongic in his major reconstruction work of 1979, but he did not reconstruct phonetic values for them there, other than to indicate that the first nineteen finals consisted of a vowel alone (with no final consonant) and that the last thirteen were some combination of vowel and nasal. Before Wang's most recent study, David Strecker orally presented a partial reconstruction of the finals (ICSTLL 1986). G. B. Downer, "Problems in the Reconstruction of Proto-Miao-Yao" (1982) analyzed some of the correspondence sets from Wang in the light of material from the Mienic side of the family and was able on that basis to reduce the number of 1979 correspondence sets somewhat and establish some phonetic values for them. Purnell reconstructed Proto-Hmong-Mien vowels as labels for correspondence sets but explicitly claimed (1970: 35) that they are not adequate as reconstructions of phonetic values.

CHAPTER TWO

TONE SANDHI COMPOUNDING

1   Tone Sandhi and Compound Formation

The term "sandhi" refers to phonetic changes occurring in words that are caused by certain phonetic characteristics of contiguous words. Thus, "tone sandhi" is the change of tone in one word caused by the tone of a neighboring word. According to Kenneth Pike (1948: 25), "regular tone sandhi" narrowly described is "forced meaningless substitutions of one toneme for another...in which one toneme is perturbed by another." Eugénie Henderson (1967: 174) refers to "tonal alternation and compounding" and differentiates "tonal alternation," which affects meaning, from "tone sandhi," which she takes in the narrow sense given above.

White Hmong tone sandhi must be understood in a broader sense. It is of Pike's "arbitrary type" (1948: 26), in which the proper phonetic environment is not sufficient to guarantee tone change. Grammatical category and the particular lexical items involved also play a role. The compounds that result from tone change are sometimes different in meaning from a phrase involving the two unaltered words, but usually they are not. I choose to call tonal alternation in White Hmong "tone sandhi" to (1) emphasize the syntagmatic nature of the alternation, and (2) to emphasize the historical connection between the White Hmong "system relic" and the "regular" (mechanical) tone sandhi system from which it came (see section 3 below). For reasons concerning the semantic unity of the members of the resultant tonally defined pairs and the behavior of a few of them as syntactic units (see section 2.5), I choose to call these pairs "compounds" after Lyman[1] and to indicate their compound status with a linking hyphen in the orthography. Inasmuch as tone sandhi serves to create new words in White Hmong, it constitutes one of the morphological functions of tone in the language.

2   A Synchronic Account of White Hmong Tone Sandhi

2.1   On the Nature of White Hmong Tone Sandhi

Many words with high falling, low level, low checked, mid rising, and mid level tones (those words marked with -*j*, -*s*, -*m*, -*v*, and -*ø* respectively) have alternate tonal realizations when they enter into a particularly close relationship with a preceding word that has either a high level or high falling tone (-*b*, -*j*). Almost five hundred pairs of words that involve alternate tonal realizations (tone sandhi compounds) are listed in appendix A. A few examples here will serve to give an introduction to the nature of these tonally defined compounds:

Noun-Verb Attribute (no change of style or meaning)	*dej siav* water cooked boiled water (H 298)[2]	*dej-sia* boiled water (H 34)
Noun-Noun Attribute (with reported stylistic difference)	*hnoob tes* sun hand sunray (B *taw*)	*hnoob-teg* sunray (B *tes*)
Verb-Noun (with reported semantic difference)	*poob dej* fall water to fall into water (native speakers)	*poob-deg* to drown (B *dej*; H 447)

---

[1] Unpublished notes of Thomas A. Lyman, 1963, quoted in Heimbach (1979: 454).

[2] "H" and "B" refer to the Heimbach (1979) and Bertrais-Charrier (1964) White Hmong dictionaries.

There are both strict phonological (section 2.2) and syntactic (section 2.3) conditions on the occurrence of tone sandhi compounding; I have also observed that certain lexical items are more likely than others, given the same phonological and syntactic environments, to enter into such compounds (section 2.4). However, even after long familiarity with the compounds that do exist and the rules that limit their occurrence, it is impossible for me to predict which pairs of words must always compound, which (of those that meet the minimal criteria) must never compound, and which, as those examples cited above, can occur either way. Of those pairs of words that have been found both in a collocation of independent morphemes and in a tonally defined compound, some have concomitant meaning differences and some do not.

Apart from a number of frozen compounds, which all sources and speakers seem to agree on (such as *teb-chaws* 'country', from *teb* 'land' and *chaw* 'place'), the sporadic appearance of these compounds in the lexicon and the equal acceptability of both the compounded and the uncompounded forms in many cases indicates to me the truth of what G. B. Downer (1967) postulates: the tone sandhi system in White Hmong is an historical relic of a system that dates back no further, probably, than Proto-West-Hmongic (the Sichuan-Guizhou-Yunnan fangyan protolanguage) and is in the process of dying out. The existence of a Proto-West-Hmongic sandhi system is inferred by Downer from a comparative study of five dialects of that branch including White Hmong, in which the system is eroded the furthest (see section 3.1 for an expanded comparative analysis). Downer believes the sandhi system may someday disappear completely: it is possible for the original forms to replace the tonally derived forms in most cases, since speakers rarely cease to identify the base form and the sandhi form as the same "word" (1967: 596). Young speakers, as represented by the two young men I have had the greatest contact with, are beginning to use words with the base tone even in the syntactic collocation that most predictably gives rise to tonal compounding: the numeral-classifier collocation. They often meet questions about which tone is acceptable or better in certain collocations with a shrug of the shoulders, meaning that either is all right and that neither will obscure communication.

Geography as well as generation seems to have something to do with the extent to which tone sandhi has eroded in White Hmong. The two dictionaries of White Hmong were both published in the 1960s, Yves Bertrais-Charrier's in 1964 and Ernest

Heimbach's originally in 1969. Bertrais-Charrier's work was done in Laos, in the provinces of Louang Prabang, Sam Neua, and Xieng Khouang, and Heimbach's dictionary is based on data collected in Thailand, in the northern provinces of Petchabun and Pitsanulok. For collocations attested in both dictionaries, Bertrais-Charrier shows a slightly higher number of sandhi compounds retained than does Heimbach. My survey of the two dictionaries reveals that Heimbach has seven sandhi compounds that appear in their uncompounded forms in Bertrais-Charrier, whereas Bertrais-Charrier has twenty-four sandhi compounds that appear uncompounded in Heimbach. Some examples follow:

Heimbach (no sandhi)	Bertrais-Charrier (sandhi)
ncej cos post treadmill	*ncej-cog* treadmill post
roj av fat earth	*roj-a* oil
qhab tsev rafter house	*qhab-tse* rafters
taub nkawm gourd hornet	*taub-nkawg* swarm or nest of hornets

Both dictionaries indicate that tonal compounding is optional in many instances.

For reasons that will be discussed fully in section 3 below, I believe that compound formation by tone change is a new use being made of an old, once more regular and thoroughgoing, phonetically motivated tone sandhi system. The points of interest in a synchronic analysis of White Hmong tone sandhi are why it occurs when it does, what kinds of words are likely to be involved within the recognized phonological and syntactic constraints, and how these tonally defined compounds may differ in meaning and behavior from collocations made of the base forms of their component parts.

2.2   Phonological Conditions

White Hmong tone sandhi is of the progressive type; that is, the trigger word precedes the word that undergoes the tone change.[3] Although the changes were most likely due to neutralization under loss of stress in non-prepausal environments originally (see section 3.3), the tones that these changes gave rise to have become associated with certain tones in the basic inventory of lexical tones, so that the system in White Hmong today is one of paradigmatic replacement of one tone by another. The "neutralization effect" is still evident in the fact that five different tones collapse into a system of three. A representation of the specific changes that take place appears below:

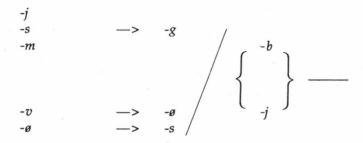

It is important to remember that the above description of the phonological environment and changes captures the necessary phonological facts about tone sandhi, but that the proper phonological conditions alone are no longer sufficient criteria for change. As mentioned above, sandhi takes place optionally, and, although its likelihood can be assessed, it takes place unpredictably. The focus is properly on its occurrence, therefore, rather than on its non-occurrence. Nonetheless, there are three important exceptions to the scheme above, which are fairly easily explained.

2.2.1   Low Level (-s) Tone Exceptions

In an account of the White Hmong tone system from a diachronic perspective, we need to differentiate two low level (-s) tones. In White Hmong, the reflex of category B2 (the second of the

---

[3] Tone sandhi in the Mienic branch, on the other hand, is regressive. See Lu Yichang (1985: 16-20); Solnit (1985: 175-191). Interestingly, tone sandhi in North Hmongic is also regressive (Ying Lin 1962: 73; Institute 1962: 5).

three Proto-Hmong-Mien tones A, B, and C; the "2" indicates an ancient, voiced initial consonant) merged with the reflex of category D1 (the D tone belongs to words that had final *-p or *-t in Proto-Hmong-Mien and arose later than the first three; the "1" indicates an ancient, voiceless initial consonant). Only the words with low level tones that can be assigned to tone category B2 on the basis of comparative evidence undergo tone sandhi. This indicates that the period when the tone sandhi process was productively generating new compounds predated the White Hmong tonal merger, since no low level (-s) tone word that can be assigned to tone category D1 undergoes tone sandhi. To illustrate the different behavior of the -s^1 tone (< B2) from the -s^2 tone (< D2), the following comparison between White Hmong and Green Hmong, which did not undergo the same tonal merger, is given below:

tone sandhi with
White Hmong -s^1 (< B2) = Green Hmong -g (< B2)

tus:	*ib-tug*	1-animate-	*tug*
tais:	*ib-taig*	1-bowlful-	*taig*
tes:	*pob-teg*	round part-hand (= wrist bone)	*teg*

no tone sandhi with
White Hmong -s^2 (< D1) = Green Hmong -s (< D1)

caws: ib caws	1 leap-	*caws*
qais: ib qais	1 skein-	*qais*
kws: pob kws	corn	*kws*

Similarly, tone sandhi does not affect the following D1 -s tone words:

nqaij dais	meat bear (= bear meat) (compare *nqaij npuas* 'pork' and *nqaij-nyug* 'beef') (H 450)
paj kws	flower corn (= popcorn) (compare *paj-npleg* 'puffed rice') (H 449)

| *sib ntaus* | (recip)-strike (= to strike each other) (compare *sib-nraus* 'to butt each other') (H 185) |
| *sib zas* | (recip)-face off (= to face off against each other) (compare *sib-zeg* 'to tease each other') (H 450) |

2.2.2 The Voiceless Aspirated Stop, Voiceless Fricative, Voiceless Sonorant/Breathy (-*g*) Tone Co-occurrence Restriction

The voiceless aspirated stops, voiceless fricatives, and voiceless sonorants constitute a natural class in White Hmong, in that they share the feature called [spread glottis], after the articulatory gesture they all have in common.[4] Since aspiration is distinctive in White Hmong, the voiceless aspirated stops have a pronounced period of aspiration before the onset of voicing in the vowel and, presumably, a correspondingly greater glottal opening than in a language where aspiration is not distinctive. The voiceless fricatives *f-*, *h-*, *s-*, *x-*, *xy-*, and voiceless sonorants *hm-*, *hn-*, *hny-*, *hl-* are characterized by the same greater than normal glottal opening that characterizes the aspirated stops. The phonological distinctions based on [spread glottis] would be difficult to maintain if the syllable in question were to be pronounced with the breathy (-*g*) tone, which phonetic studies have shown to also be characterized by [spread glottis].[5] Therefore, no Hmong word that begins with one of these initials will carry the breathy (-*g*) tone.[6] As a corollary to this fact, no word beginning with either a voiceless aspi-

---

[4] These consonants constitute a class in the Tai languages as well and are referred to as the "high consonants." Certain dialects, including Siamese, underwent a tone split on the basis of whether or not the initial was of this class (Li Fang-Kuei, *A Handbook of Comparative Tai* [Honolulu: University Press of Hawaii, 1977], 29).

[5] As was mentioned in chapter one, section 3.1.3, this tone is a more "whispered" than "murmured" breathy tone. For justification of the analysis of this cooccurrence restriction in Hmong based on a review of the pertinent phonetic studies and cross-linguistic evidence, see Ratliff (1989).

[6] Bertrais-Charrier (1964), introduction: "Les mots qui ont une aspirations ne portent jamais le tone *'neeg'*." Mottin (1978: 16): "Notons qu'aucun mot aspiré ne se prononce sur ce tone [-*g*]."

rated stop or a voiceless fricative will undergo these sandhi changes:

$$
\begin{Bmatrix} \text{-}j \\ \text{-}s \\ \text{-}m \end{Bmatrix} \longrightarrow \text{-}g \left/ \begin{Bmatrix} \text{-}b \\ \text{-}j \end{Bmatrix} \right. \text{———}
$$

Examples of this co-occurrence restriction appear below:

> *ib phaj mov*   1 plate of rice (H 448)
> 1 plate rice
> > (see *ib-roog mov* '1 tableful of rice')

> *ib phom*   1 shot (H 244)
> 1 gun/shot
> > (see *ib-nplawg* '1 blow')

Similarly:

ib chim	a little while (H 24)
ib faj	1 of a pair (H 43)
ib feem	1 part; 1 portion (H 44)
ib fij	a shift of work (Vwj 1983: 44-45)
ib hom	1 kind (H 54)
ib hwm	an ensemble of pieces (B *hwm*)
ib phaum mob	1 sickness (H 450)
ib phiaj	1 row; 1 set (H 243)
ib sas	1 spurt (H 287)
ib sij	continually; repeatedly (H 293)
ib sim neej	1 lifetime (H 294)
ib suam nag	1 shower (B *suam*)
ib thaj	1 stretch of land (B *thaj*)
ib thaj neeb	1 session of spirit worship (B *thaj*)
ib thooj	1 lobe; 1 clump; 1 packet (B *thooj*)
ib tshaj	1 case at law (H 448)
ib tshooj	1 level; 1 story (H 369)
ib txhij	at the same time (H 392)
sib fim	to know each other (H 45)
sib foom	to set a curse on each other (H 46)

Although the co-occurrence restriction between the native initials *s-*, *x-*, and *xy-* and the breathy (*-g*) tone seems to be a restriction of a solely phonological nature, the restriction on the co-occurrence of many *f-* and *h-* words and the breathy tone is apparently due both to phonology and to the fact that words with these initials are often loans from Chinese. Recent loans came into the language when the tone sandhi process was no longer productive and are, hence, less likely to undergo change (see below).

2.2.3   The Non-Involvement of More Recent Chinese Loans

Contact between the Chinese and the Hmong has existed over centuries, and the traffic in loanwords has been extensive. This is a matter of general knowledge, shared both by those who claim a genetic relationship between the two families and those who do not. The difficulty in analyzing these loans lies in identifying the dialect(s) of Chinese from which the loans came and the times at which they entered the language. The Southwest variety of Mandarin as spoken in Yunnan province is the form of Chinese used as a probable source of recent loans in Lyman's Green Hmong dictionary. Studies of Chinese loans in Hmong-Mien languages include Institute ([1962] loans in Mien Bunu, and Lakkja), Ying ([1962] loans in several Hmongic dialects), Downer ([1973] strata of loanwords in Mien), and Benedict ([1987] early Sino-Tibetan/Hmong-Mien loan relationships).

Ying (1962: 74) and Ruey and Kuan (1962: 525) both mention that Chinese loans do not undergo tone change in XIANJIN and XUYONG, respectively. The same is true in White Hmong. Such loanword exceptions in the most exceptionless environment for tone sandhi, the collocation numeral-classifier, are listed below (the Southwest Mandarin forms are from Lyman's dictionary):

> *lwm*   (< SWMan *er* 'two')
> another; times, occasions
> > *-nyeem ib lwm*
> > read one time (H 123)
> > *-dav hlau yuj ob peb lwm*
> > hawk iron hover two three
> > the plane makes 2-3 turns (B *yuj*)

tiam
generation

> *-ib tiam neej*
> 1 gen. person
> 1 generation (Downer 1967: 594; B *tiam*)

vam (< SWMan *wán* '10,000')
tens of thousands[7]

> *-ib vam; ob vam*
> 10,000; 20,000 (H 398)

yam (< SWMan *yáng* 'thing')
kind, sort, type

> *-ib yam*
> 1 thing; the same thing (H 419)

The loanword exception also explains the absence of sandhi forms in compounds such as the following:

cwj mem (< SWMan *mě* 'ink')
pointed stick ink
pencil; pen (H 21)

sib cam
(recip) argue
argue with each other (H 7)

Although I will not attempt to read too much into the fact that the six examples cited above bear the checked (*-m*) tone, I think that it suggests that a proper study of "loan-tones" in Hmong would be fruitful.

---

[7] As David Strecker points out (personal correspondence), the word for '10,000' has tone C2 in seven of the nine dialects represented in Wang 1979 and tone D2 only in White Hmong, Green Hmong, and SHIMEN. It may be that it was an early loan in the majority of the dialects and a later loan in the latter three.

2.3 Syntactic Conditions

The following word class conditions on tone sandhi were recognized by Lyman (of Green Hmong) in 1963 and were reproduced by Heimbach in his dictionary (1979: 454):

> TONE SANDHI
> At the present stage of research, it would seem that sandhi changes occur when members of certain word classes are joined syntactically, in what may be called "compounds." The following have so far been recorded:
>
> 1. Numerals joined to classifiers: *'ob-leeg'* Two persons
> 2. Numerals joined to numerals: *'ib-puas'* One hundred
> 3. Nouns joined to modifying words (these latter being either Nouns or Verbs): *'teb-npleg'* Rice field
> 4. Autotelic Verbs joined to Nouns (as locative objects): *'poob-deg'* Fall in the water
>
> (The label "Noun" is here taken to include localizers, a subgroup of nouns which correspond to English prepositions, e.g., *'qab'* Bottom or Under. The label "Verb" is here taken to include words corresponding to English adjectives, e.g., *'liab'* To be red. An "Autotelic Verb" is a verb which may or may not take a noun object. In the latter case, the object modifies the verb.)

Heimbach's only objection to the above account of Hmong tone sandhi is that it does not explain the countless times tone sandhi fails to occur in such syntactically defined compounds. In his introduction to the above quotation, Heimbach states that the two factors of word class and juncture are important in determining whether a change of tone is "required" or not. I would go further than Heimbach: to assert that word class and juncture are sufficient to insure that tone sandhi will take place ignores the frozen collocations without tone change, certainly compounds in terms of meaning and behavior, such as *pojniam* 'woman; wife' (literally 'woman'-'woman'). I think it is better to say that tone change indicates close juncture rather than that close juncture is a prerequisite of tone change. (See section 3 on why it is impossible to fully specify the conditions under which tone sandhi will occur.)

Gordon Downer (1967: 592-593) lists the following:

...constructions in which the modified tones are commonly found. As the grammatical analysis of WM [White Miao] is far from complete, all grammatical labels must be taken as purely provisional.

(1) Num. + Quant. (when the Num is i^1 'one', $ɔ^1$ 'two', pe^1 'three', plo^1 'four', $tʃi^1$ 'five', $kyua^2$ 'nine', and ti^1 'only one')

(2) Nominals (the first syllable is Noun, the second may be Noun, Verb, or Adj.; both subordinative and coordinative constructions occur)

(3) Quant. + Noun (only three examples found)

(4) VPref. + Verb (the only VPref. is $ʃi^1$ or $ʃi^4$ 'each other')

(5) Verb + Noun

Downer recognized two important constructions that Lyman omitted: the reciprocal-verb construction, and the rare, though very interesting, classifier- (Downer uses the term "quantifier") noun construction (see section 4.2).

Mottin (p. 19) recognized roughly the same constructions as Downer:

-Cela [changement de ton] semble être la plupart du temps le cas quand les mots forment une entité, un syntagme:
    -avec un numéral: ib-qho = un lieu, une chose
    -avec un verbe ou nom pris comme adjectif:
        dej sov = l'eau est chaude
        dej-so = de l'eau chaude
        kauj-ntseg = des pendants d'oreille
    -avec un verbe normalement intransitif, mais qui
        peut être directement suivi d'un nom avec
        lequel il fait comme expression:
        poob-deg = tomber (dans) l'eau
    -avec des mots comme "sib"
        sib-tog = se mordre l'un l'autre[8]

---

[8] I have added hyphens to the quotation to indicate when tone sandhi has taken place, since the base forms are not given.

2.3.1 Constructions Involving Numerals

As Heimbach observed (1979: 446) tone sandhi is "particularly noticeable in words preceded by one of the first five numerals."[9] A large number of examples involving each one of the possible changes is easy to find:

ib-rag (< raj) dej	1 tubeful of water
ib-pluag (< pluas) mov	1 meal (of rice)
ob-daig (< daim) ntawv	2 sheets of paper
peb-kw (< kwv) taws	3 shoulderloads of firewood
ib-los (< lo) lus	1 mouthful of language
	(1 word)

The above collocations are all numeral-classifier.

The collocation numeral-numeral also gives rise to tone sandhi when the second numeral is *caum* ('10s'-30 and above) or *pua* ('100') and the first numeral is 1-5 or 9 (with the interesting exception *cuaj caum* '90'[10]):

plaub-caug   40
4 ------ 10

ib txhiab cuaj-puas yim caum rau   1986
1 - 1,000 --- 9 -- 100 -- 8 -- 10 --- 6

Notice that *vam* '10,000', perhaps in White Hmong a more recent Chinese loan, does not undergo tone sandhi, as mentioned in section 2.2.3 on expected exceptions above:

ib vam	10,000
ob vam	20,000

---

[9] In at least one instance, the numerals themselves, in ordinal postposition, are changed: in the compounds referring to the days of the waxing of the moon, *xiab-raus* 'the sixth day of the moon's increase', *xiab-xyas* 'the seventh...', *xiab-yig* 'the eighth...', *xiab-cuag* 'the ninth...', *xiab-kaug* 'the tenth...'.

[10] Heimbach (1979: 457); Downer (1967: 592); Vwj (1983: 37); Xab Xyooj (personal correspondence).

A third category of words is affected by the numeral *ib* 'one': nouns used as measure words, or nouns the entirety of which is being expressed:

ib-hmos (< *hmo*)	1 night (H 452)
ib-vog (< *voj*)	1 circle (H 401)
ib-ce (< *cev*)	the entire body (B *cev*)
ib-zog (< *zos*)	the whole village (H 449)

Finally, there are two words that are "numeral-like" in meaning, bear the right tones, and can effect tone sandhi: *tib* 'single; sole; 1 blow of...' and *thawj* 'first; head':

tib-leeg (< *leej*)	sole person (B *leej*)
tib-qho (< *qhov*)	sole thing (H 315)
tib-tug (< *tus*)	sole person (B *tib* ; H 315, 325)
tib-plhaws (< *plhaw*)	1 jump (B *plhaw*)
tib-riag (< *riam*)	1 stroke of the knife (H 450)
tib-teg (< *tes*)	1 blow of the hand (H 316)
thawj-caw (< *cawv*)	head of the whiskey (B *cawv*)
thawj-zaug (< *zaum*)	first time (B *thawj*; H 335)

When I first started looking at tone sandhi in White Hmong, it seemed as though these numeral collocations came fairly close to constituting an exceptionless environment for tone change, probably because the most common classifiers (for example, *tus* 'animate, long and slender', *leej* 'human', *nkawm* 'pair', *daim* 'flat object') seem to change exceptionlessly. On a careful reading of both Bertrais-Charrier's and Heimbach's dictionaries, though, I discovered a great number of exceptions in this syntactic collocation as well, bringing it more in line with the other syntactic environments in which tone sandhi compounding may occur. A list of these exceptions follows:

ib cim	1 turn of work; 1 season (H 13, 90; B *cim*)
ib com	1 measure of 6 kilos (B *com*)
ob cum	2 sides, groups, clans (H 17)
ib cuam teeb	opium smoking utensils (B *cuam*)
ib cuam nqaij	1 stretching of meat (B *cuam*)
ib cuam nplooj	1 length of roofing leaves (H 20)
ib cuam	1 time (B *cuam*, *nrau*)

38

ib cuam neeg	1 group of people (B *cuam*)
ib chaw	1 place (B *chaw*)
ib dav hlau	1 planeful (of goods) (B *thauj*)
ib kauj hlua	1 coil of rope (H 77, 448)
ib kuam	1 hand (of bananas) (H 90; B *kuam, thij*)
ib kheev	1 bundle (B *kheev*)
ib leej	1 line (of houses) (H 110, 448; B *leej*)
ib lo lus	1 mouthful of language (B *lo*)
ib naj zia	1 gummy stick (B *naj*)
ib ncauj hniav	1 mouthful of teeth (H 145, 448)
ib ncuav pias	1 slap (H 149)
ib ntsauv	1 clump (B *ntsauv*)
ib ntsis	1 moment (H 201)
ib ntsuj teb	1 portion of field (H 204)
ib ntshua	1 cluster (B *ntshua*)
ib ntxuj	1 slab (B *ntxuj*)
ib ntxwj tsua	1 out-jutting of rock (H 448; B *ntxwj*)
ib nyuam qhuav	1 moment (H 222, 272)
ib pam quav	1 passage of defecation (H 224)
ib phau ntawv	1 book (B *phau*)
ib pheev teb	1 slope of field (B *pheev*)
ib plhaw	1 jump (H 254)
ib qhov tshiab	1 new thing (B *qhov*)
ib qhoo	1 bundle (B *qhoo*)
ib rauj rau	1 hammer blow on (B *rauj*)
ib rauv	1 cluster (of fruit) (B *rev*)
ib rauv	1 square (of embroidery) (B *rauv*)
ib rooj	1 tableful (B *rooj*)
ib ruam	1 step (B *ruam*)
ib tauv nroj	1 clump of weeds (B *tauv*)
ib tawm tsheb	1 train of cars (H 311)
ib tom	1 time (H 322)
ib twv huab	1 cloud (B *twv*)
ib tsam	1 period of several hours (B *tsam*)
ib tsum mov	1 tableful of food (Yaj, 1987)
ib txwm	a long time (H 386)
ib txwm ntawv	1 letter of the alphabet (H 386)
ib txhia	some; a portion (H 393)
ib voj-teg	a circle made with the 2 hands (B *tes*)
ib yoj thee	1 ovenful of charcoal (B *yoj*)

Many of these unmodified words have been found with the expected sandhi forms. The places where the exceptional unmodified forms were found is indicated. As of now, I have no explanation for these exceptions, except to say that a number of these words will doubtlessly prove to be Chinese loanwords (those words with initials *h-*, *f-*, *y-*, and/or tone *-m* are suspect, for example). But if tone sandhi compounding is no longer a live process in the language, it stands to reason that there would be exceptions in every eligible syntactic collocation. The proper focus here, too, then, is on the occurrences rather than the non-occurrences of the tone change.

An interesting reanalysis of tone sandhi involving the numerals was offered by Lauj Pov Vaj, who was a 21-year-old instructor in Hmong at the Southeast Asian Studies Summer Institute at the University of Michigan, summer 1985. He used the sandhi tone with the common classifier *tus* (> *tug*) after the numerals; but he said that it was not necessary to do so and that both tonal realizations sounded equally good to him. Then, seemingly as an afterthought, he added that perhaps *tus*, the base form, was the singular form (*ib tus dev* '1 dog'), and that *tug*, the sandhi form, was the plural form (*ob tug dev* '2 dogs'). His own speech did not bear out his analysis, but it was a familiar attempt to make sense out of the remains of an ancient process.

2.3.2   Reciprocal-Verb

Roughly as often as not, the reciprocal *sib* induces tone sandhi in the following verb, if it bears one of the proper tones. A list of twenty-two compounds involving the reciprocal can be found under *sib* in appendix A. It is not clear yet whether or not for some speakers there is a meaning differentiation correlated with the base form as opposed to the sandhi form of the verb. For example, with the verb *tom* 'to bite', does *sib tom* mean 'to bite each other' (the sum of its component parts), whereas *sib-tog* means 'to fight' (with specific acts of biting raised to the main event of which they are a part)?

With regard to this collocation, it is very interesting to note that *sis*, an alternate form of the reciprocal, often appears with the sandhi form of the verb in Bertrais-Charrier's examples. It is not a feature of the White Hmong of Laos to the exclusion of the White Hmong of Thailand, apparently, since Heimbach (1979: 294) mentions that *sis* is a variant form of *sib* that is "often used."

Heimbach gives fewer examples with *sis*, though, having regularized to *sib* for the most part, so that the following examples all come from Bertrais-Charrier:

sis-ceg	to argue with each other
sis-ncag	to make a line with each other
sis-nraus	to butt each other
sis-qawg	to embrace each other
sis-tog	to bite each other
sis-tuas	to kill each other
sis-tuag	to kick each other
sis-txig	the same height
sis-xyaws	mixed up together
sis-zeg	to tease each other

Note that *sis* bears the wrong tone for a tone sandhi trigger: it is extremely unusual to have the sandhi tones follow anything other than a word with a *-b* or a *-j* tone, and it always suggests something interesting about the history of the language. The other situation where this occurs is "sandhi form promotion" (section 4.1), where the sandhi form of a word, generated in the usual fashion, has, over time, become detached from the trigger that gave rise to it and has gained base form status, either co-existing with the old base (often with an accompanying semantic split), or supplanting the old base entirely. To understand the appearance of sandhi forms following *sis*, it is necessary to look at Wang's comparative data on this root (1979: 89):

YANGHAO	XIANJIN	SHIMEN
φi^{44}	$\mathfrak{z}i^{33}$	$hi^{11}/\mathfrak{z}1^{11}$
(C1)	(D1)	(D1)

GAOPO	FUYUAN	FENGXIANG
shoŋ^{13}	$\mathfrak{z}i^{31}$	φou^{33}
(B1)	(A/D)	(A1)

The tonal reflexes of this root all indicate an ancient, voiceless initial, yet all four Proto-Hmongic tones are represented. White Hmong *sib* is a reflex of category A1, and *sis* is a reflex of category D1. Although Wang writes that it is difficult to account for the vast discrepancy among the tones in the different localities, or to reconstruct the original tone, his discussion of the final [-oŋ] of the GAOPO form (1979: 124) may provide a clue as to the cause. He reports that in GAOPO the final of the reciprocal will harmonize with the final of the following verb. Accordingly,

shoŋ^{13} ʐoŋ^{43}	to be good to each other
shu^{13} tɕu^{22}	to meet each other
shə^{13} pə^{55}	to see each other
shi^{13} zi^{22}	to bind each other

The intimate nature of the relationship between the reciprocal and its verb (both Wang [1979: 124] and Downer [1967: 593] refer to the reciprocal as a "prefix") could explain the different tonal reflexes as well: in GAOPO, a live process of vowel harmony marks the relationship;[11] perhaps in ancient Hmong, a process of tone harmony marked the relationship. As this process faded out, one or another of the shifting forms became the sole form, or, as in White Hmong, two forms persisted. The connection thereafter was marked, for those languages of the West branch of Hmongic that preserved the A1 reflex reciprocal by tonal modification of the right-hand member, the verb, rather than by modification of the left-hand member, the reciprocal.

The explanation for the tone sandhi forms following the *sis* variant could be, therefore, (1) the identification of *sib* and *sis* as trivially different manifestations of the same root, with no differentiation in meaning, and (2) the need, existing through reconstructible history, to signal this semantic relationship as being an unusually close one through the deformation of one or the other of the two words.

2.3.3 Noun-Modifier

In normal White Hmong word order, modifiers follow the words they modify. When the relationship between modifier and noun is a close, common, and conventionalized one (see section 2.4 below) and the right phonological conditions obtain (section 2.2), a

---

11 We can only speculate as to how the vowel harmony in GAOPO developed. It is reported that some GAOPO prefixes also change to harmonize with the vowel of the root (nouns and ordinal numerals) to form disyllabic words (Institute 1962: 5-6).

tone sandhi compound may result. Of the two kinds of modifiers, noun and verb, compounds with noun modifiers are four times as numerous as compounds with verb modifiers in the examples presented in appendix A. Some examples follow:

ciab-mu (< muv) wax bee	bee wax
dab-npuas (< npua) trough pig	pig trough
kab-teg (< tes) line hand	lines of the hand
vaubkib-deg (< dej) turtle water	turtle
nab-qa (< qav) snake frog	lizard
nqob-npleg (< nplej) upper stalk rice	the upper part of the rice stalk[12]

Sandhi compounds with verb modifiers, however, are not unusual (there are approximately fifty in the examples presented in appendix A). It is well known that a separate class of "adjective" does not exist in most Asian languages, including Hmong, since adjective-like verbs are predicated of nouns with no need for the support of a copula. Many of the noun-verb modifier compounds involve one of these "adjective-like" verbs. A few examples follow:

dib-caug (< cauj) cucumber early	early-bearing cucumber
nkauj-mog (< mos) girl soft	young girl

---

[12] Sources for the tone sandhi compounds in this and the following three sections will be found in appendix A.

nplooj-qhua (< qhuav)	dry leaves
leaf dry	

tiab-nres (< nre)	pleated skirt
skirt to pleat	

vab-tshaus (< tshau)	sieve
tray to sift	

2.3.4   Noun-Noun

Repetition with a slight variation in four-word coordinative constructions is typical of Hmong figurative language (P'an and Ts'ao 1958; Johns and Strecker 1982). It is found in miniature in a number of two-word sandhi compounds. Here, neither word modifies the other, but together they form a coordinative construction: either a repetitive compound involving words with only slight meaning differences or a compound pair involving objects or people that belong together:

hlab-hluas	cord-rope (= viscera)
hlab-kag	cord-band (= tatters, rags)
kab-ke	custom-way (= custom, ceremony)
kwj-ha	gulley-valley (= valley)
liaj-ia	paddy field-mud (= land)
mab-sua	foreigner-foreigner
nyiaj-txiag	silver-money (= money)
plab-plaw	stomach-heart (= character, intelligence)
qeej-nruag	pipes-drums
teb-chaws	land-place (= country)
teb-nrag	land-plain (= earth)
tub-se	son-wife (= wife and children)
twj-taig	utensils-dishes (= dishes)
vaj-tse	garden-house (= house and grounds)
zeb-tsuas	stone-rock (= rock[y])

Occasionally the four-word coordinative constructions can be made up of two compounds, one or both of which involve tone sandhi. The same relationships that hold between the single words in the compounds listed above obtain here (repetition with

44

slight variation; pair membership), but in this case, the relationships hold between compounds:

hnoob-teg hnoob taw sun hand sun foot	hands and feet of the sun (= sunrays)
kauj vab kauj-le tray mat	to perform *tso plig* with basket and mat (spirit release)
khaub hlab khaub-hluas cloth cord cloth rope	ragged
liaj-ia teb-chaws field mud land place	lands (for subsistence)
lwj siab lwj-plaw soft liver soft heart	to be in turmoil
mob plaub mob-nqaig hurt hair hurt flesh	to speak harshly
muaj-kw muaj-tig have brother have brother	to have family
muaj mob muaj-nkeeg have hurt have lethargy	to be unwell
neej saub neej-see life sour life lonely	to have an unhappy life
noj-nqaig noj-hnos eat meat eat rice	a feast
nkim moo xob-hnos waste rice ? rice	to eat without working for it
npauj kub npauj-nyiag gold jewelry silver jewelry	gold and silver jewelry

nplooj xyoob nplooj-ntoos leaf bamboo leaf tree	the leaves of bamboo and trees
qub-teg qub taw[13] old hand old foot	inherited things; old things
suab-qeeg suab-nruag sound pipes sound drum	funeral music
suab-quag suab-nyia sound cry sound lament	the sound of crying and lamentation

In this discussion of sandhi compounds in figurative language, it is significant to report that my primary tutor considers the only difference between many pairs of words that can equally well exhibit sandhi or not, for example *lwj-plaw* as opposed to *lwj plawv* 'soft heart', is that the former, in which *plawv* undergoes tone change, sounds more "poetic."

2.3.5   Verb-Noun

In earlier descriptions of White Hmong tone sandhi (as reproduced in section 2.3 above) the verb-noun sandhi compounds were described as "autotelic verb [one which may or may not take a noun object]-(modifying) locative object" (Heimbach 1979: 454) and "avec un verbe normalement intransitif, mais qui peut être directement suivi d'un nom avec lequel il fait comme expression" (Mottin 1978: 19). Although it is true that many of the verb-noun compounds involve intransitive verbs, a number of the verbs in the verb-noun compounds listed in appendix A are transitive. The most heavily involved transitive verb is *noj* 'to eat', with five compounds. Transitive verbs that enter into one or two compounds include *faib* 'to divide', *laij* 'to plow', *muab* 'to grasp', *ncab* 'to stretch', *npuaj* 'to clap', *ntxuaj* 'to wave', *tshab/tshaj* 'to spread abroad', *txhib* 'to split', and *yoj* 'to wave'. Even *poob* 'to fall' in its metaphorical uses can be transitive, in which case it means 'to lose':

---

[13] Note the interesting asymmetry in this construction and in *hnoob-teg hnoob taw* above: one would expect the sandhi form of *taw* 'foot' as well (see section 2.4 on the heavier involvement of hands as opposed to feet).

46

poob-nyiag silver	lose money
poob-plhus cheek	lose face

Common to all verb-noun compounds, though, seems to be the fact that the noun involved is independent; that is, it is not a constituent of a noun phrase.[14]

A few examples of verb-noun compounds follow:

daj-ntseg yellow ear	yellow face (indicating physical problem)
kaj-ntug bright sky	morning
muaj-cag have nosebridge	to have a well-shaped (long) nose
(dab) noj-hlis spirit eat moon	an eclipse of the moon
qaij-ke lean trail	to lean to one side of the path (so that others may pass)
tshaj-xo spread message	to spread news

2.3.6   Minor Types

Although head-modifier is the dominant word order in Hmong, there are a few examples of modifier-head compounds that exhibit tone sandhi. Quite a few of these are with *qub* 'of old',

---

[14] I am grateful to James McCawley for suggesting that I consider this as the significant generalization concerning the verb-noun compounds.

which can precede the noun it modifies (Heimbach 1979: 265; Mottin 1978: 48):[15]

qub-chaws place	the old (original) place
qub-ke way	the old way
qub-teg qub taw hand foot	old (inherited) things
qub-zog village	the old village

A few other compounds were found that seem to exemplify the atypical modifier-head order:

dej-cog water treadmill	water-driven treadmill
hnoob-teg sun hand	hands of the sun (= sunrays)
noob-qes seed egg	testicles
tej-zaug other time	other times, occasions

A second minor syntactic type for which there are few examples of tone sandhi compounding is verb-verb, either in a coordinative relationship:

siab-qig high low	(to examine) high and low

---

[15] Other verbs that, as modifiers, can precede are *tuam* 'grand, great' (a Chinese loan), *me* 'small', *zoo* 'good' (Mottin 1978: 48) and *niag* 'great' (Heimbach 1979: 140).

or in a subordinative relationship:

leej-tuag willing come	willing to come
quaj-taug cry able	crybaby
qheb-tsha open bright	cleared up (of the sky)

2.3.7   Lack of Involvement of "Weak" Word Classes

Pronouns never trigger tone sandhi in a following word, despite the fact that many of them bear a sandhi trigger tone: *koj* 'you (singular)', *neb* 'you (dual)', *nej* 'you (plural)', *wb* 'we/us (dual)', *peb* 'we/us (plural)'. This serves conveniently to disambiguate the homophones *peb* 'three' (which almost always triggers tone change in a following classifier, see section 2.3.1) and *peb* 'we/us' in phrases such as:

peb-tug npua 3 clf pig	three pigs
peb tus npua we clf pig	our pig[16]

Classifiers, also a "weak" word class, have been said to be incapable of influencing a following word (Heimbach 1979: 446; Mottin 1978: 19). Although this is generally true, a number of exceptions, such as

ib lub-hlis 1 clf moon	1 month

have been found. Since this marginal involvement of classifier-noun phrases in the tone sandhi compounding process sheds light on the important topic of the nature of the Hmong classifier, I will defer discussion about it to section 4, where facts learned about dif-

---

16 Downer (1967: 594) also makes this observation.

ferent aspects of the Hmong language as a result of a study of White Hmong tone sandhi are presented.

2.4 Lexical Selectivity

An examination of appendix A, in which tone sandhi compounds are arranged by the first word of the compound, reveals typically one to three examples of compounds beginning with a particular word. This arrangement of the data would seem to indicate that tone sandhi compounding operates fairly shallowly through the lexicon, given the phonological and syntactic restrictions noted above and involves a large number of words. Through working with the data, however, I developed a feel for those words most likely to occur in a new compound. To try to substantiate this sense I had of the inequality among words with regard to their ability to enter into tone sandhi compounds, I arranged the compounds by the second word of each as well. The results for those words that were involved as the second member in a large number of compounds appear in appendix B. A combination of the information on high-frequency words in tone sandhi compounds drawn from both appendices appears in table 4. This table contains sixty words that were found in at least four compounds. Those that are especially well represented (fifteen or more compounds) are highlighted in capital letters.[17] The hyphens either before or after each word indicate whether the word appears as the left- or right-hand member of a compound (in most cases, this is predictable from the tone of the word). A number of nouns that bear the high falling (-j) tone can occur in either position and are marked with a hyphen on either side. For these nouns, the number of compounds attested has been broken into two parts: attestations as the left-hand member and ("+") attestations as the right-hand member. The last column indicates whether or not the word was included in Wang's 1979 comparative study and, for those included, the number of the reconstructed initial. It is significant that at least forty-six of these sixty words can be reconstructed for Proto-Hmongic (see section 3, where the historical development of the tone sandhi system is discussed).

---

[17] Since tone change after the numerals one through five and nine is so widespread (section 2.3.1), examples are not included in the data here.

These sixty words appear in well over three-quarters[18] of the tone sandhi compounds listed in appendix A. They are "core vocabulary" in the sense that they represent important natural items ('water', 'road', 'ditch', 'seed', 'rice', 'leaf', 'plain', 'tree', 'sky', 'flower', 'mountain', 'firewood', 'land', 'rock', 'ash', 'bamboo', 'forest'), or cultural items ('spirit', 'crossbow', 'paddy field', 'post', 'pig', 'cloth', 'silver', 'cow', *keng*, 'roof ridge', 'house', 'jacket', 'bed', 'garden', 'dragon'). Common verbs ('to have', 'to eat', 'to fall'; 'yellow', 'old', 'soft', 'dry', 'warm') are also included. Body parts included are 'mouth', 'ear', 'stomach', 'foot', and 'hand'. Certain prefix-like words that specify part, shape, or sex include 'cord', 'mouth', 'girl', 'leaf', 'middle', 'expanse (sky)', 'blob', 'behind', 'tube', 'gate', 'gourd', and 'boy'. The reciprocal comprises a class of its own (see section 2.3.2 above). Assuming that Wang's five hundred and ninety cognate sets represent important core vocabulary as well as simply the available vocabulary, it is significant to note that only fourteen of the above words are not included in his study.

Table 4: Words Appearing with High Frequency in White Hmong Tone Sandhi Compounds

dab-	spirit	5	W113
-daj	yellow	8	W116
-DEJ-	water	10 + 12	W110
hlab-	cord	5	W54
-hneev	crossbow	4	W48
-KEV	road	15	W94
kwj-	ditch	4	
-laus	old	11	W55
-liaj-	paddy field	2 + 6	W74
-mos	soft	8	W6
muaj-	to have	10	W6
-noj-	to eat	5 + 1	W49
noob-	seed	4	W59
-NCAUJ-	mouth	6 + 11	W90
ncej-	post	7	W90
nkauj-	girl	6	
-NPUA	pig	18	W7
-NPLEJ-	rice	5 + 10	W34
nplooj-	leaf	4	W34
-nqaij-	meat	4 + 3	W108
-nras	plain	4	W64

---

[18] 392 out of 494, or 79.35 per cent.

nruab-	middle	10	
ntaub-	cloth	4	W50
-ntoo	tree	12	W50
-NTUJ-	sky	7+10	W52
-ntsej-	ear	3+8	W27
-nyiaj-	silver	1+4	W87
-NYUJ-	cow	4+13	W87
-paj-	flower	9+2	W3
pob-	bump/blob	8	
poob-	to fall	7	W1
plab-	stomach	6	W28
QAB-	behind/under	18	W103
-qeej-	*keng*	1+8	W110
qub-	old	4	
-qhuav	dry	12	W104
-raj-	tube	1+3	W58
roob-	mountain	5	
rooj-	door/gate	7	W69
-ruv	roof ridge		
SIB-	(reciprocal)	22	W81
-siav	life	4	
-sov	warm	4	W81
suab-	sound	4	
taub-	gourd-like	9	W44
-taw	foot	6	W44
-taws	firewood	4	W46
teb-	land	4	W44
-TES	hand	20	W15
tib-	single	6	
tub-	son/boy	5	W44
-tsev	house	8	W22
-tsua	rock	8	
-tshauv	ash	4	W76
-tsho	jacket	4	
-txaj-	bed	1+7	
-vaj-	garden	2+4	W12
xyoob-	bamboo	4	
-zaj-	dragon	1+3	W67
-zoov	forest	8	W65

There are, however, interesting asymmetries in the list. *Tes* 'hand' enters into at least twenty compounds, whereas *taw* 'foot' enters into only six, as evidenced by the dictionaries. Of the six 'foot' compounds, my primary tutor accepts none. In a number of cases, this asymmetry does not seem to relate to the versatility and prominence of the hand over the foot, since the same trigger words yield sandhi compounds with *tes* (*pob-teg* 'wrist bone'; *taub-teg* 'fingertip'; *xib-teg* 'palm of the hand') but, for my tutor at least, not with *taw* (*pob taw* 'ankle bone'; *taub taw* 'toetip'; *xib taw* 'sole of the foot'). The particular tones involved do not seem to play a role either, since the change of mid level (-*ø*) to low level (-*s*) occurs quite commonly for my tutor with *npua* 'pig', *ntoo* 'tree', and *tsua* 'rock'.

Another interesting asymmetry is seen in the involvement of words referring to animals. *Npua* 'pig' with eighteen compounds and *nyuj* 'cow' with seventeen are heavily involved (see appendix B). On the other hand, no compounds found thus far involve *dev* 'dog' or *nees* 'horse'; only two have been found for *twm* 'water buffalo' and only three for *ntses* 'fish'. There is only one tone sandhi compound with *qaib* 'chicken' due to its tone (*npua* always, and *nyuj* most often are involved as the right-hand member of a compound, and high level (-*b*) tone words do not undergo change in this position). *Tshis* 'goat' does not participate in these compounds since -*s* changes to -*g* in the right-hand member, and there is a co-occurrence block between aspirated initials and the breathy (-*g*) tone (see section 2.2.2). Thus, we have *nqaij-npuas* 'pig meat' and *nqaij-nyug* 'cow meat', but *nqaij twm* 'buffalo meat' and *nqaij ntses* 'fish meat'. My tutor explained that the relative prominence of 'pig' and 'cow' in compounds had to do with their central role in everyday life and the time and effort expended in their care. Poultry, goats, pigs, buffalo, cattle, and horses constitute the chief domestic animals of the Hmong of highland Laos (Barney 1967: 284-285). The explanation for the involvement of 'pig' and 'cow' seems good, but still it does not explain the lack of involvement of *nees* 'horse' and *twm* 'water buffalo'. Similarly, *zaj* 'dragon' is involved in four tone sandhi compounds, but the culturally important *tsov* 'tiger', even more central a figure in Hmong folk tales, has not yet been found in one compound.

The only way to account for this selective involvement of certain lexical items in tone sandhi compounds over their semantically related cousins is to mark in the lexicon the fact that these words, namely the sixty reproduced above, or some subset thereof, are particularly powerful when it comes to inducing tone change and thereby creating a compound (if it is a -*b* or a -*j* word), or are particularly susceptible when it comes to being influenced by a preceding -*b* or -*j* word (if they bear the tones -*j*, -*s*, -*v*, or -*ø*). I think it possibly significant that no word with a low checked (-*m*) tone appears in the table of high-frequency words (which may be related to the limited involvement of *twm* 'water buffalo' mentioned above). This tone is the reflex of historical category D2, whose words can be shown to have once had a final *-p or *-t. It may be that the -*m* tone does not play as great a role in tone sandhi compounding due to its special development from checked syllables or because of its possible role as a "loan tone" for borrowed words (see section 2.2.3 above), or both.

Although a number of semantic relationships hold between the members of a tone sandhi compound, it is important to describe some of the typical relationships in order to come to an understanding of the above high-frequency words in a different way. These are specialized relationships that can be considered subordinate to the general syntactic relationship of noun-modifier described in section 2.3.3. Although it still may be desirable to analyze the syntactic relationship between the two members of the compound as noun-modifier in the following categories of specialized relationships, semantically the first member of these compounds specifies and delimits the broader category represented by the second member.

2.4.1   Part-Whole

In the following compounds, if the left-hand member is "A" and the right-hand member is "B," each can be glossed as 'the A of the B'. Thus, *nplooj-ntoos* can be understood as 'the leaf of the tree' (that part of the tree), or as 'tree leaves' (as opposed to rice leaves). This group includes spatially delimiting words also: *nrab/nruab* 'in the middle of' and *qab* 'on the underside of; at the base of; on the downhill side of'. The following examples are representative:

ncej-cog	treadmill post[19]
post treadmill	
ncauj-ke	entrance to the road
mouth road	

---

[19] Sources for the tone sandhi compounds in this and the following four sections will be found in appendix A.

nruab-ntug middle sky	in the heavens
qab-pag bottom lake	the bottom of the lake
qib-hnee trigger crossbow	the trigger of the crossbow
rooj-ntxas gate grave	the opening of the grave
taub-qeeg gourd *keng*	the body of the *keng*

2.4.2   Object-Material

Another type of tone sandhi compound in which the left-hand member delimits the right-hand member is the object-material type. As with the part-whole compounds, the relationship between the two members can be understood in one of two ways. *Khawb-hlaus* can be understood as 'a link of iron', where 'link' serves as a unit of measure of an infinite quantity of iron, or as 'an iron link' (as opposed to a silver link).

hleb-ntoos coffin tree	wood coffin
khawb-hlaus link iron	iron link
khawb-nyiag link silver	silver chain
npauj-nyiag jewelry silver	silver jewelry
nqaj-hlaus bar iron	iron bar

55

ntaub-pag cloth cotton	cotton material
roj-a fat earth	fat of the earth (= oil)
roj-npuas fat pig	pig fat
roj-nyug fat cow	cow fat
voj-hluas circle rope	circle made of rope (= lasso)
voj-teg circle hand	circle made with the two hands

2.4.3 Shape-Object

What I consider "shape prefixes" in these compounds are actually nouns, but semantically they seem to fall somewhere between classifiers, such as *lub* 'round, bulky object, *txoj* 'long object (often abstract)', and *tus* 'long, slender object (shorter than *txoj*)' on the one hand and the semantically meatier nouns with which they are paired on the other. They are not classifiers because they occur with classifiers, and, secondarily, because classifiers generally do not trigger tone sandhi (but see sections 2.3.7 and 4.2). They serve to describe what facet of a multifaceted object is under consideration. For example, *tes* 'hand' is probably better understood as 'the protuberance at the end of the forearm' because it includes a body part that we do not include in our notion of 'hand', namely the wrist. Thus, we have *dab-teg* 'wrist' and *pob-teg* 'wrist bone' as well as *taub-teg* 'fingertip' (from *dab* 'narrowing', *pob* 'round object', and *taub* 'gourd-shaped object'). Similarly, for *ntsej* 'ear' we have *nplooj-ntseg* 'the outer ear' (leaf-shaped) and *taub-ntseg* 'the ear-lobe' (gourd-shaped). A few more examples, arranged by shape prefix, appear below:

pob 'round object'

pob-a	clod of earth
earth	
pob-ntoos	tree stump
tree	
pob-ntseg	ear (the whole thing)
ear	
pob-tsuas	rock mass
rock	

taub 'gourd-shaped'

txiv taub-ntoos	papaya
fruit tree	
taub-nkawg	mass of hornets
hornet	(either swarm or nest)

tswb 'bell-shaped'

tswb-tsaig	bell jaw (= jowls)
jaw	

txoj 'long'[20]

txoj-hmoo	fortune (regarded as a length)
luck	
txoj-ke	road (regarded as a length)
road	
txoj-sia	life (regarded as a length)
life	

2.4.4   Sex/Agent Designators

Tub 'son, boy; male', *nkauj* 'girl', and *poj* 'woman' are involved in tone sandhi compounds as agentive prefixes or simply as sex designators. *Tub* 'son' is normally matched with *ntxhais* 'daughter', which cannot effect tone change. *Poj* 'woman' is matched with *txiv* 'man, father', which also is powerless to effect tone change. Thus we do not have parallel tone sandhi compounds according to sex,

---

[20] *Txoj* has been labeled a classifier, but its behavior in these compounds is much more noun-like. See section 4.2.

with the exception of *tub-qhe* 'male servant'/*nkauj-qhe* 'female servant':

Male	**Female**
tub-nkeeg	*nkauj-npuas*
boy lethargic	girl pig
a lazy person	female pig
tub-ntsog	*nkauj-qhe*
boy ?	girl servant
an orphan	female servant
tub-qhe	*nkauj-zag*
boy servant	girl dragon
male servant	female dragon
tub-txawg	
boy able	
an able person	
	poj-cuag
	woman (kin)
	mother of child's spouse
	poj-sua
	woman foreign
	foreign woman

2.4.5   Body Part Designator

Although it has been found in only one tone sandhi compound so far, the prefix *caj*, with no independent meaning (*caj dab* 'the neck', *caj tw* 'buttocks', *caj npab* 'the upper arm'), is the clearest example of a prefix-triggering tone sandhi. That one compound is *caj-pas* 'wind pipe' from *pa* 'breath'.

2.5   Compounding and Semantic or Syntactic Shift

In the majority of cases, if tone sandhi compounding is optional, it either results in no change in meaning or in only a stylistic change, the compound being perceived as "smoother," "gentler," or "more poetic" than the uncompounded collocation (see section 2.3.4). In a few interesting cases, either meaning or meaning and structure seem to be changed when the tone is changed. These five cases are discussed in some detail below:

(1) *Zaub* 'vegetable' + *ntsim* 'peppery'.

Both Bertrais-Charrier and Heimbach record *zaub-ntsig* as the name for a particular plant: Bertrais-Charrier (*zaub*) simply writes 'espèce de legumes' and Heimbach (1979: 200) describes it as 'a kind of pickled peppery vegetable prepared from the tops of mustard greens'. This is to be contrasted with the following sentence from the same entry in Heimbach:

> *Zaub ntsim ntsim li kuv tsis noj*
> vegetable peppery this way I not eat
> I don't eat peppery vegetables.

Here the subject is not a particular peppery dish but rather those vegetables of which a peppery flavor is being predicated. The semantic contrast is particular versus general, the syntactic contrast is noun-modifier versus subject-predicate.

(2) *Kub* 'horn' + *twm* 'water buffalo'.

Both Bertrais-Charrier (*twm*) and Downer (1967: 594) record a contrast in meaning between the compounded and uncompounded collocations of the above two words. *Kub twm* is a water buffalo's horn still attached to the buffalo, whereas *kub-twg* is the horn used as 'utensil', or 'coupée, devenue matière première', notably a musical horn used in funeral services or in the hunt (Bertrais-Charrier *kub*).[21] This semantic shift from the neutral designation of one of the body parts of the buffalo to the particularized, independent role it plays once separated from the body is analogous to the semantic shift of *zaub ntsim* (category of plant) to *zaub-ntsig* (a specific plant).

---

[21] Compare the same distinction marked in the opposite way with regard to animal legs: *ceg* (the sandhi form historically, now promoted to base form in White Hmong) 'leg; branch' versus *ces* (with the historical tone) 'leg separated from the body' (section 4.1).

There are three sources that do not support the analysis of 'buffalo horn' presented above, however. My primary tutor accepts only *kub twm*. In Vwj et al. (1983: 31), there are two sentences that refer to detached animal horns, neither of which shows compounding:

> *Kuam tau ib tug kub kauv.*
> Kuam get 1 clf horn deer
> Kuam got a deer horn.

> *Peb tus kuam yog kub twm.*
> we clf divining be horn buffalo
>   horn
> Our divining horns are buffalo horns.

Heimbach (1979: 450) cites *kub-twg* but notes that "this may just be poetic."

(3) *Poob* 'to fall' + *dej* 'water'.

Poob dej 'to fall into water' has been altered through compounding and semantic extension to *poob-deg* 'to drown' according to two of my tutors, although *poob-deg* can also simply mean 'to fall into water' (Heimbach [1979: 447]; Bertrais-Charrier *poob*). To indicate that 'to drown' is indeed meant, *tuag* 'to die; dead' may be added: *poob-deg tuag* 'to fall into water to death', or in other words, 'to drown' (Bertrais-Charrier *dej*). That *poob-deg* alone can mean 'to drown' is evident from the following sentence taken from Vwj et al. (1983: 44):

> *Tus neeg poob-deg lawv muab faus lawm.*
> clf person drown they take bury perf.
> As for the drowned person, they took (him) and buried (him).

This is an action they would presumably not have taken unless the person were also *tuag* 'dead'.

(4) *Muaj* 'to have' + *nyiaj* 'silver' / *txiaj* 'money'.

Downer (1967: 594) reports that tone sandhi signals a meaning difference in the following two sentences:

> *Nws muaj-txiag heev.*
> 3ps rich very
> S/he is very rich.

> *Kuv tsis muaj txiaj li.*
> I not have money at all
> I have no money at all.

The same difference between 'having money' (no tone sandhi compounding) and 'being rich' (tone sandhi compounding with semantic extension) is recorded for the collocation with *nyiaj* by Bertrais-Charrier:

> *Koj puas muaj nyiaj?*
> 2ps Q have money
> As-tu de l'argent? (B *muaj*)

> *muaj-nyiag*
> être riche (B *muaj*)

> *neeg muaj-txiag*
> personne riche (B *txiaj*)

The distinction is a fine one, however, and Heimbach cites

> *muaj muaj nyiaj*
> wealthy (H 219)

> *muaj muaj txiaj*
> wealthy (H 380)

The extension of meaning here is due to the reduplication of the verb.

(5) *Dej* 'water' + *sov* 'warm'/*txias* 'cold'.

Although Downer (1967: 593) cites both the compounded and uncompounded forms of 'warm water' and 'cold water', saying that there is "no perceptible difference in meaning," Mottin (1978: 19) makes a distinction between the two:

dej sov   l'eau est chaude

dej-so   de l'eau chaude

This distinction is the same as the one noted above for *zaub ntsim* 'the vegetables are peppery' and *zaub-ntsig* '(a particular) peppery vegetable': without tone sandhi compounding, warmth is predicated of the water; with tone sandhi compounding, warmth is attributed to the water. Bertrais-Charrier (*sov*), however, did not find this distinction and glosses both *dej sov* and *dej-so* as 'l'eau chaude'. To put this distinction on an even more tenuous footing, Heimbach (1979: 452, 381, 449) cites *dej sov* 'warm water' (no compounding), but he cites *dej-txiag* 'cold water' (compounding).

As seen in the above five examples, there is plentiful evidence that these semantic and syntactic distinctions are neither widely nor deeply felt. We may draw the conclusion that tone sandhi has the potential to encode distinctions of this type but that it is not now being used to do so in a systematic way. That it does so in a few intriguing instances, may suggest a possible line of development for this system, which was probably phonetically motivated to begin with (see section 3.3).

3   Explanations for the White Hmong Tone Sandhi System

3.1   Downer 1967

In his paper "Tone-Change and Tone-Shift in White Miao," G. B. Downer outlines a number of important tonal phenomena in White Hmong and proposes historical explanations for them. About White Hmong tone sandhi (one variety of "tone-shift," his term for syntagmatic tone change, as opposed to "tone-change," paradigmatic change that affects the basic inventory of tones), Downer (1967: 593-594) emphasizes the numerous exceptions to the phonological and syntactic "rules" described in section 2 of this chapter. He also shows how the same historical tone categories are involved in three of the five dialects he examines (p. 595):

Magpie [XUYONG]			XIANJIN			White Hmong		
A2	>	C2	A2	>	C2	A2	>	C2
B2	>	C2	B2	>	C2	B2	>	C2
—			D2	>	C2	D2	>	C2
B1	>	C1	B1	>	C1	B1	>	C1
—			C1	>	D1	C1	>	D1

On this striking correspondence of tone categories involved, despite the differences in the phonetic values of the reflexes in each dialect, and its significance for White Hmong, Downer (1967: 594, 595) writes as follows:

> Other West Miao dialects...possess much more thoroughgoing tone-sandhi systems than White Miao, which operate throughout the sentence. Such systems are suggested by the examples given of tone-sandhi in the Xianjin dialect, and are well documented for Magpie Miao. In the latter dialect, it appears that following high falling and low falling tones (the Magpie Miao reflexes of Proto-West-Miao tones [A1] and [A2]) certain tone-shifts occur regardless of the constructions involved.

> ...taking into account the fact that in nearly every way Magpie Miao and the Xianjin dialect are closer to each other than to WM, it may eventually be possible to demonstrate that the Xianjin sandhi system may be projected in its entirety back to Proto-West-Miao, although the complications of the Weining sandhi system, when it is fully described, may necessitate some modifications.[22]

> A plausible historical hypothesis that postulates some such sandhi system for Proto-West-Miao and explains both the thoroughgoing sandhi found in Magpie and Xianjin dialects as well as its limited occurrence in WM might be that WM has gone through three stages: first, a stage in which sandhi proceeded right through the sentence; second, a stage in which tone-sandhi is

---

[22] See Wang and Wang (1984) on the Weining (SHIMEN) tone sandhi system.

largely restricted to certain constructions; and lastly, the present stage of WM, in which tone-sandhi is further restricted to certain collocations within these constructions, and in which many of the hitherto modified items are apparently being gradually replaced by the basic tones of those items.

Downer's belief that the XIANJIN system "may be projected in its entirety back to Proto-West-Miao" is supported by data drawn from Wang (1979) concerning the tone sandhi systems of other West Hmongic (Sichuan-Guizhou-Yunnan fangyan) dialects.[23] The data from both sources are presented in table 5.

---

[23] In Institute (1962: 5) it is mentioned that most types of Hmong have tone sandhi, with the major exception of East Hmongic and the minor exception of the Eastern sub-fangyan of West Hmongic. As was noted in a footnote in section 2.2, tone sandhi in North Hmongic is of an entirely different type.

Table 5
West Hmongic Tone Sandhi Systems

Tone changes after an A-tone reflex	West Hmongic Dialects							
	White	Green	XUYONG (Ruey and Kuan)	XIANJIN (Wang #3)	SHIMEN (Wang #4)	QINGYANG (Wang #5)	GAOPO (Wang #6)	ZONGDI (Wang #7)
A2 > C2	X	X	X	X		X	X	X
B2 > C2	X	X	X	X		X	X	X
D2 > C2	X	X	X	X				
B1 > C1	X	X	X	X	X			X
C1 > D1	X	X	X	X	X			X
	environment: A1- or A2- _____			environment: A1- _____				

Downer's discovery that the historical category of the tone determines the Proto-West-Hmongic tone sandhi system, and his contention that the system is dying out in White Hmong, explain two important things: (1) the difficulty of describing the system in purely phonetic terms (see section 3.2 below), and (2) the sporadic occurrence of tone sandhi compounding in the language. The variation encountered in the source books, among speakers, across styles and locations can be tolerated by grammar writers who understand that they are dealing with the relic of a system[24] and, therefore, feel no need to attempt to account for every exception to the rules that govern the cases of compounding that do exist. Tone sandhi compounding can be likened to the English strong-verb system, the patterns of which can also be discerned, but which cannot be understood as part of the English verbal system without an historical perspective. Perhaps more importantly, an understanding of the English strong-verb paradigms will not allow a non-native speaker to predict whether or not any given verb will follow one of them as opposed to the weak-verb paradigm, in exactly the same way that an understanding of the Hmong tone sandhi system will not allow a non-native to predict whether or not, given the right conditions, tone sandhi compounding will occur.

The following is the standard synchronic description of White/Green Hmong tone sandhi (Heimbach 1979: 446; Mottin 1979: 18; Lyman 1974: 39):

$$
\left.
\begin{array}{l}
\text{-}j \ (52) \\
\text{-}s \ (22) \\
\text{-}m \ (21?)
\end{array}
\right\} \longrightarrow \text{-}g \ (42)
\quad
\left|
\begin{array}{l}
\left\{ \begin{array}{l} \text{-}b \ (55) \\ \text{-}j \ (52) \end{array} \right\} \quad \underline{\hspace{2cm}} \\
\\
\end{array}
\right.
$$

$$
\begin{array}{l}
\text{-}v \ (24) \longrightarrow \text{-}ø \ (33) \\
\text{-}ø \ (33) \longrightarrow \text{-}s \ (22)
\end{array}
\qquad \text{i-v}
$$

(where "i-v" outlines the eligible syntactic relationships). One inadequacy of this synchronic description is that it does not reveal the fact that there has been a tonal merger and there are, conse-

---

[24] One that may in time disappear altogether, see Downer (1967: 595-596), quoted in part above, on the preservation of the base form enabling such a system loss, and Lyman (1974: 40) on the "anti-sandhi" feeling of some status-conscious Green Hmong speakers.

quently, two -s tones, only one of which is capable of undergoing tone change (section 2.2.1). The following description, in which historical tone categories are substituted for tone values, makes this fact clear:

$$
\begin{array}{l}
\textit{-j} \quad (A1) \\
\textit{-s} \quad (B2) \qquad \longrightarrow \qquad \textit{-g} \quad (C2) \\
\textit{-m} \quad (D2)
\end{array}
\left/
\begin{array}{l}
\left\{ \begin{array}{l} \textit{-b} \\ \textit{-j} \end{array} \right\} \begin{array}{l} (A1) \\ (A2) \end{array} \quad \underline{\phantom{i\text{-}v}} \\[2mm]
\qquad \qquad \qquad \text{i-v}
\end{array}
\right.
$$

$$
\begin{array}{l}
\textit{-v} \quad (B1) \qquad \longrightarrow \qquad \textit{-ø} \quad (C1) \\
\textit{-ø} \quad (C1) \qquad \longrightarrow \qquad \textit{-s} \quad (D1)
\end{array}
$$

This configuration allows us to be more economical and more enlightening about the following points as well:

(1) The two descendants of but one historical tone—A—constitute the trigger mechanism.

(2) The prosodies of the tones involved (whether derived from a *voiceless or *voiced initial consonant) are a factor. Type 1 tones must change into type 1 tones, and type 2 tones must change into a type 2 tone.

(3) The C tone seems to be crucially involved as a sandhi (or neutral) tone. It plays this role in four of the five changes.

Future work with more data, and at a consequently greater time depth, will reveal what significance these observations may have on our ability to explain the evolution of the Proto-Hmong-Mien C tone and the proper dating of this particular tone sandhi system.

3.2 Sprigg 1975

R. K. Sprigg discusses the data on White Hmong tone sandhi presented in Downer in an article entitled "The Inefficiency of 'Tone Change' in Sino-Tibetan Descriptive Linguistics." He is interested in presenting a purely synchronic account of White Hmong tone sandhi and, of all the information presented by Downer, uses only the information about the phonetic values of the White Hmong tones and the phonetic conditioning of the sandhi changes in White Hmong. Rather than say that one tone "changes into" another, Sprigg chooses to say that each (abstract) tone may have more than one phonetic realization, that the occurrence of a particular realization is determined by the phonetic context, and that it is predictable by rule.

> I would claim for my 'phonetic-overlapping' type of analysis that it has the advantage of making a single tone classification possible for each lexical item, thereby making the distinction between 'basic tones' and 'modified tones' or 'sandhi tones' unnecessary. The price to be paid for it I believe to be modest: familiarizing oneself with two phonetic exponents instead of one for certain tones [-j, -v, -s, -ø, -m] and accepting some degree of overlapping in the phonetic exponency of, in this White Miao example at least, tones [-j, -s, -m] with each other and with tone [-g], and, though not under comparable conditions, of tone [-v] with tone [-ø] and of tone [-s] with tone [-ø]. Consequently, a single tone classification will stand, by my analysis, for each lexical item (p. 177).

> I see the variation...as a problem of pitch harmony and exponent (or realization) harmony, operating at the phonetic level, without any need to go to such drastic lengths as stating the variation as change of tone, which is, of course, a phonological change, reflecting a significant structural difference (p. 175).

> ...it is tones [-j, -v, -s, -ø, and -m] that I wish to state as having alternative pitch exponents according as these five tones harmonize, in junction, with the preceding high-register pitch (level or falling, 55 or 51) of tones [-b] and [-j]...(p. 175).

I believe that Sprigg's preference for this kind of analysis stems from his familiarity with languages with much more restricted tone inventories, where a low tone in context may become "non-low" and, therefore, much closer in phonetic value to a lexically distinctive high tone also occurring in the system. In a system with few tones, each tone has accordingly more "tone space" and an accordingly greater amount of variation can be tolerated. If the neutralized low and high tone are similar (or the same) it may be said to be an accidental case of "phonetic overlapping." But to describe the complex system of paradigmatic replacement of the reflex of one tone category by another, as so clearly elucidated by Downer, in a language of a family characterized by languages and dialects with large tone inventories as a matter of "pitch harmony," simply because the trigger tones both happen to be high, seems to deliberately ignore certain facts in order to advance a particular theoretical position.

The important question is how well his idea of "pitch harmony" works for White Hmong tone sandhi, and whether it is a simpler analysis, as he claims. I have reproduced his chart (1975: 176) of the phonetic exponents of the five tones that are borne by the right-hand members of tone sandhi compounds in table 6 below.[25] "High word" refers to a disyllabic word (tone sandhi compound) that begins, as we have seen, with a -b (high level) or -j (high falling) tone (and corresponds to the sandhi tone); "low word" refers to two syllables adjacent to each other, the first of which begins with one of the other tones of the inventory (and corresponds to the base tone).

---

[25] The chart is reproduced exactly as it appears in Sprigg's article, with the addition of the RPA tone letter equivalents to the tone numbers and values given, which appear in square brackets.

Table 6
Sprigg's Synchronic Account of White Hmong Tone Sandhi

Tone	Phonetic exponents			Pitch figure	
	'high word' (mid)	'low word'	common		
2 [-j]	mid	high	falling	31 [-g]	51 [-j]
3 [-v]	level	rising	mid	33 [-ø]	35 [-v]
4 [-s]	mid, falling	low, level	—	31 [-g]	11 [-s]
5 [-ø]	low	mid	level	11 [-s]	33 [-ø]
7 [-m]	mid	lower-mid	falling	31 [-g]	21 [-m]

Is it somehow harmonious for the pitches of tones to change in the following ways?

Tone 2   High + High > High - Mid
(lst syllable depresses 2nd)

Tone 3   High + Rising > High - Level
(lst syllable levels 2nd)

Tone 4   High + Low > High - Mid Falling
(lst syllable raises and contorts 2nd)

Tone 5   High + Mid > High - Low
(lst syllable depresses 2nd)

Tone 7   High + Lower Mid > High - Mid
(lst syllable raises 2nd)

In some cases a "high" tone raises and in some cases a "high" tone lowers the tone of a following word. Such an analysis has nothing to do with our understanding of "harmony" as exemplified by tone harmony phenomena as in downstep in African languages or by vowel harmony phenomena, for example, that of reciprocal and verb in GAOPO Hmong (section 2.3.2). There are many more problems with Sprigg's analysis as well:

(1) The fact that the reflexes of tone category A1 and A2 are high in pitch (at the outset) in White Hmong may be accidental. A glance at the chart of the phonetic values for West Hmongic tone categories given in section 3.3 below shows, for category A1, values of 53, 43, 55, 24, and 32. These A1 reflexes trigger tone sandhi in their respective dialects as well. An analysis that fails to account for the obviously related systems of near neighbors is not as good as one that does.

(2) The -b tone (55) and the -j tone (52) do not constitute a "high" class when we consider the endpoints of the two tones. It is this endpoint pitch, decidedly low in the case of -j, which should be expected to influence the pitch of the following syllable in a purely phonetic perturbation.

(3) Downer (1967: 593) writes "...any attempt to treat this process of tone-shift as an automatically occurrent feature of present-day WM will be defeated by the overwhelming number of

exceptions turning up, far outnumbering the cases of tone-shift." Sprigg simply ignores the chief characteristic of tone sandhi in White Hmong: it is sporadic, inconsistent, and idiosyncratic. This fact is elaborated at length in Downer's article and is at the heart of his argument about the nature of such cyclically rising and falling systems in the histories of Asian languages. Sprigg makes no mention of these exceptions to his system of "pitch harmony," despite the fact that Downer's article was the only source he used for his White Hmong data.

(4) It makes sense to retain the distinction between "basic tones" and "sandhi tones" since the sandhi tones represent a neutralization of the number of contrasts embodied in the basic tone inventory. In White Hmong there are seven basic tones (two of which never undergo tone sandhi), but only three sandhi tones.

(5) It also makes sense to say that one tone "changes into" another when it can be proved through comparative study, as Downer has done, that discrete tonal categories and their discrete reflexes are involved as counters in the same way in a number of different dialects, sometimes as basic tones and sometimes as sandhi tones. Although probably originally due to phonetic perturbation (see section 3.3 below), there is no denying the role of these discrete categories at some intermediate stage of West Hmongic.

This is not a system that can be reconstructed all the way back to Proto-Hmongic, however. Meng Chaoji has shown that in MEIZHU and LONGMO Bunu sandhi tones developed out of the phonetic matter of tones A1, A2, B1, and, in LONGMO B2 (Mao, Meng, and Zheng 1982; Meng 1983). The sandhi tones are in contour identical to the basic tones from which they arose, differing only in being one step higher than the corresponding basic tones. The sandhi tones do not correspond to any of the basic tones of the language. The triggering environment is the presence of a preceding word with a category A1 or A2 tone, as in the other West Hmongic dialects. "Pitch harmony" can be used to explain these Bunu dialects, but it cannot be used for White Hmong or for the dialects closely related to White Hmong.

3.3   Benedict 1985

Following a presentation I made on the topic of White Hmong tone sandhi at the Southeast Asian Studies Summer Institute Conference in Ann Arbor, Michigan, August 1985, Paul Benedict, in discussion, gave me an alternate explanation for the development of the system. I have reproduced his explanation here exactly as it was given to me but added the following caveat: this theory concerns the distant past, and many difficult questions, such as the role of stress in a tone language, are not addressed.

Benedict believes that the Proto-West-Hmongic tone sandhi system developed out of a "transphonologization of tonal close-juncture phrase" wherein initial stress on the two-word phrase was realized as high initial pitch that fell throughout the phrase. The triggering mechanism was not only a high pitch on the initial word, but a lower pitch on the second word. Coupled with this analysis of the prosodic structure of Proto-West-Hmongic compounds is Benedict's reconstruction of the Proto-Hmong-Mien tonal shapes:[26]

**A:	falling[27]
**B:	rising
**C:	mid level

Benedict does not reconstruct the D tone at this stage since it corresponds to syllables that ended in a stop consonant in Proto-Hmong-Mien. He considers the early checked syllables "tonally undifferentiated" (personal communication). When the general bipartition of these tones took place upon loss of contrastive voicing in the initial consonants, high and low allotones of the Proto-Hmong-Mien tones became distinctive:

**A1:	high falling
**A2:	low falling
**B1:	high rising
**B2:	low rising
**C1:	high level
**C2:	low level

---

[26] These are the same as Benedict's reconstructed tonal shapes for Old Chinese (c. 500 B.C.).

[27] Two stars are used to represent Proto-Hmong-Mien in this section; one star is used to indicate Proto-Hmongic.

Upon loss of the final consonants in Proto-Hmongic, the old checked syllables developed distinctive tones, also with a high-low bipartition based on the feature of voicing in the initial:

*D1: high level (+ ?)
*D2: low level (+ ?)

Benedict feels that White Hmong is remarkable in its conservation, in large part, of these original tonal values:

A1: high level (with a raised ending, as in the Cantonese A1 reflex)
A2: *high falling*
B1: *mid rising*
B2: low level (with a lowered ending)
C1: *mid level*
C2: mid falling (with whisper, a relic of the original voiced initial, < *11)
D1: low level (< *55? ; low level due to merger with B2)
D2: low falling, checked

The White Hmong tone sandhi process (compound formation process) originated as follows (bear in mind that tone change occurred only if the second word was lower in pitch in this hypothesis):

A1: High + 55 (-*b*)   >   no change
                                    (2nd word high)
A2: High + 52 (-*j*)   >   *11 (C2) > 42 (-*g*)
B1: High + 24 (-*v*)   >   33 (C1) (-*ø*)
B2: High + 22 (-*s*)   >   *11 (C2) > 42 (-*g*)
C1: High + 33 (-*ø*)   >   22 (D1) (-*s*)
C2: High + *11 (> 42-*g*)   >   no change
                                    (2nd word
                                    maximally low)
D1: High + *55? (> 22 -*s*)   >   no change
                                    (2nd word high)
D2: High + 21? (-*m*)   >   *11 (C2) > 42 (-*m*)

Benedict's analysis explains a number of things; most importantly, it provides a plausible, original phonetic motivation for a system that seems highly unmotivated in the present day. Furthermore,

(1) It explains why tones -*b*, -*g*, and -*s* (< D1) do not change.

(2) If the reconstructed shape of C is accepted and the theory of an original falling contour across the phrase is accepted, it explains the fact that four out of the five changes are changes to the C tone.

3) It supports my hypothesis that the one sandhi change that does not move toward C, C1 > D1, came later; according to Benedict's scheme above, tone C1 moves to the D1 reflex after D1 has merged with B2. That is, C1 (33) does not change to *55?, Benedict's value for the D1 tone originally, but to 22, the value of D1 following the B2-D1 merger. This cannot be determined by examination of the White Hmong data alone, of course; but in neighboring dialects where B2 and D1 are distinct, it is clear that C1 > D1.

There are, however, a number of problems, too:

(1) Although an inspection of the phonetic values of the tones of the dialects of West Hmongic (given below) does not invalidate Benedict's reconstructed tone shapes (**A falling, **B rising, **C mid level) in what way can it be said to support it, as opposed to another plausible reconstruction?[28]

	**A Falling		**B Rising		**C Mid Level	
	1	2	1	2	1	2
White	55	52	24	22	33	42
Green	55	52	24	42	33	42
XUYONG	53	21	51	11	55	33
XIANJIN	43	31	55	21	44	13
SHIMEN	55	35	55	33/11	33	53/31
QINGYAN	55	54	13	32	43	21/21
GAOPO	24	55	13	31	43	22
ZONGDI	32/22	53	42/232	11	55/35	33/13

---

[28] Benedict has recently explained to me that he started with good evidence (from Chinese) that B was originally rising and projected a falling/rising two-tone system from it on the basis of simplicity and maximal differentiation (personal correspondence).

(2) Assuming that this system developed after the loss of the initial voicing contrast in most dialects and the consequent bipartition of tones, why could C1 not have changed to C2 (33 > *11), too? Why is there a strict division of possible changes according to the feature of voicing in the Proto-Hmongic initial (type 1 > type 1; type 2 > type 2)?

(3) According to this theory, why did D2 change? It was originally *11?, maximally low. This was what was supposed to have kept C2 (*11) from changing.

(4) On the basis of the data presented in Li, Ch'en, and Ch'en (1959) and Wang (1979), I had supposed that the merger of tones B2 and D1 went the opposite way, namely, that 22 reflects the original value of D1 rather than B2. This is because in many Hmongic dialects both B2 and C2 (and, to a lesser extent, A2 and D2) are characterized by what Chinese linguists analyze as "voiced aspiration" or by what Western linguists analyze as "breathy voice" (which both would derive, in this case, from the original voiced character of the initial). Since the White Hmong B2/D1 tone is low level, clear voice, I had thought that it was more likely to have reflected an original voiceless initial, and that the original breathy voiced B2 value had been subsumed.

3.4   Conclusions

From the many problems a purely synchronic account of White Hmong tone sandhi presents, such as the ones mentioned in section 3.2 above, I would conclude that a description of tone sandhi as a system-relic is the only sensible and revealing kind of description possible. Even in a synchronic grammar, historical relics can best be described in terms of history. Both Downer and Benedict do that, and I find their explanations nicely complementary. Downer is describing the system at a more recent time (at a stage when the Sichuan-Guizhou-Yunnan subfangyan and the Northeast Yunnan sub-fangyan had not yet divided). He can prove his assertions about the tone categories involved and can support his ideas about the extent of the erosion of the system in White Hmong on the basis of comparative evidence. Benedict, typically, is comfortable speculating about an earlier state of affairs (Proto-West-Hmongic, Proto-Hmongic, and Proto-Hmong-Mien). Although his ideas cannot be proven directly, he has a plausible theory about the phonetic basis of the system.

My study of White Hmong tone sandhi has led to an under-standing of two aspects of the language that are related to, but are not central, to an understanding of the tone sandhi process itself. The first is directly derivative: the process whereby a sandhi tone form of a word can be promoted to base form status when it becomes disassociated from the A-tone trigger that gave rise to it. This pro-cess accounts for many of the words in White Hmong that have tones different from their cognates in other dialects. The second issue is the nature of the White Hmong classifier as revealed through the role it plays in tone sandhi compounds.

4.1   Sandhi Form Promotion[29]

Wang Fushi was able to account for many of the anomalous tones in his data on 590 cognates in nine Hmongic dialects by identi-fying them as promoted sandhi forms. Information about the tone sandhi systems of the dialects included in his study was presented in section 3.1 above. In addition, Wang's extensive knowledge of the dialect of SHIMEN made him more aware of the process of sandhi form promotion. In SHIMEN, A-tone prefixes are far more common than in White Hmong, so that it is possible to see the intermediate step more often:

A-tone word + sandhi-susceptible word

A-tone trigger + sandhi tone word

(A-tone trigger) sandhi form promoted to base form

All of the tonally anomalous White Hmong words that fit into one of the cognate sets presented by Wang appear in table 7. The histories of these individual words often reveal interesting semantic shifts and splits.

---

[29] As a psychiatrist, Paul Benedict prefers the term "promoted" to a term I used to use interchangably with it, "stranded," to describe these sandhi tone turned base tone forms, since it reflects a more positive mental attitude. In the interests of maintaining a positive attitude toward the inevitable and human process of language change, I have decided to adopt his preferred term exclusively.

Table 7
Promoted Tone Sandhi Forms in White Hmong[30]

1. *cag* 'root' /84 *dʐ- /   C2   <   A2

                                    A2: 12 4   8 9

                                    C2:   3 5 6 7

In White Hmong, both the historical *caj* (A2) and the sandhi *cag* (C2) occur. Although *cag* is the basic word for 'root' now, my tutor reports that *cag* is used for inedible roots, like tree roots, whereas *caj* is reserved for edible roots, like carrots. This split has not been noted in the dictionaries.

2. *ceg* 'leg' /84 *dʐ- /   C2   <   B2

                                    B2: 12   5 6 7 8 9

                                    C2:   3 4

In White Hmong, both the historical *ces* (B2) and the sandhi *ceg* (C2) occur. Although *ceg* is now the basic word for 'leg, limb, branch', *ces* persists, according to my tutor,

---

[30] In the discussions of the White Hmong words below, information will be presented in the following form:

(1) the White Hmong form, with gloss;

(2) the number (1-121) and form of the reconstructed initial from Wang;

(3) the tone category of the White Hmong word and the reconstructed tone for the word (for example, "C2 < A2," where C2 is the White Hmong promoted sandhi tone and A2 is the original Proto-Hmongic tone);

(4) the numbers of the dialects in Wang (1-9) that have the reconstructed tone and the sandhi tone respectively:

    1 YANGHAO (East Hmongic)

    2 JIWEI (North Hmongic)

    3 XIANJIN (West Hmongic)

    4 SHIMEN (West Hmongic)

    5 QINGYAN (West Hmongic)

    6 GAOPO (West Hmongic)

    7 ZONGDI(West Hmongic)

    8 FUYUAN (West Hmongic)

    9 FENGXIANG (West Hmongic);

(5) comments.

with the specialized meaning 'animal leg separated from the body' (compare English 'a lamb's leg' as opposed to 'a leg of lamb').

3. *dos* 'thumb to middle finger' (measure word) /113 *qɬ- /

D1	<	C1	
		C1:	3456789

Possibly *ib* 'one' was the trigger word in this case.

4. *hau* 'head' /11 *ẉ- /

C1	<	B1	
		B1:	12 56 89
		C1:	34 7

The probable trigger for this form is still evident in White Hmong: *taub-hau* 'gourd-head' (= 'head'). *Hau* now occurs independently as well with the meaning 'head'. *Hauv* (B1) persists with the meanings 'source; base, summit' (the 'head' part of something).

5. *kas* 'maggot' /94 *k-/

D1	<	C1	
		C1:	1 56 89
		D1:	34567

(Tone C1 and D1 have merged in dialects 5 and 6.)

6. *kua* 'liquid' /94 *k- /

C1	<	B1 ('soup')	
		B1:	56789
		C1:	234

7. *lag* 'deaf' /55 *1- /

C2	<	A2	
		A2:	1 56 89
		C2:	3
		A1:	4

8. *lau* 'cock' /53 *ʔ1- /

C1	<	B1	
		B1:	56789
		C1:	34

In the closely related Green Hmong, the form is the historically correct *lauv* (B1).

9. *liag* 'sickle' /74 *ʵ- /   C2   <   A2
                                            A2: 1   567 9
                                            A1:   34

10. *neeg* 'person' /49 *n- /   C2   <   A2
                                            A2: 12   6 89
                                            A1:   34

The probable trigger for this form is still evident in White Hmong, Green Hmong, and SHIMEN (where the tone change is A2 > A1, rather than A2 > C2): *tib-neeg* (White Hmong 'sole person'), *tuab-neeg* (Green Hmong 'individual'), [tɯ^{55}(A1)-nɯ^{55}(A1)] (SHIMEN). *Neeg* now occurs independently as well with the meaning 'person' in White Hmong. *Neej* (A2) persists in compounds with meanings such as 'the human condition', 'a male person', 'a lifetime'.

11. *no* 'this' /47 *ʔn- /   C1   <   B1
                                            B1: 123456789

Both the sandhi form *no* and the historical form *nov* (B1) persist in White Hmong with the same meaning, although the promoted sandhi form is far more common (both Heimbach and Bertrais-Charrier list only *no*, but *nov* is occasionally found in texts). The Green Hmong forms are similarly *nua* (C1) and *nuav* (B1).

12. *nplaig* 'tongue' /34 *mbl- /
                                  C2   <   D2
                                            D2: 123456789

In White Hmong, both the historical *nplaim* (D2) and the sandhi *nplaig* (C2) occur. Although *nplaig* is now the basic word for 'tongue', *nplaim* persists with the specialized meanings 'flame', 'petal', 'reed of a wind instrument'.

13. *ntsuas* 'species of sugar cane' /78 *ɳtʂ- /
                                  D1   <   C1 ('sorghum')
                                            C1:   56 9
                                            D1:   34567

(Tones C1 and D1have merged in dialects 5 and 6.)

14. *ntsws* 'lung' /26 *mpr- /

	D1	<	C1		
			C1:	2 45678	
			D1:	3	
			C2:		9

15. *plig* 'soul' /36 *bḷ- / C2 < A2

	A2:	12		89
	C2:		3 567	
	A1:		4	

16. *plhws* 'to stroke' /29 *phl- /

	D1	<	C1	
			C1:	1234 7 9

17. *qeg* 'short' /105 *G- / C2 < B2

B2: 1 3456789

In White Hmong, both the historical *qes* (B2) and the sandhi *qeg* occur. Although *qeg* is now the basic word for 'short (in stature)', *qes* persists with the meaning 'low to the ground' and in measurement comparisons for people: *qes dua* 'short-more' (= 'shorter').

18. *quas* 'to marry (a husband)' /103 *q- /

	D1	<	C1	
			C1:	1 345 78

Strecker (personal communication) has suggested that the sandhi form in White Hmong may be traced to the verb phrase *muab-quas* 'take-marry' (= 'to take [someone] and marry [him/ her] off [to someone else]').

19. *rau* 'claw' /56 *t- / C1 < B1

	B1:		56	
	C1:	234	7	

20. *tag/tog* 'half' /46 *d- /C2   <   B2
                                               B2: 1   9
                                               C2:   34567

Wang (1979: 62) believes that sandhi form promotion in most dialects was due to the effect of a preceding 'one' (*ib* in White Hmong) in the phrase 'one-half'. See also number 31 below.

21. *taus* 'ax' /44 *t- /   D1   <   C1
                                               C1:   12   56789
                                               D1:   34

22. *tog* 'to sink' /46 *d- /   C2   <   A2
                                               A2:   1   5 7 9
                                               C2:   34   8

Wang (1979: 62) writes that although this looks like sandhi form promotion, verbs do not usually change, and the change in SHIMEN should be to tone A1, not to tone C2. Although I have nothing to say about the SHIMEN form, it does seem to be the case that verbs are involved in tone sandhi compounds as the right-hand member in White Hmong (see sections 2.3.3 and 2.3.6 and examples 16 and 18 above) and may prove to be in other dialects as well.

23. *tw* 'tail' /44 *t- /   C1   <   B1
                                               B1:   123   56789

In White Hmong, both the historical *twv* (B1) and the sandhi *tw* (C1) occur. Although *tw* is the basic word for 'tail' now, *twv* persists with the specialized meaning 'to compete' (play out 'to the end') and as a minor variant of *tw* (Bertrais-Charrier *tw*).

24. *-tsi* 'what' /75 *ts̬- /   C1   <   B1
                                               B1:   1   5   8
                                               C1:   34
                                               D1:   7

The trigger for this form is still evident in White Hmong: *dab-tsi* 'what'. Since *tsi* never appears as an independent form, it cannot be said to be fully "promoted." The historical form **tsiv* (B1), however, does not occur.

25. *tsos* 'armpit' /75 **tʂ-* /

	D1	<	C1				
			C1:	12	56	8	
			D1:		34567		9

(Tones C1 and D1 have merged in dialects 5 and 6.) Both *tsos* (D1) and *tso* (C1) exist in White Hmong with the same meaning, 'armpit'. Heimbach records only *tsos*, whereas Bertrais-Charrier records *tsos* as a variant of *tso* .

26. *tsuag* 'rat' /24 **br-* /

	C2	<	A2			
			A2:			9
			C2:	3	567	
			B2:			8

27. *txia* 'crop (of a bird); goiter' /13 **pʐ-* /

	C1	<	B1			
			B1:	1	56	89
			C1:		34	7

28. *txos* 'cooking stove' /37 **tʂ-* /

	D1	<	C1			
			C1:	1	567	9
			D1:		34	

29. *txuas* 'chopper' /37 **tʂ-* /

	D1	<	C1			
			C1:	1	456	89
			D1:		3	7

30. *txha* 'bone' /38 **tsh-* /

	C1	<	B1		
			B1:	12	56789
			C1:		34

A possible trigger for this form is still evident in White Hmong: *pob-txha* 'bone', where *pob* is a shape prefix mean-

ing 'round object' (see section 2.4.3). *Txha* now occurs independently as well with the meaning 'bone'.

31. *txhais* 'half of a pair' /14 *phẓ- /
                      D1   <   C1
                               C1:   56 89
                               D1:   34567

Wang (1979: 35) believes that sandhi form promotion may
have been due to the effect of a preceding 'one' (*ib* in White
Hmong) in the phrase 'one-half'. See number 20 above.
(Tones C1 and D1 have merged in dialects 5 and 6.)

32. *xyuas* 'young' /92 *ç- / D1   <   C1
                               C1:   56 8
                               D1:   34567

(Tones C1 and D1 have merged in dialects 5 and 6.)

Occasionally, a promoted sandhi form other than one of the
thirty-two discussed in table 6 will turn up in the dictionaries or in
the literature. An account of those that I have discovered follows,
with either an explanation or an educated guess as to their derivation, if possible. For a number of these forms I have no comments to
offer, and I hope that others will find their inclusion here helpful
as part of a compilation of problems yet to solve.

The most important and interesting group of promoted sandhi
forms in White Hmong are a small set of words referring to male
humans or to people related through the father. I had been aware
of a small number of male-female pairs, sex-coded by tone, for
almost two years, but only recently have I come to consider the possibility that the origin of the contrast may be nothing other than
sandhi form promotion. The relevant pairs are:

ntxawm	youngest daughter
ntxawg	youngest son
npaws	female lst cousin,
	different clan
npawg	male lst cousin,
	different clan

yawm	maternal grandfather
yawg	paternal grandfather
poj	maternal grandmother
pog	paternal grandmother

A few other forms that seem to fit a pattern of -*m* "female," -*g* "male" are not accounted for by sandhi form promotion and will be discussed in chapter three, section 6.

I propose that the lost A-tone trigger word that gave rise to *ntxawg* 'youngest son' was *tub* (A1) 'son', 'boy', the male prefix discussed in section 2.4.4 above. *Tub* operates in a limited way as a prefix in White Hmong (*tub-nkeeg* 'a lazy person', *tub-ntsog* 'an orphan', *tub-qhe* 'a male servant', *tub-txawg* 'an able person'). It is also a common prefix to a boy's given name.[31] The compound *tub-ntxawg* 'youngest son' exists according to my tutor, although the truncated *ntxawg*, with the meaning *tub* transferred to the -*g* tone (historically, *ntxawm* simply meant 'youngest'), is now more common. By default, the -*m* tone has acquired the meaning "female" in *ntxawm* 'youngest daughter'. *Ntxawm* is also used as a given name for a girl. It is never used as a name for a boy, even though many given names can be used for either sex.

The compound that gave rise to *npawg* 'male 1st cousin, different clan; friend, fellow' was, I believe, **tij-npawg*, literally 'brother-outside'. Although this compound does not now exist in White Hmong according to my tutor and to the published sources, there is good comparative evidence to suggest that it did earlier (see chapter three, section 6). For both *ntxawm/ntxawg* and *npaws/npawg*, comparative evidence establishes the "female" form as the historical form, the "male" form as derived. This is also true of the doublets *yawm/yawg* 'maternal grandfather'/'paternal grandfather' and *poj/pog* 'woman'/'paternal grandmother', although there is no longer any trace of the compounds that gave rise to *yawg* and *pog*. The comparative evidence establishing the male/paternal forms as recent derivations is also to be found in chapter three, section 6.

---

[31] My tutor Xab Xyooj's middle son was named Tub Cawm 'rescue son'. (Note that *cawm*, a Chinese loan, does not undergo tone sandhi.)

Accounting for *npawg* 'male cousin' as a sandhi form of *npaws* 'female cousin' also takes care of what I had perceived as an annoying asymmetry in the pattern of *-m* "female"/*-g* "male." If sandhi form promotion is responsible for generating the *-g* tone forms, which come to be regarded as "male" upon the loss of the A-tone trigger, we need not anticipate that the contrasting female forms will be exclusively *-m* tone words but rather, according to the rules of tone sandhi, that they will be *-j* tone, *-s* tone, or *-m* tone words. Thus, *npaws/npawg* fits the pattern directly, rather than obliquely as I had once thought.

There are also some interesting cases of reduplication with tone change in the second word that may be explained as cases of sandhi form promotion. The tone change in each of the four examples below is one of *-v* to *-ø*:

> *ntxoov-ntxoo* (< *ntxoov* 'to shade')
> cloudy, overcast (H 213)
>
> *khov-kho* (< *khov* 'steady, hard')
> strong (H 98)
>
> *qhov-qho* (< *qhov* 'thing')
> business (B *qhov*)
>
> *sov-so* (< *sov* 'warm')
> warm(er) (H 299)

It is difficult to be precise about the meaning differences between the base form and the reduplicated form. Reduplication is used for, among other things, intensification, and that seems to be the difference between *sov* and *sov-so*, at least.[32] Both David Strecker (personal communication) and I hypothesize that the lost A-tone sandhi trigger in these cases was a poetic or intensive infixed word. Words of this type are not common in everyday speech, but they may be encountered in the folk tales and in ritual texts. It may be that they once played a greater role in more ordinary language. There is one intensive infixed word, though, that is

---

[32] My primary tutor and his wife told me that *sov-so* represented a distinct temperature range between *sov* 'warm' and *sov sov* 'extremely warm'.

widely used today in informal situations: *tsis* .[33] Thus, *rog* means 'fat', *rog rog* means 'very fat' and *rog tsis rog* means 'unbelievably fat'. The infixed word *tsis* is very productive and can be used to further intensify any reduplicated verb. The more literary and less frequently encountered infixed words so far discovered include *-lis-*; *-qab-, -qas-, -qam-; -tib-*, with indeterminate meanings. Two of the words, *-qab-* and *-tib-*, have an A-tone, and it may be from the loss of such words that the interesting reduplications above resulted.

The following is an alphabetically arranged list of miscellaneous words with anomalous tones that may have arisen through sandhi form promotion:

dag < daj yellow	in *qhiav daj* 'yellow ginger' (Xab Xyooj) ginger yellow
deg < dej water	in *pliag deg/piag deg* 'clam' (H 251)
	Xab Xyooj says *pliaj-deg* for 'clam', which may either be the source of *deg* or a regularization in *cws deg* 'shrimp, prawn' (B *dej*)
ke < kev path	in *ua ke* 'together' (B *ke*, H 81) make
	via *ua ib-ke* (literally 'make one path')[34]
leeg < leej seam	independent word meaning 'vein, line; artery, seam' (B *leeg*, H 110)
luag < luaj like	in *yuav luag ib yam* get same 1 thing almost exactly the same (H 120)

---

[33] *Tsis* is homophonous, interestingly enough, with the preverbal negative. Further study may reveal the semantic development of one of these from the other.

[34] *Ua ke* is mentioned here because it is a very common phrase. In many cases, however, the numeral *ib* 'one' is omitted when it can be inferred from the sandhi form of the classifier (Mottin 1978: 19).

nkeeg < nkees lethargy	in *kev mob kev nkeeg* way hurt way sickness and lethargy (H 154)

perhaps the second member can influence the
fourth: *mob-nkeeg*

ntiag < ntiaj (in compound)	independent word meaning 'the earth front surface' (H 189)

possible origin is compound *sab-ntiag* 'the front
surface'—literally 'side-front'

ntseg < ntsej	independent word meaning 'ear' in ear
	  lag ntseg 'deaf' (H 102), *qhws ntseg*
	  'earring' (H 199)

probably via *pob-ntseg* 'round-ear'

ntsig < ntsim ?	in *txuag txiaj txuag ntsig* 'gifts' (H 381) care for money

probably via *txiaj-ntsig* 'gifts' (H 381)

puas < pua 100	in *txhiab niag tim puas xyoo* 1,000 great 100 year 100s + 100s of years (B *puas*)

qhia < qhiav ginger	in *ntiv qhia* 'one piece of ginger' (B *qhiav*) finger ginger

possibly via *tsob-qhia* '[classifier]-ginger'

riag < riam knife	in *ntaus ib nplhos riag* strike 1 puncture knife to make a knife puncture (B*nplhos, riam*)

on analogy with *ntaus ib roob-riag* 'to make a
blow with the flat of the knife'?

so < *sov*   in *dej sem so* 'lukewarm water' (H 299)
warm   water ? warm

                    possibly via *dej-so*

taws < *taw*   in *taws siab taws qis*
foot   foot high foot low
                              step high step low (B *taw*)

tsaig < *tsaim*   in *tawv ncauj tawv tsaig*
jaw   hard mouth hard jaw
                              indocile (B *tsaim*)

                    probably via *ncauj-tsaig*

tse < *tsev*   in *plag tse*
house   central part of the house (B *tsev*)

tshos < *tsho*   in *ntiag tshos* 'front edge of jacket' (H 450)
jacket   front jacket

zag < *zaj*   in *nws hais zag pib zag xaus*
story   3ps speak   start   finish
                              he tells stories one after another (B*zaj*)

zaug < *zaum/zaus* in *lwm zaug*
time   next time
                              next time (Lauj Pov Vaj)

zog < *zos*   in *nyob ua zej ua zog*
village   live as ? as village
                              to live in villages (B *zej*)

                    probably via *zej-zog*

4.2   On the White Hmong Classifier

Both Heimbach and Mottin agree that classifiers do not have
sufficient power to affect tone change in a following word:

89

No classifier (or noun used as a classifier) regardless of its own tone, affects a tone change in a following word (Heimbach 1979: 446).

Un classificateur n'affecte...jamais un nom auquel il se rapporte (Mottin 1978: 19).

Nonetheless, the following exceptions have been found:

hnub
day (as measure)
>   *ib hnub-ke* (< *kev*)
>   1 day   trail
>   a day's journey (Downer 1967: 593)

khaub
stick
>   *ib khaub-nplawg* (< *nplawm*)
>   1 stick   blow
>   1 stick-blow (B *nplawm*)

leej
human classifier
>   *leej-txi* (< *txiv*)
>   father
>   father (Downer 1967: 593)

lub
bulky or round object classifier
>   *lub-deg* (< *dej*) *pluam*
>   water release
>   the bag of waters breaks (B *dej*)

>   *lwm lub-hlis; ib lub-hlis* (< *hli*)
>   next   1   moon
>   next month; 1 month (B *hli*; tutors)

>   *lub-loog* (< *loom*)
>   basin
>   park; walled garden around house
>   (B *loog*; Mottin 1978: 18)

90

lub-ncaug (< *ncauj*)
           mouth
mouth (H 453)

lub-qeeg (< *qeej*)
           keng
keng (B *qeej*)

lub-tee (< *teev*) *phaj yeeb*
       balance plate opium
the dish of the balance (B *teev*)

lub-tiag (< *tiaj*) *lub-dawg* (< *dawm*)
         level   pass
level places and gaps in a mountain ridge (H 319)

nrauj lub-txag (< *txaj*)
share   bed
to share a bed (B *nrauj*)

tsob
plant classifier
     ib tsob-qhia (< *qhiav*)
                        ginger
     1 root (?) of ginger (B *qhiav*)

tshooj
classifier for stories, levels
     cuaj tshooj-ntug (< *ntuj*)
     9   sky
     9 heights of heaven (H 369)

txoj
length classifier
     txoj-hmoo (< *hmoov*)
                  fortune
     fortune (H 67, 451)

     txoj-ke (< *kev*)
                 path
     path (B *kev*)

txoj-sia (< *siav*)
          life
   life (H 298)

Even allowing for the possibility that some of the above examples may have been due to recording errors or typing mistakes, there is enough evidence to show that classifiers may sometimes trigger tone sandhi.

These exceptions are due, I believe, to what David Strecker (personal communication) has explained as a "noun scale" in classifier languages that does not cleanly differentiate classifiers from nouns but places both on a scale that ranges from concrete (independent nouns) to abstract (dependent nouns, or classifiers). The independent nouns that are also used as classifiers (for example, *cev* 'body', *rooj* 'table', *tsev* 'house') have to be count nouns and have to be able to quantify the following noun: *ib-tse neeg* '1-house-people', or '1 household'. Under the concept of classifier as "noun-adjunct," one would anticipate that the classifiers more like independent nouns (and therefore more powerful) would be the ones most likely to trigger tone sandhi in the following noun. It is interesting to note, therefore, that the most general and abstract classifier in the language, *lub* (not only 'round' or 'bulky', but used for places, buildings, clothes, machines, times, body parts, and abstractions) has accounted for the greatest number of classifier-noun tone sandhi compounds in the list above.[35] This may force us to a reanalysis, or a more flexible analysis, of *lub*. When the roundness or bulkiness of an object is being stressed (roundness being the dominant feature of the moon, for example, or of the bag of waters), perhaps, the word can effect change in the following word; although in most cases (*ib lub tsev* '1 house'), very little in meaning is added to the noun phrase by the use of *lub*, and there is, consequently, no tone change. In any case, the behavior of the classifiers listed above with regard to tone sandhi supports the idea that classifiers are best understood as noun-adjuncts that usually, but not always, play a subordinate role.

---

[35] It would be of interest to determine the semantic nature of the ancestor of this form in the proto-language. An ancient meaning such as 'fruit' or 'ball' would give the right results. This may be impossible to determine, however, since the cognate to *lub* in Iu Mien, [nɔm], is even more abstract: it refers to all that *lub* refers to, plus the "lower animals" (Court 1986).

CHAPTER THREE

TONALLY DEFINED FORM CLASSES

1   Tonally Defined Form Classes in White Hmong

The employment of tone to signal membership in a word class, semantically and/or syntactically defined, is not an expected function of tone in Asian languages but one that has been manifested from place to place and from family to family throughout the area, as outlined in Henderson (1965a and 1967). Tonally defined form classes are typically small and self-contained: for example, a pronoun, demonstrative, or anaphoric pronoun class. Large word classes are usually not designated by overt morphological markers, either tonal or segmental, in monosyllabic-word Asian languages. The only exceptions to this that I am aware of are (1) a group of Tibeto-Burman languages[1] exemplified by Tiddim Chin, in which an indicative/subjunctive verb distinction and a direct/oblique noun distinction are tonally marked,[2] and (2) SHIMEN Hmong, in which the distinction noun/non-noun is marked by a tone split in tone categories B2, C2, and D2 (Wang 1979: 9).

White Hmong is more typical of the area in that its tonally defined form classes are of modest size. The numeral class contains five members; the pronoun class only two. The denominal preposition class has ten members, as does the class derived from it, the demonstrative noun class. This latter class is defined by a "new"

---

[1] For Mpi, see Srinuan Duanghom (1976: xii-xiv); Henderson (1967: 171) mentions other Chin dialects (Laizo, Tashon, and Lushai); and David Bradley discussed Ugong in this respect in "Phonological Convergence in a Minority Language: Ugong in Thailand," paper presented at the Conference on Southeast Asia as a Linguistic Area, Chicago, April 16, 1986.

[2] E. J. A. Henderson (1965b: 22, 69-84).

tone, -*d*, which is not one of the seven basic tones, and this new tone has been extended in its use in various ways from its base in the demonstrative noun class. The male and female noun classes have at least four members each. These words can be shown either to have changed to the "correct" tone for the sex of the referent, or to have developed a male or female association upon the formation (by tone change) of the opposite member of a male-female pair.

It is important to determine what conditions are favorable to the development of tonally defined form classes in a tone language. As I explained in chapter one, section 2.3 above, my impression is that it is related to the structure of the word in the particular tone language. In a strictly monosyllabic-word tone language, the main function of tone, lexical discrimination, would necessarily be its only function, because of the need to avoid more homophony than is already inherent in such a language. If a tone language is beginning to move toward the polysyllabic word in its development at least as an alternate word type, though, tone need not be held as strictly to this one task. Tone can be put to other tasks if words are some-what longer and easier to differentiate: the organization of seman-tic and syntactic classes could be one of these new tasks. I believe that this is what is happening in Hmong. This is a large issue, properly a study of its own, though, which is beyond the scope of this primarily descriptive work.

2   Numerals 1 Through 5

An obvious and unproblematic tonally defined form class in White Hmong is the set of the first five numerals: *ib* 'one', *ob* 'two', *peb* 'three', *plaub* 'four', *tsib* 'five'.[3]   The high level (-*b*) tone is the reflex of tone category A1. Since the first five numerals in prac-tically all recorded Hmongic dialects have reflexes of tone cate-gory A1, this form class can be reconstructed for Proto-Hmongic, as shown in table 8.

The few seeming exceptions to this form class in the data can be explained as

---

[3] Ballard (1985: 75) also noticed this form class in White Hmong.

(1) probable errors

KAITANG (East Hmongic) 'two' [ʔau²³] (C2) (Cao 1961: 188) —23 was probably erroneously recorded for 33 (A1).

SHIDONGKOU (East Hmongic) 'one' [ʔei³³] (C2) (Kwan 1966: 29) —33 was probably erroneously recorded for 44. Li Fang-kuei (1977) discerned five level tones for this dialect, and Kwan (1966: 27) notes that this caused "momentary indecisiveness when taking the field notes."

WENJIE (Pa Hng) 'two' [va⁵³] (D1) (Mao, Meng, Zheng 1982: 123) —35(A1) was probably miscopied as 53(D1). Wang (1986a) cites the form [va³⁵] (A1) for WENJIE 'two'.

(2) different roots for 'one'

IWEI (North Hmongic) 'one' [ʔa⁴⁴] (B1/D1) (Wang 1985: 197); WENJIE (Pa Hng) 'one' [jɦu³²] (D2) (Wang 1986a).

There is evidence that initial consonants are involved as well as tones in small form classes within the set of the first nine numerals:

(1) The words for 'one' and 'two' had glottal initials in Proto-Hmongic, and that initial persists in most of the modern dialects.

(2) The words for 'three', 'four', and 'five' have reconstructed voiceless labial stop clusters, as shown in table 9.

(3) The words for 'eight' and 'nine' have reconstructed palatal or palatalized lamino-alveolar initials, as shown in table 10. Furthermore, the numeral 'seven' has developed a palatal initial in White Hmong *xya* [ça³³], XIANJIN [ɕaŋ⁴⁴], and SHIMEN [ɕaɯ³³], even though the regular reflexes of the reconstructed retroflex initial *dʐ- in these dialects are [tʂ-], [tʂ-], and [dʐ-], respectively. Wang (1979: 85) attributes the unusual initials for 'seven' in these dialects to the change of tone (C2 > C1, which places 'seven' in a pair with 'six' as described below) because he is focusing on the voicing anomaly in SHIMEN, one of the few dialects that has split the original four tones according to the feature of voicing in the initial, and has yet kept the voicing distinction. What seems more significant to me is that the place of articulation change puts 'seven' into a group with 'eight' and 'nine', as shown in table 11.

In addition to the main tonally defined form class 'one' through 'five', which is quite old as we have seen above, there is another more recent shift in White Hmong and its most closely related dialects. This is the shift of tone in the numeral 'seven' from a reconstructed C2 to C1. This serves to bring 'seven' into line with 'six' in the dialects shown in table 12.

We may speculate that these numeral form classes developed to serve some pragmatic function, for example ease of recitation, although I know of no way of proving this. The tonally defined form class 'one' through 'five' is, nonetheless, strikingly long for a "number run"[4] and cannot be dismissed as an accidental similarity.

---

[4] Term coined by James A. Matisoff, "Sino-Tibetan Numerals and the Play of Prefixes," paper presented at the 17th ICSTLL, Eugene, Oregon, September 1984.

Table 8
Tone A1 Numerals

	YANGHAO	SHIDONGKOU	JIWEI	FENGXIANG	MEIZHU
1	ʔi^{33}(A1)	ʔei^{44}(A1)	—	ʔi^{33}(A1)	ʔi^{33}(A1)
2	ʔo^{33}(A1)	ʔɔ^{44}(A1)	ʔɯ^{35}(A1)	ʔa^{33}(A1)	ʔau^{33}(A1)
3	pi^{33}(A1)	pje^{44}(A1)	pu^{35}(A1)	tsi^{33}(A1)	pe^{33}(A1)
4	ļu^{33}(A1)	ļo^{44}(A1)	pei^{35}(A1)	plou^{33}(A1)	tļa^{33}(A1)
5	tsa^{33}(A1)	sai^{44}(A1)	pʐa^{35}(A1)	tsa^{33}(A1)	tsu^{33}(A1)

Table 9
Initial Consonants in Numerals 3 through 5

	White	GEZHENG	FUYUAN
Wang 13 *pz- "three"	pe^{55} (*peb*)	pa^{44}	pzi^{31}
Wang 28 *pl- "four"	plau^{55} (*plaub*)	plo^{44}	plou^{31}
Wang 22 *pr- "five"	tʃi^{55} (*tsib*)	prai^{44}	pja^{31}

Table 10: Initial Consonants in Numerals 8 and 9

	White	SHIMEN	FUYUAN*
Wang 93 *ʐ– 'eight'	ʐiʔ²¹ (yim)	ʐɦi³¹	ʐa³¹
Wang 84 *dʐ– 'nine'	ʈuɑ⁵² (cuɑj)	dʐɦa³⁵	ʐa³¹

Table 11: Initial Consonants in Numerals 7 through 9

	White	XIANJIN	SHIMEN
Wang 77 *dʐ– 'seven'	ɕa³³ (xyɑ)	ɕaŋ⁴⁴	ɕaɯ³³
Wang 93 *ʐ– 'eight'	ʐiʔ²¹ (yim)	ʐi²⁴	ʐɦi³¹
Wang 84 *dʐ– 'nine'	ʈuɑ⁵² (cuɑj)	ʈʐuɑ³¹	dʐɦa³⁵

Table 12: Tone C1 Numerals

	White	XUYONG	XIANJIN	SHIMEN
Wang 68 *tɭ– 'six'	ʈau³³(Cl) (rau)	ʈau⁵⁵(Cl)	ʈou⁴⁴(Cl)	ʈɭau³³(Cl)
Wang 77 *dʐ– 'seven'	ɕa³³(Cl) (xyɑ)	ɕaŋ⁵⁵(Cl)	ɕaŋ⁴⁴(Cl)	ɕaɯ³³(Cl)

---

* Now that tones A and D have merged in FUYUAN, "eight" and "nine" are homophonous. Wang (1979: 15) tells of field workers asking speakers how they distinguished between the two, and reports that they were told "nine" had to be expressed by the phrase "eight and one more."

All of the numeral sub-groups in White Hmong, both tonally and consonantally defined, are as follows:

1	*ib*:	⎡ *ʔ-	>	⎡ ʔi	55 ⎤	<	*A1 ⎤
2	*ob*:	⎣ *ʔ-	>	⎣ ʔɔ	55 ⎦	<	*A1
3	*peb*:	⎡ *pʐ-	>	⎡ pe	55 ⎤	<	*A1
4	*plaub*:	*pl-	>	plau	55	<	*A1
5	*tsib*:	⎣ *pr-	>	tʃi	55 ⎦	<	*A1 ⎦
6	*rau*:			ʈau	33 ⎤		
7	*xya*:			⎡ ça	33 ⎦		
8	*yim*:	⎡ *ʐ-	>	ʑiʔ	21		
9	*cuaj*:	⎣ *dʐ-	>	⎣ ʈua	52		

3   Dual and Plural Pronouns

In dialects of West Hmongic and East Hmongic, tonally contrastive dual and plural pronouns for the second and third person appear. It can be said that the reflexes of the A1 tone category in these dialects have become morphotonemes with the meaning "dual" and that the reflexes of the A2 tone category have become morphotonemes with the meaning "plural." The tonally contrastive pairs found to date appear below:

West Hmongic
White Hmong (Heimbach, Bertrais-Charrier, Mottin)

	dual	plural
2nd	ne^{55}(A1) (*neb*)	ne^{52}(A2) (*nej*)
3rd	—	—

Green Hmong (Lyman, Xiong)

	dual	plural
2nd	me^{55}(A1l) (*meb*)	me^{52}(A2) (*mej*)
3rd	—	—

XUYONG (Ruey and Kuan 1962: 532, 541, 544)

	dual	plural
2nd	—	ne^{11}/me^{11}(B2)
3rd	me^{53}(A1)	ne^{11}/me^{11}(B2)

MEIZHU (Mao, Meng, Zheng 1982: 85)

	dual	plural
2nd	mi^{33}(A1)	mi^{12}(A2)
3rd	mu^{33}(A1)	mu^{12}(A2)

East Hmongic
YANGHAO (Wang 1985: 48)

	dual	plural
2nd	$maŋ^{33}$(A1)	$maŋ^{55}$(A2)
3rd	—	—

As more Hmongic dialects are fully described, more dual pronouns are likely to come to light. The dialects cited above have been more fully described than others. In the basic word list used by both Mao, Meng, Zheng (1982) and Wang (1985) in their overview descriptions of the languages of the "Yao" and "Miao" peoples, only singular and plural pronouns are included. The MEIZHU Bunu and YANGHAO Mhu forms were part of fuller grammatical descriptions of those dialects in particular in the Mao, Meng, and Zheng and Wang works, respectively.

There are two possible explanations for the origin of the dual forms presented above. The first explanation was offered by Herbert Purnell (1970: 78), and it is based on the reconstruction of an initial consonant contrast, which would place the origin of the dual forms as far back as Proto-Hmongic. My explanation would allow for the sporadic development of dual forms in scattered dialects and is based on tonal assimilation of the plural pronoun(s) with the following numeral 'two' in attested constructions meaning 'you (we/they) two people'.

(1) Purnell (1970: 236) reconstructs a glottalized nasal (*ʔmn-) for the dual in Proto-Hmongic and a plain nasal (*mn-) for the corresponding plural. This reconstruction was suggested "with some degree of hesitancy...because of irregularities in both sets" (1970: 78). His table is as follows:

	you (dual)	**you (pl)**
Cheng-feng [ZHENFENG]	—	mye (A2)
Hua-yuan [JIWEI]	mɨ (A2) T	—
Petchabun [White Hmong]	ne (A1)	ne (A2)

Tak [Green Hmong]	me (A1)	me (A2)
Su-yung [XUYONG]	me (B2) T	ne (B2) T
PM [Proto-Miao]	*ʔmn–	*mn–

The irregularities in JIWEI and XUYONG (marked with "T" for unexpected tone) disappear upon a reexamination of both the sources Purnell used and consideration of a new source (Wang 1985) for JIWEI:

	you (sing)	you (dual)	you (pl)
JIWEI	mu (A2)	—	me (A2)
XUYONG	ne/me (B2)	—	ne/me (B2)

The "dual" form Purnell found for JIWEI is actually the second person singular form, which eliminates the dual category/tone category mismatch he worried about; a reexamination of Ruey and Kuan shows that the only dual in the XUYONG system is a third person dual and that the original A2 tone second person pronouns (both singular and plural) have merged with the B2 tone third person pronouns (both singular and plural).

Purnell's reconstruction of an ancient glottalized/non-glottalized initial contrast is evidenced by only White Hmong and Green Hmong, then, in his collection of dialects. However, we can bring in the second person forms from MEIZHU and YANGHAO cited above to support his reconstruction. The YANGHAO dual form extends the reconstruction of the dual/plural contrast to include another of the three major branches of the Hmong family. The origin of the glottalized initial for the dual, under this theory, may well have been the preposed word 'two'. Wang (1979: 120) reconstructs a glottal initial for this word, as it has a glottal initial in the nine dialects included in his comparative study.[5] Numerals precede

---

[5] The initial for 'two' in LUSHAN Mhu and KAILI Mhu and in BAO-LAC is [w–] and in dialects of the Pa Hng branch is [v–]. Both Benedict (forthcoming) and Strecker (personal correspondence) believe the initial in these forms is a conservative feature. Strecker (personal correspondence) tentatively reconstructs *ʔwi A for 'two' in Proto-Hmong-Mien.

objects enumerated in Hmong. The possible development of the tonal contrast under this theory would be as follows:

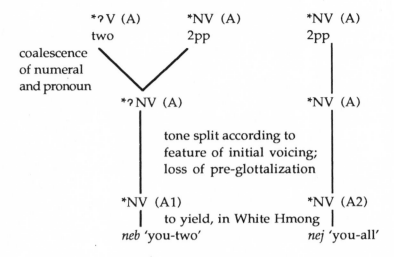

The same development would be proposed for the third person dual/plural contrast in MEIZHU.

(2) The second explanation is based on an examination of Hmong phrases that contain a "resumptive noun phrase" (this term on analogy with "resumptive pronoun" in English phrases such as "my brother and I, we..."). The numeral 'two' follows the plural pronoun in SHIMEN, the only way the dual can be expressed in that dialect (Wang, personal correspondence):

mi^{31}(A2)   ʔa^{55}-lɯ^{55}(A1)   you two
2pp   2   person

In White Hmong and Green Hmong, exactly the same construction is found—but with a dual pronoun instead of a plural pronoun:

White Hmong (Bertrais-Charrier *wb*)

wb   ob-leeg   we two
1pd   2 person

wb   ob   kwv   tij   we two brothers
1pd   2   y-bro   e-bro

Green Hmong (Lyman: 73, 181)

> *meb ob leej* you two
> 2pd 2 person

> *wb ob leej* we two
> 1pd 2 person

I hypothesize that White Hmong and Green Hmong once expressed duality exactly as SHIMEN expresses it now, with a construction containing a plural pronoun and a noun phrase beginning with the numeral 'two'.[6] The dual pronouns arose in White Hmong, Green Hmong, XUYONG, MEIZHU, and YANGHAO when the tone of the plural pronoun assimilated to the tone of the numeral 'two', A1. It will be recalled that the XUYONG dual is a third person dual with tone A1 and contrasts with a B2 third person plural. I have reproduced the XUYONG pronouns below:

	singular	**dual**	**plural**
1st	kȯ (B1)	—	pe (A1)
2nd	ka (A2)	—	ka (A2)
	ne/me (B2)	—	ne/me (B2)
3rd	ne/me (B2)	me (A1)	ne/me (B2)

This dual form can be accounted for by my explanation (the A1 dual tone came from the assimilation of the plural pronoun to the following word 'two') but not by Purnell's explanation (in which case we would expect the dual and the plural to be marked by A1 and A2, or by B1 and B2, respectively).

Tonal assimilations have been used to account for at least two other phenomena. Wang hypothesizes that such tonal assimilations took place in SHIMEN (see his discussion of the word for 'head', for example [1979: 31]), and I have hypothesized that tonal assimilation accounts for the tonal variants of the reciprocal throughout the family (see chapter two, section 2.3.2 above).

---

[6] I am grateful to Gérard Diffloth for first proposing that I look for traces of an analytic construction with the word 'two' to explain the dual forms.

The first person duals present a special problem. They also may be the result of an assimilation of the first person plural pronoun and the word for 'two'.

West Hmongic
White/Green Hmong

	dual		plural
1st	ʔɯ^{55}(A1) (*wb*)		pe^{55}(A1) (*peb*)
('two'	ʔɔ^{55}(A1) (*ob*))		

MEIZHU

	dual		plural
1st	ʔa^{33}(A1)		pe^{33}(A1)
('two'	ʔau^{33}(A1))		

East Hmongic
YANGHAO

	dual		plural
1st	ʔo^{33}(A1) (*ob*)		pi^{33}(A1) (*bib*)
('two'	ʔo^{33}(A1) (*ob*))		

Simple inspection of the first person dual forms above suggests that the White/Green Hmong and MEIZHU forms are modifications of the word for 'two' in either dialect, but whether or not the modification is in the direction of the first person plural form is hard to say. The YANGHAO words for the first person dual and the numeral 'two' are homophonous.[7]

4   Denominal Prepositions

The space and time words that serve as the first words of prepositional phrases in White Hmong and are marked by the morphotoneme -*m* (the low falling checked tone, reflex of tone category D2) comprise an important tonally defined form class. I call

---

[7]   In YANGHAO, the forms for 'we (plural)' and 'three' are also homophonous. This is true of many Hmongic dialects, although differences in initials in some dialects leads Wang to reconstruct *p- for 'we', *pẓ- for 'three'; finals and tones are identically reconstructed (Wang 1979: 23, 33).

these prepositions "denominal" because five of them are cognate with nouns in White Hmong that have different tonal realizations, and all but two of the others are cognate with nouns in different dialects that have different tonal realizations. They are:

nram 'down' (< *nras* 'plain')

mus nram suav [8]	go down to where the others live
go down	

nraum 'outside' (< *nrau* 'place beyond')

nyob nraum toj nraum pes	on the other side of the mountains
be outside hill outside mountain	

ntawm 'here/there (nearby)'

nyob ntawm kuv sab xis	on my right
be here I side right	

pem 'up' (< *pes* 'mountain')

mus pem hmoob	go up to where the Hmong live
go up Hmong	

saum 'above'

nyob saum ntoo	up in the tree
be above tree	

tim 'opposite'

nyob sab dej tim ub	on the other side of the river
be side river opp. far	

tom 'over there (less far than *tim*)'

---

[8] All of the above example phrases are taken from Bertrais-Charrier (1964) and can be found under the entries for their respective denominal prepositions.

mus tom khw go there market	go to market

txhaim 'on the far side' (< *txhais* 'outside')

peb ua teb puag txhaim ub we make field very far far side	we make our fields far on the other side of the mountain

thaum 'time when'

puag thaum kuv tseem yau very when I still young	when I was young

zaum 'time when' (< *zaus* 'time')

peb yuav mus zaum no we will go time this	we are going to leave now

This word class exists in White Hmong, SHIMEN, and, to a lesser extent, in Green Hmong.[9] In all three, the morphotoneme is the reflex of tone category D2. The closely related dialects to those above for which we have good word lists, XUYONG and XIANJIN, do not show the development of such a class.

Below are comparative data on the ten members of the denominal preposition form class, showing the origin of each, insofar as possible. This information is essentially a union of the information presented in Downer (1967: 596) (checked against Ruey and Kwan [1962: 517-80] for XUYONG and the Hmongb-Shuad dictionary for XIANJIN), Wang's 1979 comparative study, and Wang and Wang's 1982 article on SHIMEN localizers, with the addition of the Green Hmong forms from the Lyman and Xiong dictionaries and some miscellaneous additional forms from other dialects.

---

[9] In syntactic role, lexical items involved, tone category involved, and even with phonetic manifestation, the similarity of the White Hmong and SHIMEN denominal preposition and demonstrative noun classes is striking. Wang and Wang (1982: 31) and Downer (1967: 597) believe that the development of these classes is an innovation in these dialects. If genetic subgrouping is to be determined on the basis of shared innovations, it may be necessary to place White Hmong and SHIMEN within the same sub-branch.

1. DOWN (*nram* < *nras* 'a plain')

White	ɳɖa^{21}(D2)/ɳɖa^{22}(B2)	down/plain
Green	ɳɖan^{42}(B2) (*nraag*)	over there; plain
XUYONG	ɳʈan^{11}(B2)	plain
XIANJIN	ɳɖɦaŋ^{21}(B2)(*ndrangl*)	plain
SHIMEN	ɳɖaɯ^{33}(B2)	plain
QINGYAN	ɳʈaŋ^{32}(B2)	plain
FUYUAN	ɳʈʐoŋ^{55}(B)	plain
FENGXIANG	ɳʈɕaŋ^{13}(B2)	plain

The semantically equivalent SHIMEN preposition is derived from a C2 noun as represented by the XIANJIN form below. It would correspond to a White Hmong **nrom* .

XIANJIN	ɳɖɦau^{12}(C2) (*ndraos*)	
SHIMEN	ɳɖɦu^{31}(D2)	'on the slope, lower'

Downer (1967: 596) writes that White Hmong *nram* and SHIMEN [ɳɖɦu^{31}] (D2) are cognate, but this seems not to be true.

2. OUTSIDE (*nraum* < *nrau* 'place beyond')

White	ɳɖau^{21}(D2)/ɳɖau^{33}(C1)	
		outside/place beyond
Green	ɳɖau^{33}(C1) (*nrau*)	outside
XUYONG	ɳʈau^{55}(C1)	
XIANJIN	ɳʈou^{44}(C1) (*ndrout*)	outside
		(Wang 1985: 161)
GAOPO	ɳʈo^{53}(C1)	outside
		(Chang 1947:108)
GEZHENG	ɳʈau^{33}(C1)	outside
		(Chang 1947: 108)
YAOLU	ntjuŋ^{33}(C1)	outside
		(Chang 1947: 108)
RONGJIANG	tjɔ^{24}(C1)	outside
		(Chang 1947: 108)
JIWEI	ʈei^{53}(C1)	outside
		(Wang 1985: 161)

3. NEARBY (HERE/THERE) (*ntawm*)

White	ndaɯʔ²¹(D2)	nearby
Green	ndaɯʔ²¹(D2) (*ntawm*)	there
XIANJIN	ntɛɯ¹³(C2) (*ndeus*)	

Downer (1967: 596) writes that White Hmong *ntawm* and SHIMEN [vɦai³¹] (D2) are cognate, but this is surely not true. Wang and Wang (1982: 20) write that [vɦai³¹] 'here/there' has no cognates in any dialects of West Hmongic.

4. UP (*pem* < *pes* 'mountain')

White	peʔ²¹(D2)/pe²²(B2)	up/mountain
Green	pe⁴²(B2) (*peg*)	up
XUYONG	pi¹¹(B2)	
XIANJIN	pe²¹(B2) (*bel*)	mountain
SHIMEN	bɦi³¹(D2)	higher on the slope
QINGYAN	pa³²(B2)	mountain
GAOPO	pæ³¹(B2)	mountain
ZONGDI	pe¹¹(B2)	mountain
FUYUAN	vei⁵⁵(B)	mountain
FENGXIANG	pi¹³(B2)	mountain
YANGHAO	pi¹¹(B2) (*bil*)	mountain
SHIDONGKOU	pje²²(B2)	slope
		(Kwan 1966: 12)

5. ABOVE (*saum*)

White	ʃauʔ²¹(D2)	above
Green	ʃau³³(C1) (*sau*)	above
XUYONG	ʐo⁵⁵(C1)	
XIANJIN	ʐau⁴⁴(C1) (*shout*)	

6. OPPOSITE (*tim*)

White	tiʔ²¹(D2)	opposite
Green	tiʔ²¹(D2) (*tim*)	opposite
XUYONG	ti²⁴(C2)	
XIANJIN	dɦi¹³(C2) (*dis*)	
SHIMEN	dɦi³¹(D2)	opposite

7. OPPOSITE (*tom*)

White	tɔʔ²¹(D2)	there
Green	tɔʔ²¹(D2) (*tom*)	there

XUYONG	tau^{12}(D2)	
XIANJIN	dɔ^{24}(D2)	
SHIMEN	dɦu^{31}(D2)	opposite-far

8. ON THE FAR SIDE (*txhaim* < *txhais* 'outside')
White   tshai?^{21}(D2)/tshai^{22}(D1)

on far side/outside

XUYONG	tshai^{44}(D1)	
XIANJIN	tshai^{33}(D1) (*caik*)	
SHIMEN	tshai^{31}(D2)	on the side; out of sight

9. TIME WHEN (*thaum*)
White	thau?^{21}(D2)	time when
Green	thau^{22}(D1)/thau?^{21}(D2) (*thaus/thaum*)	
		time when

XUYONG	thau^{44}(D1)	
XIANJIN	thou^{33}(D1) (*touk*)	
SHIMEN	thau^{33}(C1)[10]	time when

10. TIME WHEN (*zaum* < *zaus* 'time')
White	ʒau?^{21}(D2)/ʒau^{22}(B2)	time when
Green	ʒa^{42}(B2) (*zag*)	time when

The development of this class through tone shift was described by Downer (1967: 596-597) for White Hmong and SHIMEN, was mentioned by Wang (1979: 26) with regard to Downer's analysis of the root for 'mountain' > 'up', and then was fully described by Wang and Wang (1982) for SHIMEN. Both Downer and Wang and Wang agree that this class was formed by analogical extension ("analogical tone-shift" is Downer's term), in which "all members of a small, closed word-class acquire the same tone" (Downer 1967: 597). Downer does not attempt to say what the model for this analogical shift was, but he refers to the Cantonese and Hakka personal pronoun classes, where tones have also been leveled in favor of one or another of the pronouns, as representative of this kind of tone shift.[11] Wang and Wang, on the other hand, do

---

[10] Note the anomalous tone.

[11] Another example of analogical leveling in a "small, closed word class" is the Thai (Siamese) demonstratives. See Noss (1964: 103).

attempt to identify the model. The "prepositional localizers"[12] [ŋɖɦu³¹] (D2) (which would correspond to a White Hmong *nrom) meaning 'on the slope, lower' and [dɦi³¹] (D2) (which corresponds to White Hmong *tim* 'opposite') were originally tone C2 words, as determined by Wang and Wang through comparative analysis. Tones C2 (non-noun) and D2 (non-noun)[13] are both mid falling (31) in SHIMEN; the only difference between the two being "voiced aspiration" of the initial in D2 words. Wang and Wang hypothesize that the analogical process had two parts:

(1) the other prepositions developed the same contour as hypothetical C2 *ŋɖu³¹ and *di³¹, and then,

(2) on analogy with two different prepositions, originally B2 and A2, both categories associated with "voiced aspiration" in SHIMEN, all of these words developed voiced aspiration, the result being a class of words with mid falling pitch and voiced aspirated initials, which makes them indistinguishable from category D2 words.

My objections to this hypothesis are, first, that if voiced aspiration is analyzed as a phonation-type contrast in the vowel, a correlate of tone (albeit originally due to voicing of the initial consonant), the shift becomes much simpler and more believable: the shift is then to the D2 (non-noun) category from a number of different tone categories. If the shift is to D2 rather than to mid falling, though, the C2 forms Wang and Wang propose as models for the analogical shift can no longer be considered as candidates for that role. Second, the SHIMEN and White Hmong classes are extremely close in that they involve the reflex of the same tone and four of the words in the two classes are cognate (corresponding to White Hmong *pem* 'up', *tim* 'opposite', *tom* 'there', and *txhaim* 'on the far side'). The origin of the preposition class in each dialect is probably the same. A hypothesis that depends on the phonetics of the non-noun C2 and D2 tones in SHIMEN will not be able to account for the White Hmong facts as well.

I have no strong counter hypothesis, but I think a more likely candidate for the model for this form class would be a word that has a reconstructed tone D2. Of the words common to both White

---

[12] This translation is by Jiang Zixin, as are all others from Wang and Wang (1982) and Wang (1979).
[13] For the split of three tones according to word class in SHIMEN, see section 1 above.

Hmong and SHIMEN, that could only be *tom* 'there'. Wang and Wang scarcely discuss this preposition because it is, according to them, merely an ablaut form of the counterpart of *tim* and has the same origin. As cognates for both *tim* and *tom* exist in both XUYONG and XIANJIN, with C2 forms for the *tim* cognates and D2 forms for the *tom* cognates, it may be that their common origin, if there is one, lies fairly deep, and the vowel and tone differentiation took place long enough ago for the ancestor of *tom*, as an independent D2 form, to serve as the nucleus for the development of this class in both SHIMEN and White Hmong. On semantic grounds, *tom* is a good candidate in that it is a very general, abstract, multipurpose locative in White Hmong and Green Hmong, with meanings such as 'side; place, location, area; at, towards, in, on, by, out' (Lyman 1974: 314). In SHIMEN, however, it is reported to mean simply 'farther than *tim*' (Wang and Wang 1982: 22). I can understand why Wang and Wang, on the basis of SHIMEN, believe that *tim* is basic and *tom* derived, but White Hmong would suggest just the opposite: here *tom* is closer and *tim* is further away (and much more restricted in its use).[14]

Since the D2 reflex in White Hmong is characterized by a final glottal stop, Eric Hamp proposed that I look for an analytic construction or a locative suffix that may have given rise to a tone with such a shape upon absorption into the preceding word. It is precisely such an "absorption theory" that can best account for the demonstrative nouns derived from these prepositions, to be discussed in section 5 below. It is not as good a theory for the development of this form class for the following reasons:

(1) no likely construction has been found that may have served as the link between a word like 'plain' and its derivative 'down', something like 'the plain where...' and

(2) two alternate explanations for the final glottal stop in the morphotoneme *-m* exist:

—it could be very old, a trace of the final stop consonants *-p and *-t which characterized the ancient syllables corresponding to all D tone words (other than loanwords); or

---

[14] The fact that *tim* is farther away than *tom* in White Hmong belies the easy generalizations often made about the sound symbolic properties of vowels: that high vowels have "close" and "small" associations and low vowels have "far" and "large" associations.

—it could be a phonetic outgrowth of a low tone falling to "over-low," that is, to a point below the range where it is possible to sustain voicing.

In the absence of any evidence for a locative suffix or word that could have served as a source for the final glottal of the -*m* tone, I conclude that the glottal stop in itself is not a significant clue to the origin of this word class and can probably be attributed to one of the alternate explanations mentioned above.

Gérard Difflotth has proposed that stress may be involved in the tone shift to D2 in this form class in White Hmong and SHIMEN, since prepositions are normally unstressed words. The checked -*m* tone is indeed shorter than the other tones, but it is also at least as perceptually salient as the other tones because of the final glottal stop. Also, the fact that the same tone category (D2) is involved in both White Hmong and SHIMEN, and SHIMEN D2 (31) is not short or neutral in any way, makes me think that analogical tone change is the best explanation for the development of this form class.

5   Demonstrative Nouns

5.1   Description and Development of the -*d* Tone Class

When one of the ten denominal prepositions discussed above is used independently at the end of a phrase, it becomes a demonstrative noun that points out a place or time known to both speakers, either from previous discourse or from the speech situation. The syntactic change is accompanied by a tone change: the regular reflex of D2, the low falling checked (-*m*) tone changes to a derivative form, the -*d* tone, which is characterized by a low fall-rise contour and is somewhat longer in duration than the seven basic tones of the dialect. The -*d* tone is not an independent lexical tone in the language; it is almost always related to an -*m* tone form. Examples of tonal doublets corresponding to eight of the ten denominal prepositions follow:

nram /nrad 'down'

nyob nram teb[15]   down below in the field
be   down field

nyob nrad   down there

nraum /nraud 'outside'

nyob nraum zoov   outside
be   outside forest

nyob sab nraud   outside; on the other side
be   side outside

ntawm /ntawd 'here/there (nearby)'

nyob ntawm kev   on the trail
be   here trail

nyob ntawd   there (a small distance away)

pem /ped 'up'

nyob pem roob   up on the mountain
be up mountain

nyob ped   up there

saum /saud 'above'

nyob saum nthab   on the storage platform
be above platform

nyob saud   above there

---

[15] All of the above example phrases are taken from Bertrais-Charrier (1964) and can be found under the entries for their respective denominal prepositions.

tim /*tid* 'opposite'

> *nyob tim nej* at your place
> be opposite you
>
> *nyob tid* over there

tom /*tod* 'there'

> *mus tom khw* go to the market
> go there market
>
> *mus lawm tod* go over there
> go distance there

thaum /*thaud* 'time when'

> *thaum ntawd* at that time
> time there
>
> *puag txheej thaud* in the old days
> many generation time

Txhaid (< *txhaim*) is not attested; *zaud* (< *zaum*) does occur, but it stands in a somewhat different relationship to *zaum* than that of the *-d* forms to the *-m* forms above (see section 5.2 below).

A few *-m* tone words have been attracted into the pattern established by the space/time words above and have developed *-d* tone demonstratives as well. For these words, D2 is the historical tone; an earlier shift to D2 from some other tone has not taken place.

qaum /*qaud* 'back; top part of'

> *qaum tes* the back of the hand
> back hand (B *qaum*)
>
> *nyob nraum kuv sab nraub qaud* behind my back!
> be outside I side middle back (B *nraub*)

114

sim /*sid* 'time'

> *tam sim no*   right away (B *sim*)
> time this

> *tam sid*   right away
>   (B *sim*; H 293, 304)

chim /*chid* 'moment'

> *ib chim kuv tuaj*   I'm coming in a minute
> 1 moment I come   (B *chim*)

> *thawj chid*   at the beginning (B *chim*)
> first moment

npaum /*npaud* 'measure'

> *koj yuav npaum li cas?*   How much are you
> you take measure like how   taking? (B *npaum*)

> *kuv yuav tsis tas npaud*   I am not taking as
> I   take not all measure   much as that (B *npaum*)

tshuam /*tshuad* 'to fork; to join'

> *nyob tom kev tshuam*   where the roads meet
> be there road join   (B *tshuam*)

> *tom ob txog kev tshuad*   there where two roads
> there 2 clf road join   meet (Xab Xyooj)

menyuam /*menyuad* 'child'

> *nws muaj ob tug menyuam*   she had two children
> s/he have two clf child   (Downer 1967: 598)

> *ces ob tug menyuad chis chis*   then the two children
> then two clf child angry angry   were very angry
>   (Downer 1967: 598)

Sim and *chim* must be relative latecomers to this pattern since they are Chinese loans. This is to be suspected from the mismatch of initial and tone: *-m*, the White Hmong reflex of tone D2, corresponds to words with ancient voiced initials, while *s-* comes from [*ʒ-] and *ch-*, because of the aspiration, always patterns with the voiceless initials in native words.[16]

White Hmong and SHIMEN share not only the denominal preposition class but also this class, the demonstrative noun class (Wang and Wang 1982: 30-34). In SHIMEN, the members of the latter class are also derived from members of the former class by tone change. Just as the preposition class in each dialect is marked by the reflex of tone category D2 (in both cases a low falling tone), the demonstrative class in each dialect is marked by a rising tone. In SHIMEN, this rising tone has merged with the reflex of A2 (35, breathy voice). In White Hmong, this tone has not merged with the one rising tone in the inventory of basic tones (the reflex of B1, 24) but has stayed a distinct minor tone, low falling as its "mother tone" *-m*, with a rise to mid at the end:

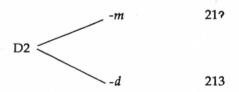

Downer (1967: 597-598) and Wang and Wang (1982: 30-34) disagree about the origin of the demonstrative noun class. Downer believes the *-d* tone is due to the absorption of a following demonstrative (for example, *ped* 'up there' is a portmanteau of *pem no*, where *no* is the demonstrative adjective meaning 'this') because

(1) a noun is obligatorily preceded by a classifier if it is followed by either a denominal preposition plus a demonstrative

---

16 David Strecker (personal correspondence) has pointed out to me that these words should be compared to Mandarin *shí* 'season; era, epoch, age; time; hour' and *qí* 'period, time; designated time; to expect'. Having begun a study of Chinese loans in Hmong, he and Brenda Johns have noted that the Mandarin second tone usually corresponds to White Hmong *-j*. The fact that it corresponds to White Hmong *-m* in these two words lends some support, they believe, to my theory that the *-m* tone plays a role as a "loantone" in White Hmong (see chapter two, section 2.2.3).

adjective or by a noun with tone -*d* in the White Hmong nominal phrase:

> *lub tsev pem no*   this house up here
> clf house up this
> > (but **tsev pem no*)

> *lub tsev ped*   this house up here
> > (but **tsev ped*)

(2) the -*d* words correspond to demonstrative adjectives in other dialects.[17]

(3) all -*d* words carry "the common semantic feature of definite reference" Downer (1967: 598), and

(4) "compensatory tone shift," or tone shift due to the absorption of one word by another, leaving only a tonal perturbation as its trace, "has been plausibly suggested as the origin of the Cantonese "changed-tones" and the Vietnamese anaphorics in the Saigon dialect, and serves equally well here" Downer (1967: 598).[18]

Wang and Wang (1982: 21), on the other hand, state that this class arose the same way the denominal preposition class (the -*m* tone class) arose: by analogy. As was mentioned above, the rising tone in SHIMEN, which corresponds to the -*d* tone in White Hmong, has merged with the A2 tone (35). Wang and Wang therefore look for a word with an original A2 tone as the model for this class. There being none, they hypothesize that [vɦai^{31}] (D2)/[vɦai^{35}] (A2) 'here/there' (semantically similar to White Hmong *ntawm/ntawd*) was originally A2. For this word alone they

---

[17] I specifically looked for this kind of cross-dialectal correspondence, but since most of my information on other dialects consists of words in isolation, I was unable to find it. SHIMEN does have many more demonstrative adjectives corresponding to the White Hmong *no* 'this' and *ub* 'that', and they indicate spatial relation to speaker in more detail than the two White Hmong demonstrative adjectives; but SHIMEN also has a class of nouns corresponding to the -*m* class of White Hmong, as we have seen.

[18] Other examples of "compensatory tone shift" include (1) possessive nouns and nominalized forms in Burmese (Thurgood 1981); (2) diminutives in Lahu (Matisoff 1986); (3) tone shift and definite reference in the Wenzhou dialect of Chinese and diminutives and nominalizations in the Wenling dialect of Chinese (Ballard 1985: 80).

were unable to find cognates among the dialects of the Sichuan-Guizhou-Yunnan fangyan, and so it became the model by default.

Of the two theories of the development of the -*d* tone and its counterpart in SHIMEN, Downer's theory seems the better to me for the following four reasons:

(1) As Downer mentions, "all examples can occur with the tone [-*m*] allomorph and followed by Demonstrative, with little difference in meaning (more precisely, with the added meaning of "contrast"...)" (1967: 598). I checked this statement with my primary tutor, who was able to affirm the identity of the following:

nram no	=	*nrad*	down there
nraum no	=	*nraud*	out there
ntawm no	=	*ntawd*	right here
pem no	=	*ped*	up there
saum no	=	*saud*	above there
tim no	=	*tid*	over there
tom no	=	*tod*	there
thaum no	=	*thaud*	at that time
qaum no	=	*qaud*	back there
tam sim no	=	*tam sid*	at this time (= right away)
chim no	=	*chid*	at this moment
npaum no	=	*npaud*	as much as this
...tshuam no	=	*...tshuad*	at that place (where two roads) meet
menyuam no	=	*menyuad*	this child

For the -*m*/-*d* pairs presented this far, the only exceptions to this equivalence were *txhaim no*/*txhaid* 'on the far side there', which is not part of my tutor's vocabulary (and is by far the least frequently encountered locative of the group) and *zaum no*/*zaud* 'that time' (*zaud* exists but not as the equivalent of *zaum no*, see section 5.2 below). Nonetheless, the equivalence of the -*m* form plus *no* 'this' (or *ub* 'that', I would imagine, although I did not check for it systematically) and the -*d* form is striking. What is more, my tutor rejected collocations, such as **thaud no* (=**thaum no no* 'that that time'), as ungrammatical.[19]

---

[19] Folk tales and stories of the past often begin with *thaud ub* 'long ago', though; a bit of counterevidence.

(2) The development of a rising tone in both SHIMEN and White Hmong upon absorption of a following demonstrative makes sense phonetically. In SHIMEN, it is easy to see how the D2 tone of the denominal prepositions (31) plus the B1 tone of the demonstratives [ɲi⁵⁵] 'this' and [i⁵⁵] 'that' could yield the high rising tone of the demonstrative nouns:

$$31 \quad + \quad 55 \quad = \quad 35$$

In White Hmong, the equation -*m* plus -*ø* equals -*d* works equally well:

$$21 \quad + \quad 33 \quad = \quad 213$$

(3) Both Downer and Wang and Wang translate and interpret the demonstrative nouns in the same way: Downer: "definite reference" (1967: 598); Wang and Wang: translate [vɦai³⁵], [bɦi³⁵], [ɳɖɦu³⁵] as "pointing at the place..." (1982: 32-33); state that these forms were derived from the denominal prepositions "in order to make the locations even clearer" (1982: 31).

The correspondence of the interpretation of these forms suggests a common development in the two dialects: from denominal preposition plus demonstrative adjective to independent demonstrative noun.

(4) There are certain weaknesses in the argument that the SHIMEN demonstrative nouns were formed on analogy with an original rising tone [vɦai³⁵] (A2) 'here/there'. First is the obvious problem that an original A2 form has not been established through comparative evidence; since the word exists only in SHIMEN, the antiquity of its tone is inferred. The authors are well aware of this weakness in their hypothesis (Wang and Wang 1982: 21). Second, since there is no counterpart to [vɦai³⁵] in White Hmong, it cannot be invoked as the model for an analogical shift in that dialect, but we would expect the development of this form class in the two dialects to be the same, since they are almost identical in function, form, and composition. Similarly, we would expect the demonstrative noun class in White Hmong to be characterized by the -*j* tone (A2) rather than by a variant of the -*m* tone (D2), if [vɦai³⁵] (A2) had been the model. Third, Wang and Wang explain that the demonstrative adjectives [ɲi⁵⁵] and [i⁵⁵] (corresponding to White Hmong *no* and *ub*) are not attracted into the demonstrative noun

class because they do not have aspirated initials (under my analysis, because they do not bear a tone characterized by breathiness or do not have aspirated initials) like the other words so changed (1982: 31). A better explanation for their non-involvement in this tone shift is that their absorption is the cause of the shift and that they would, of course, never be the affected words since it is their trace we see in the rising tone of the other demonstratives. The White Hmong demonstrative nouns are not characterized by any particular class of initial consonant, and, again, we would expect most explanations for phenomena related to this form class to hold for both dialects.

A third explanation for the development of this tone has to do with its occurrence in words in phrase final position.[20] This phrase final (if often sentence internal) position is the primary locus for the interaction of tone and intonation. Impressionistically, I have always felt an iconic relationship between this tone's length and rising contour, its deictic function, and its phrase final position. This is especially clear in the vocative use of *-d*, to be discussed below. The study of intonation in Hmong has not yet begun, however, so nothing definite can be said now about this important topic.

5.2   Extensions of the Use of the *-d* Tone

Downer reported two *-d* tone forms that are not related to *-m* tone forms but rather to words with other tones: *hnoob hmod* 'day-night' (= two days ago) and *tag kid* 'yesterday' from *hnoob hmo* and *tag kis*, respectively. These unusual forms were not confirmed by my primary tutor. The inference Downer draws from them, "that tone [*-d*] now functions independently as a morpheme of definite reference, no longer tied to the original derivation" (1967: 598) is nonetheless true for other reasons. If the "original derivation" was *-m* tone form plus demonstrative adjective, the following *-d* tone forms have broken away. They cannot be equated with the corresponding *-m* tone form plus demonstrative adjective, unlike the group of "secondary-members" attracted into the demonstrative noun class (*qaum, sim, chim, npaum, tshuam, menyuam*).

---

[20]   The suggestion that phrase final position might be related to the development of the *-d* tone was made by Gérard Diffloth.

120

lawm /*lawd* (≠ **lawm no*) perfective marker

> *Thaum yuav tau pojniam lawd, nws ua tus txiv kiag.*
> when marry get   wife   perf.   he make clf man true
> When he marries, a man becomes a "real man."

pom /*pod* (≠ **pom no*) 'to see'

> *Tos pod lawv twb nres nrheev ntawd.*   (B *tos*)
> ?   see they truly stop short   there
> Before they were seen, they were already there.

thwjtim /*thwjtid* (≠ **thwjtim no*) 'disciple'

> *Thwjtid coj peb mus.*   (Xab Xyooj)
> disciple take we go
> The disciples took us away.

The use of *-d* in all of the above is hard to characterize as "definite reference," but it is clear that the *-d* tone is now operating independently of its origin. There are at least three extended functions and meanings of the *-d* tone in White Hmong today:[21]

(1) as Downer observes, as a morpheme of definite reference,

> —*Nws muaj ob-tug menyuam.*
> S/he have two clf child
> She has two children   (Downer 1967: 598)

> —*Ces ob-tug menyuad chis chis*
> then two clf child angry angry
> Then those two children were very angry.
>   (Downer 1967: 598)

(2) in an extension of the definite reference for animate *-m* tone words, as a "mid-range" vocative:

---

[21] Matisoff (1986) discusses the exploitation of rare or "secondary" tones for grammatical or affective purposes (Lahu high rising tone, Jingpho falling tone, and Burmese creaky tone, for example).

—Menyuad!
Children!   (Xab Xyooj)

—Menyuam 'aw!!
Children!!   (Xab Xyooj)

   (3) as a stylistic variant of certain *-m* tone words, which has
the effect of either (a) revealing something about the attitude of
the speaker in difficult to define ways, much like intonation in
English does, or (b) imparting a certain literary or formal flavor.[22]
Some examples follow:

niam	mother
niad!	mother!
	("rude" "one would not call one's own mother that way," Yang Dao, personal correspondence)
tej zaum	maybe
	("60% likely," Xab Xyooj)
tej zaud	maybe
	("40% likely," Xab Xyooj)
muam	sister (man speaking)
leej muad	person-sister = Miss
	("polite, respectful" as used in courtship or in folk tale, personal correspondence to David Strecker from Mim Yaj)

The implications of these extended uses of the *-d* tone can probably
only be understood in light of a thorough knowledge of Hmong soci-
olinguistics and Hmong intonation, neither of which we have now.
The phonetics of the *-d* tone should also be studied and compared to
such stylistic variants as the above to see if in fact they can be
equated or whether a roughly similar intonation pattern has been
regularized in the orthography to match the demonstrative *-d*.

---

[22] Xab Xyooj consistently interprets *-d* tone forms as "literary" in folk
tales.

5.3   The Third Person Dual *nkawd*

It seems to me quite clear that the third person dual pronoun *nkawd* 'they two' developed out of the corresponding *-m* tone noun meaning 'pair; couple', which is attested for each of the nine dialects in Wang's comparative study (1979: 107). This is Mottin's analysis as well (1978: 20). My primary tutor accepts the equivalence of *nkawm no* and *nkawd*. Perhaps due to the fact that this pronoun is quite commonly used, two of my tutors have regularized the tone from the marginal *-d* (213) to *-v* (24), the one rising tone among the seven basic tones. I would be interested to see how widespread this regularization to *nkawv* has become. The semantic generalization that has accompanied the development of the third person dual pronoun is as follows:

> *nkawm*   pair; couple
>   (two unlike people or objects that go
>   together)
>
> *nkawd* (> *nkawv*) two
>   (either like or unlike: two brothers,
>   for example, or a man and a wife)

It is surprising to me that both Heimbach and Downer missed the connection between *nkawm* and *nkawd*. Heimbach cites *nkawd* as one of the two *-d* tone words that is almost always heard with that tone and not with *-m* (the other being *thwjtid* 'disciple', which, according to my tutor, is acceptable but does not sound as good as the corresponding *thwjtim*) (1979: 446). On the basis of these two words, he sets up *-d* as the eighth phonemic tone of White Hmong (1979: xxiii), which I find unnecessary to do since these words prove to be not at all exceptional. Downer cites *nkawd* as an exceptional word that cannot be equated to the corresponding *-m* tone form plus demonstrative (1967: 598); moreover, not only was *nkawm no* acceptable to my tutor, the meaning of the third person dual pronoun is a good example of the "demonstrativization" of a noun: 'a twosome' becomes 'these two (of whom we have been speaking)'.

I am intrigued by the possibility that the third person plural pronoun *lawv* may have arisen in a similar way. Many different words are used for the third person plural among the Hmong dialects: in Green Hmong, *puab*; in XUYONG, XIANJIN, and

SHIMEN, a compound with the third person singular; in MEIZHU, the third person dual and plural share the same root, [ɱu³³] (A1)/[ɱu¹²] (A2) (see section 3 above). I have not found a cognate for *lawv* in the pronoun systems of the other Hmongic dialects. What may its origin have been? The verb *lawm* 'to leave' in White Hmong has many varied extensions. It is used not only as a main verb but also as a perfective marker: 'the action is accomplished' as in *kuv noj mov lawm* 'I-eat-rice-perfective', or *'I am finished eating'* (often it indicates that "the action is underway," that is, has left the starting point). This word can also be used in reference to a place a certain distance away from the speaker, as in these sentences from Mottin (1978: 75, "a preposition used before others indicating a certain distance") and Bertrais-Charrier (*lawm* 'there'):

> *Cia peb mus lawm tom lawv.*
> let we go distance there they
> Let's go to their place.

> *Nws khiav lawm pem Tsheej Maim.*
> s/he run distance up Chiang Mai
> He escaped to Chiang Mai.

> *Koj mus lawm nrad.*
> you go distance down
> You are going down there.

> *Yes Xus mus lawm pem ntuj.*
> Jesus   go distance up sky
> Jesus went up into heaven.

Note that *lawm* in these sentences is unlike either the verb 'to leave' or the perfective marker and is more like a locative. I believe that an attempt to strictly categorize multifaceted words of this type in Asian languages according to part of speech is counterproductive and that a broader view based on the semantic thread that runs through all the uses of the word is more revealing.[23]

---

23 This bias of mine against strict part of speech categorization in Asian languages is due in large part to my interest in historical explanations for synchronic phenomena. In this larger framework, the word endures, but

What is common to the three uses of *lawm* above is that they all are concerned with a line between a home center and a certain distant point: the beginning of movement along the line (*lawm* 'to leave'), the accomplishment of either the outset or completion of such a movement (*lawm* perfective aspect marker), and the point at the end of the line (*lawm* 'there'). The next steps are not hard to take: 'there' to 'over there' to 'those over there'.[24] The supposition here is that White Hmong speakers in the not too distant past derived a *lawd* '(those) over there' form from *lawm* 'there', which has been regularized to *lawv* 'they', just as my tutors have regularized *nkawd* to *nkawv* 'they two'. This hypothesis is proposed with some hesitancy since the intermediate *lawd* '(those) over there' has not been attested. Such a form exists, but it is related to the perfective marker manifestation of the root (as exemplified in section 5.2 above). I propose it here in the absence of another explanation for the appearance of a form in the personal pronoun system that has no counterpart in any of the closely related dialects, even the mutually intelligible Green Hmong.

6   Male and Female Nouns

In White Hmong there are three pairs of words consisting of a male member and a female member that are distinguished phonologically by tone alone. Two more tonally contrastive pairs of words seem to be related to this small system, and a number of unpaired words seem to lend support to the idea that male words are often associated with the breathy (*-g*) tone and that their female counterparts are often associated with the low checked (*-m*) tone. The relevant words appear below:

Female	Male
ntxawm	*ntxawg*
youngest daughter;	youngest son
> *Ntxawm* (given name)	

---

its functions shift over the course of generations. I have nonetheless benefited greatly from the insights of Marybeth Clark, who has argued well over the years for the "synchronic derivation" of adverbs from verbs and prepositions from verbs within a purely synchronic framework.

[24] Benedict (1975: 209-210) claims to have found relationships between locatives and third person pronoun forms in Austronesian languages.

(muam) npaws female lst cousin different clan	*npawg* male lst cousin, different clan; peer, friend
(poj) ntsuam widow	*ntsuag* widow(er); orphan
yawm (txiv) maternal GF; older men in M's line	*yawg* paternal GF; older men in F's line; man, sir
niam (tais) wives of men designated by *yawm*	*pog* wives of men designated by *yawg*
muam sister (man speaking); female peer relation	
maum female	
niam mother; older female relation	
	nraug young unmarried man

The existence of the four form classes discussed previously, the numeral class, the dual/plural pronoun class, the denominal preposition class and the demonstrative noun class are certainly not controversial; only particular explanations for them may be disputed. In the case of the proposed "male class," marked by tonal morpheme -*g*, and "female class," marked by tonal morpheme -*m*, however, it is important to ascertain whether or not this is a pattern that actually exists in the language. Are new words entering this pattern or are old words being adapted to it? Are speakers avoiding -*g* tone words to designate females and -*m* tone words to designate males (in selecting names for children, for example)? Since there are questions in my mind about whether -*g* and -*m* are morphotonemes that have psychological reality for speakers or are merely artifacts of my analysis, the information about these words that follows is offered more as an intriguing possibility than as a discovery.

Since the shift of -*m* and -*s* tone words to the -*g* tone (categories D2 and B2 to category C2) is one of the tone sandhi shifts that can be reconstructed for Proto-West-Hmongic (see chapter two, section 3.1), I have proposed that the male members of four of the above pairs have arisen through sandhi form promotion (chapter two, section 4.1). This is the process whereby the dependent sandhi forms are elevated to independent form status upon the loss of the preceding -*b* tone or -*j* tone (category A1 or A2) trigger word. The male words for which tone category C2 (corresponding to -*g*) can be reconstructed and the female words for which tone category D2 (corresponding to -*m*) can be reconstructed may have been attracted into these developing male and female classes due to an accidental identity of tone. The crucial cases in the lists above are those cases where a word has unaccountably developed the "proper" sex coding: namely *ntsuam* 'widow' (the historical form corresponds to *ntsuag* 'widow(er), orphan') and *muam* 'sister (man speaking)'.

(1) *ntxawm* 'youngest daughter'/*ntxawg* 'youngest son'

This pair undoubtedly arose through sandhi form promotion. The youngest son in a family is often called *tub* (A1)-*ntxawg* (C2) (< *ntxawm* D2) 'son-youngest'. *Tub Ntxawg* is also often a given name for the youngest boy, just as *Ntxawm* is a common name for the youngest girl. Historically, *ntxawm* by itself simply meant 'youngest' without sex specification. This is still apparent in the kinship terms for father's younger brother and father's younger brother's wife, *txiv ntxawm* 'father-youngest' and *niam ntxawm* 'mother-youngest'.

Heimbach, Bertrais-Charrier, and Mottin all report that the identification of the -*g* tone with the male ('youngest son, pet name for little boy' Heimbach [1979: 210]; 'benjamin' Bertrais-Charrier [*ntxawg*]; Mottin [1978: 171]) and the identification of the -*m* tone with the female ('youngest daughter, pet name for little girl' Heimbach [1979: 210]; 'benjamine' Bertrais-Charrier [*ntxawm*];

127

Mottin [1978: 171]) have already been accomplished. As was reported in chapter two, however, the choice to use tone sandhi or not is often an individual matter. My primary tutor's father calls his youngest son *tub ntxawm*, without tone sandhi (or sex coding), although *tub-ntxawg* sounds better to his middle son, my tutor. Could it be that the younger generation is beginning to develop a feel for these tonally defined sex classes and in the process is restoring part of the generally decaying tone sandhi system?

(2) *npaws* 'female 1st cousin, different clan'/*npawg* 'male 1st cousin, different clan; peer, friend'

In this pair a good case can be made that the male (-*g* tone) form arose through sandhi form promotion, although the evidence is not quite as strong as that for the origin of the male form *ntxawg* 'youngest son' given above, where the tone sandhi trigger *tub-* 'son' is still in evidence in a White Hmong compound.

Historically, the word for 'cousin' (better translated as 'outside' according to Ruey 1958: 623) has tone B2, corresponding to the female form *npaws*:

MOSHICUN	$mp'e^{33}$(B2)
XUYONG	$mpeu^{11}$(B2)
SHIMEN	$mboey^{33}$(B2)

The word corresponding to *npaws* in White Hmong enters into a number of compounds in these dialects, the first parts of which are all sibling kinship terms. This makes sense, since *npaws* is in the same generation as ego. My tutor rejected **tub-npawg* as an impossible compound. It is clear to me now that *tub-* 'son' could not have triggered the shift to *npawg* because *tub* is in a younger generation than ego and would not be appropriate here simply as a sex designator. We must look, then, to one of the sibling kinship terms as the most likely trigger. The following 'sibling-cousin' compounds exist:

Woman speaking
   —sister-cousin:
      XUYONG ve^{51}(B1) $mpeu^{11}$(B2) 'older sister-cousin'
      XUYONG $ntʂau^{11}$(B2) $mpeu^{11}$(B2)
                              'younger sister-cousin'

Green Hmong *viv ncaug npawg*   'sister-cousin'

> Note that the possibility of sex coding arising through tone sandhi promotion does not exist in this case because in Green Hmong tones B2 and C2 have merged and are both realized by the breathy (*-g*) tone.

—brother-cousin:

XUYONG no^{11}(B2) mpeu^{11}(B2)

Green Hmong *nug npawg*

> See note above on *viv ncaug npawg* in Green Hmong

White Hmong *nus npaws*

> Note that Bertrais-Charrier (*npawg*) does not record *npawg* in this case, which may be due either to incomplete systematization of sex coding or to some retention of the meaning of the lost trigger in the word *npawg* (< *tij-npawg* 'brother [man-speaking]-cousin')

Man speaking

—sister-cousin:

XUYONG ma^{33}(C2) mpeu^{11}(B2)

Green Hmong *muam npawg*

> See note above on *viv ncaug npawg* in Green Hmong

White Hmong *muam npaws*

—older brother-cousin:

XUYONG ti^{21}(A2)-mpeu^{33}(C2)

> Note sandhi form

—younger brother-cousin:

XUYONG ku^{51}(B1) mpeu^{11}(B2)

> Note no tone sandhi here and compare XUYONG 'older brother-cousin' compound above

MOSHICUN kv^{55}(B1) mp'e^{33}(B2)

Green Hmong *kwv npawg*

> See note above on *viv ncaug npawg* in Green Hmong

White Hmong *kwv npawg*

The only sibling kinship term that could have acted as the trigger for the sandhi form *npawg* is *tij* 'older brother (man speaking)' in White Hmong, by virtue of its tone (A2). The compound **tij-npawg*, however, does not exist in White Hmong currently, according to my tutor (but the similar *kwv npawg* 'younger brother [man speaking]-cousin' compound does occur). What leads me to think that the origin of the "male form" was an earlier *tij-npawg is (1) the freedom of sibling terms to enter into compounds with 'cousin', as attested by Ruey's data for XUYONG (1958), and by pieces of that fuller system in White Hmong, Green Hmong, and MOSHICUN; and (2) the existence of this compound in XUYONG (which belongs to the same fangyan and sub-fangyan as White Hmong), with the sandhi form of 'cousin' here alone, of all the forms that Ruey cites.

(3) *poj ntsuam* 'widow'/*ntsuag* 'widow(er); orphan (either sex)'

Inspection of this White Hmong pair alone would lead one to think it another example of the male form arising from the female through tone sandhi promotion, especially since *tub-ntsuag* is a common term for 'boy orphan'. This seems not to be the case, though, since the word 'bereft one' (widow[er], orphan) bears the reflex of tone C2 (corresponding to White Hmong *ntsuag*) in every one of the nine dialects included in Wang's comparative study.[25] The only explanations for the -*m* form I can suggest are, therefore, (1) that it arose as a back-formation; *tub-ntsuag* perhaps looks and "feels" like a tone sandhi compound and a base form *ntsuam* has been inferred; or (2) the highly restricted *ntsuam* meaning 'widow' in the phrase *poj ntsuam* 'woman bereft' developed as a result of sex coding. In deciding between these two explanations, it is important to note that both Heimbach (1979: 205) and Bertrais-Charrier (*ntsuag*) list both *poj ntsuam* and *poj ntsuag* for 'widow'. The -*m* form does not dominate, apparently, even within its own semantic realm. The back formation theory would not explain why we encounter the form *ntsuam* only in a phrase that is a likely candidate for tone sandhi compounding itself (compare *poj-cuag* and *poj-sua*, appendix A) and not in isolation. The sex-coding theory, however, would explain the marginal appearance of the -*m* tone form and its use only by certain speakers or at certain times when used in reference to a woman, on analogy with *muam* 'sister', *niam* 'mother,

---

25 'Bereft one' is homophonous with the word for 'bamboo shoot' and interestingly cognate with it, according to Wang (1979: 43), because a bamboo shoot, without leaves or branches, is a symbol of loneliness.

woman' and *muam* 'female'. For these reasons, I would attribute the development of *ntsuam* to sex coding.[26]

(4) *yawm (txiv)* 'MGF...'/*yawg* 'PGF...'
   niam (tais) 'MGM...'/*pog* 'PGM...'

The words for maternal and paternal grandparents may be related to the tonally defined form classes I have been discussing with an interesting twist: referents are not coded by tone for sex, but the relationship to ego, through mother (*-m*) and father (*-g*). The paternal grandparent forms could also be promoted tone sandhi forms. There are two problems involving these pairs, however: (1) in the closely related XUYONG dialect the same doublet for 'grandfather' exists (with C2 and D2 tone category reflexes) but with a different semantic distinction, and (2) there is no trace of the trigger words that may have given rise to the forms *yawg* (<*yawm*) or *pog* (<*poj*).

In XUYONG [ʤeu^{13}] (D2) (corresponding to White Hmong *yawm*) is the unmarked form and is used to refer to grandfathers and many other older male relatives on either the mother's or the father's side. [ʤeu^{33}] (C2) (corresponding to White Hmong *yawg*) is the marked term: by itself it means 'husband' (as in Green Hmong *quas yawg*), in compounds, it refers to men related to the husband through his wife (Ruey 1958: 618). XUYONG [pɔ^{21}] (A2) (corresponding to White Hmong *poj*) by itself is used for 'wife' (as in White Hmong *poj niam* and Green Hmong *quas puj*), and in compounds it is used to refer to the wives of different uncles, [pɔ^{33}] (C2) (corresponding to White Hmong *pog*) is used to refer to either grandmother (Ruey 1958: 612-622). The asymmetry in the application of these terms in XUYONG is characteristic of the Hmong kinship term systems as discussed by Ruey (1958) and Lemoine (1972). The following passage from Ruey (1958: 632), describing the complexity and instability of the kinship term system; it also helps explain why such closely related dialects should utilize the same terms so differently:

---

[26] An unexplained doublet characterized by these same two tones with the same distribution (*-g* tone historical, in general use, *-m* tone confined to one compound) is *ntswg* 'nose'/*caj ntswm* '(body part)-nose' (H 206).

This brief analysis of the Miao kinship system shows it to be a complicated and unbalanced system of classifying relatives....Thus we see that first, it recognizes the biological differences between persons of the same and separate generations, and between lineal and collateral relationship on the one hand, but uses single terms to designate several relatives of different generations and of separate lineages on the other. Secondly, it recognizes the social phenomena of marriage on the one hand, but uses several single terms to designate both consanguineal and affinal relatives on the other. Thirdly, it recognizes sex differences of the relatives referred to, of the speaker, and of the person through whom relationship exists, but these distinctions are expressed only partially and rather unbalancedly. Fourthly, it recognizes age difference within one generation, but this distinction is made only between older and younger relatives of the same sex to ego and not those of the opposite sex. In short, the Miao kinship system recognizes criteria of generation, collaterality, affinity, sex, speaker's sex, bifurcation, and relative age within one generation, but carries them out inconsistently.

The significance of the fact that the *-m*/*-g* distinction is used to mark maternal/paternal ascendant relations in White Hmong may be that this is an extension of a growing tendency toward sex coding in this dialect. In Green Hmong, *yawm* and *yawg* are used to indicate maternal and paternal ascendant relations, as in White Hmong, but the corresponding female terms are *tais* (literally 'in-law', according to Ruey (1958: 626) and *puj* (corresponding to the "uncoded" White Hmong *poj*). To establish that *yawg* and *pog* were derived from *yawm* and *poj* via sandhi form promotion, we need to have evidence that allows us to reconstruct tone D2 for 'grandfather' and tone A2 for 'woman', and we would like to have evidence of probable tone sandhi trigger forms that, in compounds with *yawm* and *poj*, would have given rise to the *-g* forms. The following cognate forms have been found for 'grandfather' > 'husband; man':

	grandfather	husband	man
White Hmong	jaɯʔ²¹(D2)/jaɯ⁴²(C2)		jaɯ⁴²(C2)
Green Hmong	jaɯʔ²¹(D2)/jaɯ⁴²(C2)jaɯ⁴²(C2)		
XUYONG	jeu¹³(D2)	jeu³³(C2)	
XIANJIN	ʐeu²⁴(D2)		

Although few in number, these forms seem to confirm tone D2 (the *yawm* tone) for Proto-West-Hmongic. The following cognate forms have been found for 'woman, wife' > 'grandmother':

	woman	wife	grandmother
White Hmong	po⁵³(A2)	po⁵³(A2)	po⁴²(C2) (paternal)
Green Hmong	pu⁵³(A2)	pu⁵³(A2)	pu⁵³(A2)
MOSHICUN	—	po³¹(A2)	po³¹(A2)
XUYONG	po²¹(A2)	po²¹(A2)	po³³(C2)
XIANJIN	po³¹(A2)	po³¹(A2)	po¹³(C2)
SHIMEN	bɦo³⁵(A2)		
FUYUAN	vu³¹(A)		

These forms similarly confirm tone A2 (the *poj* tone) for Proto-West-Hmongic. It is interesting to note the mirror-image semantic development of the male and female terms: the male term in sandhi form is extended through generalization (grandfather > honorific > man), while the female term in sandhi form is extended through specialization (woman > grandmother).

The second kind of evidence that would show that *yawg* and *pog* are promoted tone sandhi forms, however, has not been found. The tone sandhi trigger forms that gave rise to the *-g* forms would have appeared to the left of *yawm* and *poj*, and, of the many compounds involving these terms that I have seen, *yawm/yawg* and *poj/pog* always appear as the first member.[27] The only compound I have been able to imagine as a possible source is *poj-yawg* 'grandparents' on the model of *niam txiv* 'mother-father' or 'parents' (but see Bertrais-Charrier *yawg: niam txiv poj yawm* 'ancestors' with no tone sandhi). After the shift of *yawm* to *yawg*,

---

[27] The only exception is White Hmong *phauj pog* 'paternal grandfather's sister', which does not seem relevant.

one might then imagine an assimilatory shift of *poj* to *pog*. In the absence of a truly strong candidate for the compound that gave rise to the sandhi form *yawg*, however, we may entertain the idea that the pair *yawm* / *yawg*, already existing in the family (as represented by XUYONG), whatever its origin, came to be identified with the emerging male and female classes in White Hmong. Similarly, *pog*, which in XUYONG and XIANJIN seems to be applicable to either the paternal grandmother or the maternal grandmother, is used solely for the paternal grandmother in White Hmong. I look forward to future descriptions of the kinship term systems of related dialects to provide the data that will eventually explain these interesting White Hmong doublets.

Hereafter follows the comparative data on the one unpaired male term and the three unpaired female terms that may reinforce developing tonally defined male and female form classes in White Hmong.

(1) *nraug* 'young, unmarried man'

White Hmong	$ɳɖau^{42}$(C2)
Green Hmong	$ɳɖau^{42}$(C2)
XIANJIN	$ɳtou^{13}$(C2)
SHIMEN	$ɳɖau^{53}$(C2a)
ZONGDI	$ɳto^{13}$(C2)
FUYUAN	$ɳtʑu^{24}$(C)
FENGXIANG	$ɳtɕou^{31}$(C2)
MEIZHU	$ɳtau^{22}$(C2)
YANGHAO	$ŋo^{13}$(C2)

There is a word meaning 'man' in a number of Hmong dialects, with a reconstructed tone C2 that would correspond to a White Hmong *cag*, but it certainly plays no role in the development of these classes. What is of significance is that both *npawg* and *yawg*, originally 'male cousin' and 'paternal grandfather', have become quite general in their use. *Npawg* is now used to refer to any male friend or acquaintance who is not in one's clan or who is believed to be outside one's clan. *Yawg* is now used to refer to any older man whose name one does not know, and one of my tutors reports that it is also used in slang to address peers ("Hey, man").

(2) *niam* 'mother'

White Hmong	$nia?^{21}$(D2)	mother
Green Hmong	$na?^{21}$(D2)	mother
MOSHICUN	na^{13}(D2)	mother
XUYONG	na^{13}(D2)	mother
XIANJIN	na^{24}(D2)	mother/female
SHIMEN	$ɲɦie^{31}$(D2)	mother/female
QINGYAN	mje^{54}(D2)	female
GAOPO	$mε^{55}$(D2)	female
ZONGDI	mi^{21}(D2)	female
FUYUAN	men^{24}(C)	female
FENGXIANG	men^{13}(D2)	female
MEIZHU	mi^{21}(D2)	mother
YANGHAO	mi^{31}(D2)	female

(3) *maum* 'female'

White Hmong	$mau?^{21}$(D2)
Green Hmong	$mau?^{21}$(D2)

(4) An important case is *muam*, the word for 'sister (man speaking)'. The data are as follows:

White Hmong	$mua?^{21}$(D2)
Green Hmong	$mua?^{21}$(D2)/mua^{42}(C2)
	(the C2 form is limited to the compound *muag nug* 'sister-brother', Lyman 1974: 186)
XUYONG	ma^{33}(C2)
XIANJIN	mua^{13}(C2)

The XUYONG, XIANJIN, and marginal Green Hmong forms allow us to reconstruct C2 as the historical tone for White Hmong *muam* 'sister (man speaking)'. This reconstruction is supported by cognates in the Mien family that have tone C2 (Purnell 1970: 180). The appearance of the D2 forms in White Hmong and Green Hmong supports the idea that tonally defined sex classes are emerging in these dialects. In both the case of *muam* (D2) 'sister' and the case of *(poj) ntsuam* (D2) 'widow', the change of tone may best be understood as a combination of a move toward the female -*m* tone and away from the (historical) male -*g* (C2) tone. If the historical tone for these two words had been neutral with respect to sex coding, perhaps the tone change would not have taken place.

135

CHAPTER *FOUR*

TONAL MORPHOLOGY AND TONAL ICONICITY IN TWO-WORD EXPRESSIVES

1   Expressive Language in Hmong

Expressives constitute a formally and syntactically distinct word class in White Hmong. Early descriptions of White Hmong expressives include Heimbach (1979: appendix 8), Ratliff (1986), and Pederson (1985). Studies of expressives in other Hmongic languages include P'an and Ts'ao (1958), to the extent that they occur in four-word coordinative constructions, and Ts'ao (1961), both concerning dialects of East Hmongic, and Wang and Wang (1983), concerning the SHIMEN dialect of West Hmongic. The term "expressive" is taken from the work of Gérard Diffloth (1972, 1976, 1979) and is used to describe the White Hmong word class because of similarities between the words Diffloth discusses (in various Mon-Khmer languages and Korean) and the Hmong words herein discussed in terms of (1) their importance in everyday expression, (2) their characteristic position outside the main structure of the phrase, (3) their morphology, (4) their meaning, and (5) the greater exploitation of the sound symbolic properties of the components of these words as opposed to "prosaic" words.[1]

Although one-word expressives and four-word coordinative constructions are quite common in Hmong, I have focused on the two-word expressives, examples of which appear listed in appendix C, because it is only at the level of the two-word phrase that we can begin to talk about morphology in a language that is characterized by monosyllabic words bare of affixes. The interaction of the tones,

---

[1] I use the term "prosaic" after Diffloth (1979) to refer to all other except expressive words, where the connection between sound and meaning is largely, but certainly not wholly, arbitrary.

consonants, and vowels in these two-word phrases constitutes their morphology. Furthermore, the resemblance perceived between sound and meaning is revealed more surely in these two-word phrases, where there is more phonological "stuff" to establish the iconic connection with the particular sound, movement, or attitude being described. Although the breathy (-g) tone in the exclamation *poog!* 'boom!' (derived from the verb *poob* 'to fall', according to one Green Hmong speaker) is doubtlessly chosen because its inherent properties recall the impact of the fall in some way, the other tones, which involve clear phonation, cannot in isolation be associated with aspects of the real world as easily. In unison with another tone, however, the possibility of symbolic exploitation becomes greater: two low level (-s) tones can be used to suggest humming, droning, or an unending sight; a high falling (-j) tone followed by a mid rising (-v) tone can be used to suggest a back and forth movement or mental vacillation. The choice of initial consonant (which must be identical in the two words) from the rich Hmong inventory of initials, and to a lesser extent the choice of the second vowel (the first being determined by the tone pattern as I will show), together with the choice of tone pattern allows a great deal of precision in fit between sound and meaning in these expressive phrases. I will not have much to say about the iconic properties of the segmental phonemes, however, since the tone patterns are fewer in number and simpler to characterize and since the focus of my study of Hmong has been tone as a tool for organization.

Expressives in Hmong, as in the languages described by Diffloth, are of central importance to the language as a whole. According to Ts'ao (1961) who studied the expressives of the KAITANG dialect of East Hmongic:

> These syllables are sometimes incomprehensible to the Chinese comrades who study Miao. Even when they do understand these syllables, it is very difficult for them to translate the Miao meaning into Chinese. Nevertheless, the expressive power of these syllables is great. In some linguistic environments they are practically indispensable. Without such syllables the language would be much less colorful. On the one hand, a speaker would be unable to express his specific thoughts and feelings. A hearer, on the other hand, would consider the conversation dull.
> (translated in Purnell 1972: 187)

The little stories and practice sentences in the *White Hmong Literacy Primer* published by the Center for Applied Linguistics (Vwj Tsawb et al. 1983) are full of these expressive phrases, testimony to the importance of these words: the *Primer* was designed by literate Hmong to be the first written Hmong encountered by native students and was carefully planned to reflect ordinary, everyday speech as opposed to oral literature (Barbara Robson, CAL coordinator, personal correspondence).[2]

Syntactically, Hmong expressives are differentiated from the language of propositions, the language proper, where utterances can be reduced to predicate and arguments and where words participate in relations of synonymy and antonymy. Expressives can be neither questioned nor negated. They stand post-verbally and generally phrase finally. A goal or source verb may follow, however, as in:

> *tus nqaij maub nuj nuag los*   (B *nuj*)
> clf game grope   come
> the wild animal comes...(manner)...through the underbrush;

a prepositional phrase may follow:

> *tsov quaj mlig mlog tim roob*   (*Primer* 112)
> tiger cry   over on mountain
> the tiger calls *"mlig mlog"* over on the mountain;

or a sentence adverb such as *xwb* 'only' may follow:

> *Foom ua tib tug fee duj das xwb* (*Primer* 43)
> Foom make single clf turn   only
> Foom merely turned his head, shaking his head and shoulders "I don't know."

---

2 There may be a predisposition toward these alliterating two-word expressives in the *Primer*, however, since the organizational focus of this and all other literacy primers I have seen is the initial consonant: with each lesson a new initial is introduced, and the stories written are limited to words beginning with that consonant and those introduced previously. The early stories are, hence, highly artificial and heavily alliterative. On the advice of Robson, I began to pay close attention to these prose samples at a point about halfway through the book for that reason.

The onomatopoeic expressives are often, but not always, preceded by the word *nrov* 'sound', which has the force of 'goes' in English: "the whistle goes 'pfweet'." Otherwise, they are preceded by a verb that will give an indication of what sensory experience is being appealed to: for example, *poob* 'to fall', *txav* 'to move', *nrog* 'to drip', *sawv* 'to rise', *quaj* 'to cry'.

Expressives capture the speaker's perception of the essence of the thing described, not only its sound but also its movement, its persistence, its visibility, and other innate characteristics, through his determination of the resemblance between sound and meaning. The speaker's sensory experience related to sound and movement and his attitude toward what he is describing predominate in the White Hmong expressives I have collected (see appendix C). Except for the interesting *nrhij nrhawj,* which, according to Bertrais-Charrier (*nrhij*) is used to describe the sensation of cracking nerves, and perhaps *lis loos,* which seems to be used to describe the smoothness of machine woven fabric (Xab Xyooj), neither kinesthetic sensations nor the sensation of touch plays a great role.

The multiple associations I was given for some of these expressives are fascinating but are also sometimes very difficult to reduce to a "common core":

> The meaning of expressives seem to be extremely detailed and idiosyncratic, describing a situation perceived as a whole, as an independent clause would. On the other hand, the same expressive can be used to describe a variety of situations which at first glance seem to be quite different but share a common core which could be defined as a cluster of elementary sensations. For instance, /klknare:l/ is used to describe an arrow or knife stiffly vibrating after embedding itself into a piece of wood; it can also describe the walk of a tall, skinny old man. The cluster of sensations common to both meanings (and recognized by informants) are: stiffness, perpendicularity, and repeated small oscillations. (Diffloth 1976: 257)

Accordingly, in the sources and in this study, either a very specific association will be given, for example, *txij txej* 'a rat crying out in a snake's mouth', or an attempt at the "common core" will be offered, for example, *nkhis nkhoos* 'the sound of hollow things'. Neither alone gives enough information for the expressive to be well understood. I have included, therefore, all information at my disposal, at whatever level of abstraction, to elucidate the two-word expressives in appendix C, and I am conservative in advancing judgments as to the unifying concept underlying a number of different associations for one expressive.

One reason for this conservatism is that there remains a question in my mind as to whether the meaning of an expressive can always be reduced to a "cluster of elementary sensations," with all sensations having equal status with regard to each other. Perhaps one sense is basic and the others derived. For example, *hawv huav* has the following associations: (1) the sound of animals growling, getting ready to bite, (2) human panting, and (3) nervous, tense pacing—the sense of sound may be basic and the apprehension of the related behavior may be secondary; similarly, the behavior of the animals may be basic, and the behavior of the humans may be perceived as animal-like.

Expressives seem to be characteristic of the Hmongic family, as evidence by the studies by Ts'ao and Wang and Wang cited above. Heimbach made good lists of expressives in his White Hmong dictionary (1979: 468-479), although a number of unrelated things are included there (all of which are difficult to translate and come at the ends of phrases). He calls these words "post-verbal intensifiers," a term that I feel should be dropped. These words particularize; they are eye witness accounts of the passing scene and, as such, give immediate apprehension to characterizations. They do not intensify in the sense of giving more of some aspect of meaning that is already in the utterance without the expressive. That is the function of reduplication in Hmong. Although the single richest source of expressives in White Hmong is Bertrais-Charrier's dictionary, he denigrates his contribution, and the word class itself for that matter, when he writes in his preface: "Délibérément nous avons omis les onomatopées, très nombreuses, mais aussi très fantaisistes et variables d'un individu à l'autre." What is surprising to those acquainted with English comic-book expressives, which are fanciful and variable, to some extent, from one individual to another, is the remarkable agreement as to the precise situation when a particular Hmong expressive is appropriate from one individual to another. The subject of unanimity of interpretations will be discussed further in section 3.1.2.

Iconicity in Hmong expressives, or the direct reflection of meaning in phonological representation, is apparent in other parts of speech and other aspects of language in the Hmongic family: (1) in the reduplication of prosaic words to convey the idea of augmentation, (2) in the vowel gradation in the classifiers of SHIMEN described by Wang (1957), and (3) in the vowel gradation and tone patterns in the second and fourth member of the four-word coordinative constructions described by P'an and Ts'ao (1958), Mottin (1978), and Johns and Strecker (1982). Since in these instances an effort is made to bend the prosaic language to mirror the natural world, a language that has a well-developed expressive system can be expected to have other kinds of "word play," or evidence of the language craftsman's skill: this is certainly true of Hmong, in which pig latins (secret languages) have been encountered and a highly sophisticated and elaborate oral literature exists.

2   The Morphology of Two-Word Expressives

2.1   The Two Basic Forms

The White Hmong two-word expressives have one of two basic forms. In each, the two words have identical initial consonants or consonant clusters but dissimilar vowels. In the first form, the tones of the two words are the same, and the vowel of the first word is -i-, with -aw- being a less common alternative. In the second form, the tone of the first word is high falling (-j); the tone of the second word is some other tone, and the vowel of the first word is -u-. From the semantic associations I was given by my tutors, there seems to be clear tonal iconicity in the more well-represented patterns. For that reason, the data in appendix C are organized by tone pattern, and impressions of the meanings associated with the patterns are given where possible. The two basic forms can be represented as follows:

(1) $C_1 / i / T_1$ $C_1 V_2 T_1$
       $(C_1 / aw / T_1$ $C_1 V_2 T_1)$

(2) $C_1 / u / T_{-j}$ $C_1 V_2 T_2$

The variant of the first form with -aw- has so far been identified only for the tone patterns -g/-g, -s/-s, and -v/-v. It is a minor variant with the first two tone patterns, but it accounts for about half of the examples with tone pattern -v/-v.

Given the basic tone inventory of seven tones, there are thirteen possible patterns:

(1)   *-ø/-ø   (2)   -j/-ø
       -b/-b   -j/-b
       -g/-g   -j/-g
       -j/-j   -j/-m
      *-m/-m   -j/-s
       -s/-s   -j/-v
       -v/-v

Of these thirteen possibilities, two do not occur: -ø/-ø and -m/-m.[3] Further field work of the kind described in section 3.1.2 below, where hypothetical expressives are presented to speakers for evaluation, is necessary to determine if these are impossible patterns or if the absence of examples here is simply fortuitous.

2.2   The Derivative Nature of the First Word

In both of these two-word expressive forms, it is important to note that the second word is likely to be the core of the phrase and the first word is likely to be an artificial construct. As can be seen from the formulae above, the initial, vowel, and tone of the first word can be predicted from the initial, vowel, and tone of the second (although it is impossible to predict, unless the tone of the second word is -ø or -m, which of the two forms, reduplicative tone or falling tone, will be chosen). In this respect, and even with respect to details about initial, vowel, and tone, White Hmong two-word expressives are very much like the SHIMEN "bisyllabic manner words":

> The variant of a monosyllabic manner word is its basic form plus another syllable in front of it. The initial of the added syllable is the same as that in the basic form and its final is /u/ and its tone is high level....If the basic form has /u/ as its final, then the final of the

---

[3] I am grateful to Terrence Kaufman for calling my attention to this gap in the data.

added syllable will dissimilate into /i/... (Wang and Wang 1983: 194)

Although many two-word expressives seem to have existed in this form ab origine, others can most profitably be thought of in terms of Wang and Wang's "basic form" and "added syllable." These are the two-word expressives in which the second word can be used independently, either as a "prosaic word" (noun, verb) or as a one-word expressive. Of the two types of incorporation, the one involving prosaic words is the most interesting because here the line between the two broad categories of words in the language, prosaic and expressive, is blurred. Where the two meet, speakers demonstrate sensitivity to the latent iconic possibilities of "real words."

In the sections that follow, examples of both prosaic-word incorporation and one-word expressive incorporation are given.

2.2.1   Prosaic-Word Incorporation

Since the number of examples of prosaic-word incorporation I have is small, I present all of them below:

(1) *dig*   to be blind

tus neeg dig muag   a blind person   (H 35)
clf person blind eye

> *ua duj dig*   to feel one's way with feet and
make   hands like a blind person   (B *dig*)

> *maub duj dig*   to go along, feeling one's way
grope   like a blind person   (B *dig*)

(2) *nthav*   to detach, separate

mov txua nthav   mandarin rice separates
rice non-separate   (is not sticky)   (B *nthav*)
   glutinous

> *nag poob nthiv nthav*   the rain falls in
rain fall   large, distinct drops
                                   (B *nthiv*)

(3) *teev*   drop (n.)

teev ntshav no liab   this drop of blood is red
drop blood this red   (B *teev*)

> *dej nrog tuj teev*   the water drips drop by drop
water drip   (B *teev*)

(4) *vias*   to hang, balance, swing

ua ib-viag   to make one swing (H 400)
make 1 swing

> *ua vuj vias*   to go back and forth on a swing
                                                          (Kuam Yaj)
                                            (of a drunk's or a toddler's way of
                                            walking) (Kuam Yaj)

(5) *xuav*   to whistle

xuav yij   to whistle for game birds
whistle game bird   (B *xuav*)

> *nplooj zeeg nrov xuav*   when the leaves fall
leaf shake sound whistle   off in great number
                                            they make a whistling
                                            sound (B *xuav*)

> *los nag xuj xuav*   a long, light, all-day rain
come rain   (H 412, Kuam Yaj)

> *xuj xuav*   (of a snake's slow wriggle)
                                                          (Xab Xyooj)

In the following example, the basic word has been tonally altered:

(6) *hlu*   to drag out, delay

Txhob hlu!   Don't stall! (H 65)

> *xuab taw hluj hluav* to drag the feet; delay in
rub foot   taking action (H 412)

144

In the following example, the prosaic word, because of its tone and vowel, better fits the slot of the first word:

(7) *yuj*   to hover, fly in slow circles

dav yuj saib qaib   the eagle hovers, watching
eagle circle watch chick   the chickens (B *yuj*)

> *ua yuj yees*   to have vertigo (B *yees*)
  make

> *cov ntses ya ua yuj yees*   the fish flash by in
  clf fish fly make   circles (*Primer* 120)

> *qav taub ya ua yuj yeev*   the little frog flies
  frog short fly make   around (*Primer* 25)

> *piav yuj yeev*   to balance oneself lightly
  dawdle   (B *yuj*)

> *kuv nyob yuj yeev*   I'm fooling around (B *yuj*)
  I stay

2.2.2   One-Word Expressive Incorporation

Since there are many examples of one-word expressives preceded by "added syllable," I will list only six illustrative examples here:

(1) *dhev*

quaj dhev   to cry a little (H 40)
cry

> *quaj dhuj dhev*   to whimper (B *quaj*)
  cry

> *quaj nqus ntswg dhawv dhev*   wept loudly
  cry inhale nose   and bitterly (H 266)

(2) *nkaus*

145

nthos nkaus   snatch   (H 196)
grasp

> *nthos nkuj nkaus*   snatch and put back quickly
  grasp   (Xab Xyooj)

(3) *nrhawj*

tu nrov nrhawj   to break with the sound . . .
break sound   (H 182)

>*tu nrov nrhij nrhawj*   to break with the sound . . .
 break sound   (B *nrhij*)

(4) *nhreev*

sawv nrheev   to stand straight up   (H 182)
rise

> *sawv nrhuj nrheev*   to stand up with difficulty
   rise   (H 182)

(5) *qees*

hais qees   to continue talking   (H 262)
speak

> *hais quj qees*   to speak slowly
                                            and deliberately   (H 263)

(6) *tsuaj*

tsuj av nkos nrov tsuaj   when one walks in the step earth
mud sound   mud, it goes... (B *tsauj*)

> *lwg zeeg nrov tsij tsuaj*   the dew shakes off . . .
   dew shake sound   (B *tsuaj*)
        off

3   Impressions of Tonal Iconicity

In this section, I will set forth the initial impressions I
formed about resemblances perceived by speakers between certain

aspects of the major tone patterns and certain phenomena in the real world. Tone is used as a focus for my discussion of the White Hmong two-word expressives because (1) tone defines the two basic forms of these expressives, (2) tonal iconicity involves fewer contrasts than consonantal iconicity and is, therefore, easier to isolate and discuss, and (3) tonal iconicity simply seemed clearer and more consistent than that involving either consonants or vowels. My impressions grew out of an examination of the associations I had been given for the two-word expressives as organized by tone pattern (as in appendix C) and were first presented in Ratliff (1986). Of the ten attested patterns at that time (there are now eleven, with the addition of seven examples of expressives with the *-uj/-ø* pattern), impressions as to the nature of the tone/meaning connection were attempted for only six. This was due to the limited number of examples and the heterogeneous nature of the associations for the *-iv (-awv)/-v, -uj/-b, -uj/-g,* and *-uj/-m* patterns. The six patterns for which impressions of iconicity were formed as follows:

-ib/-b   (high level/high level)
        high pitched, short sounds

-ig/-g   (breathy fall/breathy fall)
        low pitched, echoic, hollow, airy sounds

-ij/-j   (high falling/high falling)
        energetic, fast, short sounds; surface contact
        as opposed to contact and penetration

-is/-s   (low level/low level)
        flat, continuous, unending sights and sounds

-uj/-s   (high falling/low level)
        suggests both aspects of *-uj/-v* (back and forth) and
        -is/-s (level and steady): sounds, movements,
        attitudes

-uj/-v   (high falling/mid rising)
        a double orientation (back and forth, up and down,
        in and out): movements, sounds, attitudes

3.1   Verification Techniques

The two "experiments" I used to verify the accuracy of my initial impressions of tonal iconicity as represented above were not particularly rigorous. They were conducted under informal interview conditions, embedded in a context of conversation, with a number of interruptions and digressions. Nonetheless, I found them both to be a valuable check on my analysis. It is of importance that both are replicable by any other interested party. Such verification techniques as the two discussed here and their implementation by more than one investigator are necessary to insure that flights of one particular investigator's fancy are not imposed on an analysis of expressives, which already belong to the more fanciful part of language.

3.1.1 Expressive Elicitation

In 1983, when I first discerned the morphology of the two-word expressives and had formed an initial idea as to the meanings associated with the major tone patterns, I wrote a list of some natural phenomena that I felt were of the type to be described by an expressive in Hmong. I also made a guess as to which tone pattern would characterize the expressive, if there were one. Keeping my predictions about tone patterns to myself, I asked my tutors (in a joint session) if there were expressives for these phenomena. Usually, there was no expressive for a particular meaning I proposed. However, if one did exist, its tone pattern matched my prediction with more than chance frequency. Some examples of expressives elicited in this fashion follow:

(1) the sound of thunder
    prediction: *-ig/-g*
    given: *ntig ntwg*

(2) the sound of a typewriter
    prediction: *-ij/-j*
    given: *nrij nrawj* or *ntij ntawj*

(3) the sound of a little animal running over an empty box
    prediction: *-ig/-g* (hollow)
    given: *kig kuag*

(4) the sinuous movement of a snake
    prediction: *-uj/-v* (back and forth)
    given: *xuj xuav*

(5) the sound of hiccups
    prediction: either *-iv/-v* or *-ij/-j* (short, energetic)
    given: *iv awv* (Xab Xyooj only) and
          ij awj (Kuam Yaj and Xab Xyooj)

3.1.2 Expressive Paradigm Completion

Following a suggestion by Gérard Dif, I conducted a more extensive check on my initial impressions of tonal iconicity in the winter of 1985, the results of which were presented at a conference on sound symbolism at the University of California at Berkeley in January, 1986. I met with the same two people who had participated in my earlier investigation in individual sessions.[4] To each, I presented twenty expressive paradigms built on at least one attested expressive. The consonants and second vowel were held constant and only the tone patterns (and the dependent first vowel) were changed. For example, I had already received the expressives

> *plib pleb* (the sound of wood crackling)
> *plij plej* (the sound of popcorn popping)

from these speakers before. What associations, if any, did they have for the following hypothetical expressives (which I predicted should exist, or should at least sound Hmong-like, based on my understanding of the morphology of White Hmong two-word expressives)?

> *?plig pleg*
> *?plis ples*
> *?pluj plev*
> *?pliv plev* or *?plawv plev*

(Note that only the major patterns, the most productive and/or the ones for which I had formed an impression of the tone/meaning connection were included.) This experiment served to accomplish three things: (1) to support and refine my impressions of tonal iconicity (its original purpose), but also (2) to confirm my description of the morphology of these expressives, and (3) to provide insight into consonantal iconicity.

---

[4] One of my tutors, Xab Xyooj, kindly took lists of my hypothetical expressives home with him and discussed them with an older (60-65) monolingual male speaker, Txawj Tsab Xyooj. Xab made notes on his comments and shared them with me.

As a check of my account of the morphology, this procedure worked very well. Almost all of the hypothetical expressives were judged well-formed (they "sounded like Hmong") whether or not the speakers were able to give me contexts and associations for them. As a control, I randomly inserted poorly formed hypothetical expressives into the paradigms (such as *mus mes, based on the attested expressive mij mej, where the vowel of the initial word is wrong). These poorly formed expressives were almost all immediately rejected, whereas the unfamiliar well-formed expressives were generally pondered over for a period of some minutes, whether or not clear associations were forthcoming.

It is important to note that the morphological constraints on the two-word expressives demonstrate that these words are not simply sound imitative. The onomatopoeic expressives have a highly stylized character because of their morphology, which aligns them more closely to the more abstract expressives conveying other sensory impressions and emotional attitudes rather than to the natural sounds they attempt to capture.

The original purpose of this procedure, to serve as a check on my initial impressions of tonal iconicity, was also accomplished, if not quite as successfully, as it served as a check on the morphological description. As will be seen below from an examination of the associations I was given for the expressives I constructed, some supported and some did not support my generalizations about the meanings of different tone patterns.

On the supportive side, cuj cov, constructed on the basis of the attested cij coj, was judged descriptive of something swaying back and forth when used with the verb co 'to hang' by Kuam Yaj. Xab Xyooj gave an association for cuj cov that also supports my hypothesis that the -uj/-v pattern is associated with things that have a double orientation: he said he would use it to describe the movement of a "baboon" [sic] who is making a serpentine route through the forest to avoid contact with a potential enemy. Similarly, Xab Xyooj reported that the attested mij mej was the sound of a mosquito flying around one's ear, whereas the constructed mis mes was the sound of a mosquito landing on one's ear and staying there. Although mosquitoes who do that are generally quiet because they are getting ready to bite, I think he was emphasizing the continuous nature of close buzzing as opposed to now and again buzzing, which would support my hypothesis about the -is/-s "continuous" pattern. He also gave the association "footsteps heard from the apartment above" for the constructed *tig taug*, which would support the theory that -*ig*/-*g* is used to characterize low-pitched, hollow, echoic sounds. Kuam Yaj reported no precise context for *tig taug*, but said that it sounded "big" and "heavy" to him.

To give a sense of the ratio between supportive and nonsupportive associations given, I have reproduced the twenty paradigms and the responses of both speakers below. The previously attested expressives appear in boldface and the previously attested associations given for them are in parentheses. A question mark indicates that the hypothetical expressive "sounded good" but no association could be given; "X" indicates that the hypothetical expressive was not acceptable.

	Xab Xyooj	**Kuam Yaj**
	(1) *c-* + -*o*-	
(a) *cig cog*	elephant or wild pig, walking slowly	X
(b) *cij coj*	(chicks chirping) many	
(c) *cis cos*	a group of monkeys coming directly, but not very fast	X
(d) *cuj cov*	baboon moving serpentine through woods to avoid enemy	something hanging, swaying back and forth
	(2) *dh-* + -*e*-	
(a) *dhij dhej*	sound of water boiling	baby crying with stuffy nose
(b) **dhis dhes**	water boiling	X
(c) **dhiv dhev**	dog's hunting bark	X
(d) **dhawv dhev**	(whimpering) 2 sounds	in sleep: cry-stop-cry

(e) *dhuj dhev*   (continuous whimpering)
                              or of doing something
                              you don't want to do

(3) *h- + -ua-*

(a) *hij huaj*   girls' laugh: X
                  fast, giggle

(b) *his huas*   (manner of laughing)
                  men: not fast

(c) *hawv huav*   (growling, panting, pacing)
                  old men's laugh: grunting
                  very slow

(d) *huj huav*   (manner of breathing)
                  old men's laugh:
                  very slow

(4) *ø- + -aw-*

(a) *ig awg*   (wild pigs gobble: breathy growl)
                  or dogs fighting
                  over bone

(b) *ij awj*   (hiccup or dog's hunting bark)
                  many dogs

(c) *iv awv*   (hiccup or dog's hunting bark)
                  few dogs

(d) *is aws*   continuous mixed
                  sound: baboon [sic]

(e) *uj awv*   stop-start sound   2 separate sounds,
                                              high and low

(5) *kh- + -ua-*

(a) *khij khuaj*   (wild chicken running)
                  a lot of fruit falling

(b) *khis khuas* chicken scratching;   ?
                  running through dry leaves

152.

(c) *khawv khuav*

jogging, steady   fast walking
run: run-stop-run-stop

(d) *khuj khuav*   (deliberate, slow manner)

few fruit falling   something with
hand

(6) *m-* + *-e-*

(a) *mig meg*   cats fighting   ?

(b) *mij mej*   (mosquito near your ear)

passing by   skinny, long wings

(c) *mis mes*   mosquito lands on   small bee, short,
your ear and stays   round wings

(d) *miv mev*   horse   ?

(e) *mawv mev* ?   X

(f) *muj mev*   horse   ?

(7) *m-* + *-o-*

(a) *mig mog*   (mooing or civets fighting)

dogs fighting   "/i/ too high for
over bone   cow"

(b) *mij moj*   high moo?   X

(c) *mis mos*   sound of cows or   X
horses pulling up grass

(d) *miv mov*   X   X

(e) *mawv mov* baby's crawl:
slowly, no purpose

(f) *muj mov*   also of baby's crawl   of motion

(8) *ml- + -o-*

(a) *mlig mlog*   (tiger growling)
cats fighting

(b) *mlij mloj*   2 separated cats   X
meowing before fight

(c) *mlis mlos*   (cat's cry)
very slow

(d) *mliv mlov*   higher
mlawv mlov   lower

(e) *mluj mlos*   (cat's cry)

(9) *nph- + -oo-*

(a) *nphij nphooj*   (bamboo, popcorn popping)
action of pigs fighting   continuous

(b) *nphis nphoos*
drip from pipe   big drum
into tank   very low

(c) *nphiv nphoov*   (sound of gunfire)
from afar

(d) *nphawv nphoov*   (manner of hitting)

(e) *nphuj nphoov*
male pigs circling   bamboo
one another   popping:
start-stop, high-low

(f) *nphuj nphoos*   (boar grunting; negative manner of
action)

(10) *nr- + -aw-*

(a) *nrig nrawg*   ?   cows stampeding

(b) *nrij nrawj*   tapping   hammering

(c) *nris nraws* running away, continuous sound
 continuous of cow bells or
   pots and pans
(d) *nruj nrawv* tapping with one sound repeated
 pauses between with pauses;
   motion of scupltor's arm
   andresultant "chink"

(11) *nrh- + -aw-*

(a) **nrhij nrhawj** (splitting, cracking, tearing)
 rope, fast sound

(b) *nrhis nrhaws*
 wheezing—liquid
 in throat

(c) *nrhiv nrhawv*
 tearing, slow sound ?

(d) **nrhuj nrhawv** (slowly, with difficulty)
 hopping; 1 thing breaking
 unwilling manner after another

(12) *pl- + -aw-*

(a) *plig plawg* (bird rising from nest)
 many big birds birds flying
 flying

(b) *plij plawj* pigeons flying or birds flying
 dry husks falling
 off bamboo

(c) *plis plaws* ? sight of birds
   hopping sideways
   on distant fence

(d) *pliv plawv*
 ? ?

(e) **pluj plawv** (heavy bubbles)
   ? - not a sound

155

(13) *pl-* + -*e*-

(a) *plib pleb*   (wood crackling)
grass burning

(b) *plig pleg*   cow snorting,   cow's bilabial trill
heavy exhale   before fighting

(c) *plij plej*   (a little popcorn popping)
fast, many sounds

(d) *plis ples*   sound of playing flute   ?

(e) *pliv plev*   sound of toy airplane   ?
or small real airplane

(f) *pluj plev*   sound of small   separate pops
explosions in a burning
field: a few sounds
here and there

(14) *pl-* + -*o*-

(a) *plib plob*   (bamboo exploding)
small bamboo

(b) *plig plog*   (bodies jumping into water)

(c) *plij ploj*   (bamboo bursting or bullet impact)
high, close sound

(d) *plis plos*   water running   sound of people
fast downhill;   talking at a
stick hitting leaves   distance

(e) *pliv plov*   machine gun fire,   X
heavy rain

(f) *pluj plov*   intermittent gunfire   X

(15) *pl-* + -*oo*-

(a) *plig ploog*   big sound, many   X
bodies jumping in water

156

(b) *plij plooj*   ?   ? - something to do
                                                            with water

(c) *plis ploos*   hand touching water,   ?
                    going back and forth

(d) *pliv ploov*   (ducks diving or bottle filling up
                                under water)
                                            slow continuous
                                        water sound: bubbles

(e) *pluj ploov*   touching water   kid playing in
                    or fruit falling   bathtub: separate
                    in water   sounds

(16) *rh-* + *-e-*

(a) **rhij rhej**   (light and sound: lightning or grease)
                    close

(b) *rhis rhes*   grease spattering   ?

(c) **rhawv rhev**   (response of wild hen to bird call)
                    rendering fat   crying sound

(d) **rhuj rhev**   (lightning and thunder: light-pause-
                                sound)
                                            slow sound,
                                            far away

(17) rh- + -ua-

(a) **rhij rhuaj**   (foilage, grass rustling; crackling
                                leaves; chicken scratching)
                    sharp steps

(b) *rhis rhuas*   bird, rat moving   ?
                    through dry leaves;
                    dragged out steps

(c) *rhiv rhuav*   people shuffling   ? (sound)
                    through dry leaves
                    with force

157

(d) *rhuj rhuav* (bird shuffling through leaves; cutting vegetation)
distinct steps, but slow

(18) *t-* + -*au-*

(a) *tig taug*   footsteps from   big, heavy sound
the 2nd floor

(b) **tij tauj**   (raindrops)
loud, like hail   soft, high,
separate sounds
(finger-knuckle on dry
surface)

(c) *tis taus*   ?   X

(d) *tiv tauv*   rain on umbrella   on wet surface

(e) **tuj tauv**   (dripping water; flattery)
slow manner

(19) *ts-* + -*ua-*

(a) **tsig tsuag**   (downpour; monkeys jumping)
waterfall

(b) **tsij tsuaj**   (splashing sound)
chopping banana
tree with water
inside

(c) *tsis tsuas*   ?   X

(d) *tsiv tsuav*   walking in mud   ? - not a sound
or shallow water

(e) *tsawv tsuav*
manner and sound   baby's slow
of a gorilla walk   side-to-side
walk

(f) *tsuj tsuav*   pig or dog eating   2 sounds
alone, slowly;
sound of river at night

(20) *tx- + -e-*

(a) *txig txeg*   ?

sucking through big
hole; match taking
light; firecracker
after lit, but before boom

(b) *txij txej*

(sucking sound; rat in snake's mouth)

burning hole in	small, high sound
wood with hot	small mice biting
steel awl; burning	each other
chemicals	

(c) *txis txes*   ?   ?

(d) *txiv txev*

(rats or birds chirping)

(e) *txuj txev*   water or oil   1 discontinuous sound
leaking; pigs under
the house on a
cold night—the
little one squeals as
he tries to get between two others

I have concluded that the reason why the associations given did not match my impressions of the meanings of the tone patterns more clearly is that the consonants and vowels contribute to the iconic equation to the same extent that the tones do. If the consonants or vowels have particularly strong iconic force, as I believe is true of *rh-* [tʐʰ] (associated with tearing, splitting), *ploo-* [ploŋ] (associated with water), *nqh-* [Nqʰ] (associated with dryness or thirst), and *ø-* [ʔ] (associated with involuntary sounds originating from within), they will dominate, and the tone pattern will serve merely to refine and subtly modify. But if the tone pattern has particularly strong iconic force, as I believe is true of *ig/-g* and *-uj/-v* patterns, the consonants and vowels serve mainly to refine and subtly modify the basic meanings of "big, low, echoic" and "back and forth," respectively. This procedure would reveal my tone pattern/meaning impressions purely only if the consonant and vowel consistently comprised the core of the expressive, in which case the tone pattern changes would merely reveal different approaches or aspects of that core meaning. The interaction among the phonological components is more complex than that, and the percentage each

159

component contributes to the overall meaning of the expressive differs from case to case. The contribution of each component needs to be assessed in the way that I have assessed the contribution of the tones, and then these separate icons must be taken together in order to properly understand the meaning of these expressives.

The additional expressives generated by this procedure did serve to refine my initial impressions of the tone pattern meanings somewhat. To the characterization of *-ig/-g*, I would add "big"; to the characterization of *-ij/-j*, I would add "many, high, close"; to the characterization of *-uj/-v*, I would add "separate (of sounds)." The *-iv/-v* pattern seemed to represent slow sounds or movements often, and the pattern *-awv/-v* was relatively even slower.

A last lesson learned from this procedure, which as I have said was conducted in series of individual sessions with two tutors, is that the meanings of these expressives are shared by the community and do not vary greatly from one speaker to another. Both men I worked with were quick to eliminate situations that were very close to the one they were trying to describe but which were not quite right as an occasion when the expressive under discussion could be used. Expressives have precise, if somewhat elusive, meanings. That these meanings are not idiosyncratic, as Bertrais-Charrier maintains, but are shared was strikingly demonstrated by the associations I was given by each man separately to the following expressives: (1) *khawv khuav* XX: of jogging, a steady run, yet with pauses; KY: of a steady run or a fast walk, with pauses; (2) *nruj nrawv* XX: tapping with pauses between; KY: one sound repeated, with pauses; (3) *plig pleg* XX: of a cow snorting; KY: of a cow snorting before a fight (both demonstrated what the cow looked and sounded like, and both gave a loud bilabial trill).

4   Exceptions—Spurious and Real

While in the process of collecting the data, I came across a number of examples of two-word expressive or expressive-like phrases that did not conform to the morphology with regard to vowel and/or tone, even though the initials of the two words, being identical, did conform. The meanings (insofar as given) and the position of these phrases with relation to other words make them seem like expressives. After a great deal of checking on the meanings of these words taken individually, a number of these exceptions can be explained as an attempt to incorporate two independent words into the expressive mold. Two-word expressives, as we have seen, are generally either (1) two-word (or perhaps better, two syllable) constructs made of segmental icons in which the individual words have no independent life, or (2) two-word constructs made of an independent second word (either prosaic or expressive) and a wholly determined first word (see section 2.2 above). The exceptions that I contend are merely seeming exceptions (sections 4.1. and 4.2. below), can be understood as approximations of the general case.

4.1   Prosaic Word Plus One-Word Expressive

The following phrases can be shown to contain two independent forms, a prosaic word and a one-word expressive:

cus ciav	*cus*: bustling, vital, spirited
laug laws	*laug*: to sustain a note
nkig nkuav	*nkig*: dry, brittle
nphau nphwv	*nphau*: to boil over
npliag nplaws	*npliag*: to be soaking
nrawm nroos	*nrawm*: quickly
ntsuag ntseb	*ntsuag*: runs down (of water)
qaj qug	*qaj*: to snore
qis qawv	*qis*: to clench
qos qawv	*qos*: to close (the mouth)
qhuav qhawv	*qhuav*: to be dry
yoj yees	*yoj*: to swing; to quiver
zaj zes	*zaj*: classifier for sayings, stories

4.2   One-Word Expressive Plus One-Word Expressive

The following phrases can be shown to contain two independent forms, two one-word expressives:

daws duam
dhawv dhi
hlawv hlias
hlawv hlo
nqaj nqug
nqhawv nqho

4.3   Vowel Reversal

In both of the basic forms of the two-word expressives, the first vowel is usually high, either *-i-* or *-u-*. There are three expressives that reverse the expected order and have either the pattern *-o-/-i-* or *-o-/-e-*. I would not have thought this remarkable, given the other exceptions in which almost anything goes in terms of vocalism, except for the fact that the meanings of these expressives seem to be related: "sloppy, careless; off balance." I propose that in these cases the basic morphology may have been altered purposively to indicate "sloppy work." Analogs for this kind of diagrammatic iconicity (where the relation of the parts of the action represented corresponds to the relation of the parts of the phonological string, given our expectations concerning that which is orderly) exist in other languages: in Semai (Diffloth, personal correspondence), if there is a vowel disharmony between corresponding morphemes in a two-word expressive, the associated meanings have to do with randomness, sloppiness, or imbalance, for example, /klicwŭc-klicwĕc/, 'random kicking, as of a turtle in sand'. In Bini, a Nigerian Kwa language,[5] polysyllabic expressives with alternating high and low tones are associated with "irregular shape or motion," for example, the expressives for "staggering," "fluttering," "twisted," "crippled," and "jerky." The three White Hmong expressives that seem to be of this type follow:

> *doj de*   in *quag doj quag de*
>   weak   weak
> tottering, unsteady, reeling from side to side (H 259)

> *dog dig*   in *ua dog ua dig*
>   make make
> to do sloppily, carelessly (H 35; very commonly heard)

---

5 Wescott (1973: 197-205, esp. 200-201).

nkog nkig   in *ua nkog ua nkig*
                  make make
vacillating, unsteady; to do carelessly or poorly (H 154)

4.4   Exceptions

As testimony to the fact that language is never tidy, I list here those seeming expressives that do not follow the morphology of the majority and for which insufficient data exists to explain them away as the union of two independent forms.

daj dawg
fab fo
khaws khiam
nuj nus
ncub nciab
nplem nplig
nqhug nqhos
nrag nrig
nrawv nroos
ntshawv ntsheeb
ntxej ntxaum
qog qees
qos qees
qhaws qhem
qhaws qhoom
soj si
taj tauv
tsuj tsus
vaj vos
vej vuam
yaj yees
zij zev
zom zaws

APPENDIX A

Tone Sandhi Compounds Arranged by
First Word[1]

TRIGGER	Base	Compound	Source	Type
AUB ?	ncauj mouth	(q)aub-ncauj saliva	B ncauj, phuj	
CAB to lead	*kev* trail	*cab-ke* to lead forcibly	H 451	V-N
CAJ body part	*p a* breath	*caj-pas* throat	B *caj, pa* H223, 453	Pref-N
CAJ vine	*qhuav* dry	*caj-qhua* serpent	B *caj, qhuav*	N-Mod
CIAB wax	*muv* bee	*ciab-mu* bee wax	B *muv*	N-Mod

---

[1] This appendix includes all the examples of tone sandhi compounds known to me at the time of this study. "Exceptions" to these compounds, that is, collocations of the component words without tone change, are not exceptional: often both compounded and uncompounded collocations are given in the same source. For reasons of space, not all sources are listed for a particular compound. The most accessible source, generally a dictionary, is listed if there are a number of sources. The primary sources are: H (Heimbach), B (Bertrais-Charrier), P (Vwj et al., *Primer*), XX (Xab Xyooj, tutor).

164

TRIGGER	Base	Compound	Source	Type
COJ to follow	*kev* way	*coj-ke* to observe	XX	V-N
CUB fire	*taws* firewood	*cub-tawg* fire	B *taws* H 17	N-Mod
	tshauv ash	*cub-tshau* fireplace	B *tshauv*	N-Mod
CUAB to lay hold of	*nplua* slippery	·*cuab-npluas* to have good footing	B *nplua*	V-N
DAB spirit	*ntuj* sky, layer	*dab-ntug* spirits that live inside the earth	XX	N-Mod
	qua spirit	*dab-quas* spirit	TC Thao	N-N
	rooj door	*dab-roog* spirit of the door	H 27, 280	N-Mod
	tshau to sieve	*dab-tshaus* (evil spirit)	B *tshau*	N-Mod
	zaj dragon	*dab-zag* dragon spirit	XX	N-Mod
DAB ?	*tsho* jacket	*dab-tshos* embroidered patch on jacket	B *tsho* H 29, 367, 453	
DAB ?	*ros* to laugh	*dab-rog* to laugh	B *ros*	

165

TRIGGER	Base	Compound	Source	Type
DAB (kin term)	*laus* old	*dab-laug* mother's brothers	B *laus* H 29, 449	N-Mod
DAB narrowing	*taw* foot	*dab-taws* ankle	H 29, 453	N-Mod
	tes hand	*dab-teg* wrist	H 29, 449	N-Mod
DAB trough	*npua* pig	*dab-npuas* pig trough	H 452	N-Mod
	nyuj cow	*dab-nyug* cow trough	B *nyuj*	N-Mod
DAJ ?	*deev* to make love	*daj-dee* to make love	B *daj, deev*	
DAJ yellow	*mos* soft	*daj-mog* light yellow	XX	V-V
	ntsej ear (face)	*daj-ntseg* yellow face (sick)	B *ntsej*	V-N
DAJ unit of meas.	*tes* hand	*daj-teg* outstretched arms	B *daj, tes*	
DAJ ?	*duav* back	*daj-dua* (kind of horse)	B *duav*	
DAUJ pestle	*cos* treadmill	*dauj-cog* treadmill pestle	H 16, 448	N-Mod

TRIGGER	Base	Compound	Source	Type
DAWB white	*mos* soft	*dawb-mog* soft white	XX	V-V
	pliaj forehead	*dawb-pliag* white spot on forehead	B *pliaj*	Mod-N
DEJ water	*cawv* alcohol	*dej-caw* whiskey	H 9	N-Mod
	cos treadmill	*dej-cog* water-run treadmill	B *cos* H 16, 34	Mod-N
	daj yellow	*dej-dag* turbulent water	H 34, 447	N-Mod
	liaj paddy field	*dej-liag* canal water	B *liaj*	N-Mod
	npua pig	*dej-npuas* pig water	XX	N-Mod
	siav cooked	*dej-sia* boiled water	H 34	N-Mod
	sov warm	*dej-so* warm water	B *sov* H 452	N-Mod
	teev standing	*dej-tee* standing water	N-Mod	
	tsev house	*dej-tse* water in eaves	B *dej, tsev*	N-Mod
	txias cold	*dej-txiag* cold water	B *txias* H 381, 449	N-Mod

TRIGGER	Base	Compound	Source	Type
DIB squash	*cauj* early	*dib-caug* an early- bearing squash	B *cauj, dib*	N-Mod
	txaij striped	*dib-txaig* a striped squash	B *txaij*	N-Mod
DUB black	*ncauj* mouth	*dub-ncaug* (of enemy; one who doesn't talk)	XX	V-N
FAIB to divide	*kev* trail	*faib-ke* a split in the road	XX	V-N
	siav life	*faib-sia* to share life (of dawn)	B *ntuj*	V-N
HWB ?	*tes* hand	*hwb-teg* (whistle) through hands	B *tes*	
HLAB cord	*hlua* rope	*hlab-hluas* guts	B *roj*	N-N
	kaj band	*hlab-kag* rags	B *kaj*	N-N
	pa breath	*hlab-pas* wind pipe	B *pa* H 60, 223, 453	N-Mod
	sev apron	*hlab-se* apron ties	B *sev*	N-Mod
	tsho jacket	*hlab-tshos* type of bean with long casings	B *tsho*	Mod-N

168

TRIGGER	Base	Compound	Source	Type
HLEB coffin	*ntoo* tree	*hleb-ntoos* wood coffin	H 191, 453	N-Mod
HMAB vine	*daj* yellow	*hmab-dag* little tree with white flowers	XX	N-Mod
HMOOB Hmong	*suav* others (Chinese)	*hmoob-sua* Hmong living in China	Vaaj Lwm[2]	N-Mod
HNAB bag	*nplej* rice	*hnab-npleg* rice hull	XX	N-Mod
	tsho jacket	*hnab-tshos* jacket pocket	B *tsho*	N-Mod
HNOOB/HNUB day (sun)	*tes* hand	*hnoob-teg* sunray	B *tes*	Mod-N
	hmo night	*hnub-hmos* night of day before yesterday	H 71	
KAB way	*kev* way	*kab-ke* ceremony	B *kev* H 74, 451	N-N
KAB insect	*laum* cockroach	*kab-laug* kind of spider	H 73, 449	N-Mod
	rws ?	*kab-rwg* termite	B *rws*	N-Mod

[2] Preface, *Grandmother's Path, Grandfather's Way*, ed. Lue Vang and Judy Lewis (Rancho Cordova, CA, 1984), 2.

TRIGGER	Base	Compound	Source	Type
KAB line	*tes* hand	*kab-teg* lines of the hand	B *kab, tes*	N-Mod
KAB ?	*ntxau* ?	*kab-ntxaus* acne	B *ntxau*	
KAB ?	*noj* eat	*kab-nog* cavity	B *noj*	
KAJ bright	*hli* moon	*kaj-hlis* moonlight	H 75	V-N
	ntuj sky	*kaj-ntug* morning	H 75, 192, 447	V-N
	zoov forest	*kaj-zoo* bright forest	XX	V-N
KAUJ ring	*ntsej* ear	*kauj-ntseg* earring	B *ntsej*	N-Mod
KAUJ ?	*lev* mat	*kauj-le* (part of soul calling ceremony)	B *lev, vab*	
KAWB bent	*tsaim* jaw	*kawb-tsaig* (of person with no chin)	B *tsaim*	V-N
-KIB turtle	*dej* water	*vaubkib-deg* turtle	H 399, 447	N-Mod
KUB horn	*twm* buffalo	*kub-twg* buffalo horn	B *kub, twm* H 450	N-Mod

TRIGGER	Base	Compound	Source	Type
	txhuav to cup	*kub-txhua* cupping horn	B *txhuav*	N-Mod
KUB ?	*nyuj* cow	*kub-nyug* variety of large peach	B *nyuj*	
KWJ gulley	*dej* water	*kwj-deg* gulley	B *dej* H 34, 447	N-Mod
	hav valley	*kwj-ha* valley	B *hav* H 90, 451	N-N
	liaj paddy field	*kwj-liag* canal	B *kwj, liaj*	N-Mod
	tsev house	*kwj-tse* house drainage ditch	B *tsev* H 90, 452	N-Mod
KHAUB cloth	*hlua* rope	*khaub-hluas* rags	B *khaub*	N-Mod
KHAWB link, chain	*hlau* iron	*khawb-hlaus* iron link	B *khawb*	N-Mod
	nyiaj silver	*khawb-nyiag* silver chain	B *khawb,* *nyiaj*	N-Mod
LAJ ridge	*zoov* forest	*laj-zoo* forest ridge	B *laj, zoov*	N-Mod
LAIJ to plow	*liaj* paddy field	*laij-liag* to plow paddy fields	B *laij* H 113, 447	V-N

171

TRIGGER	Base	Compound	Source	Type
	ŋyuj cow	*laij-nyug* to work non- irrigated fields	B *laij, ŋyuj*	V-N
LEEJ willing	*tuaj* to come	*leej-tuag* willing to come	H 110	V-V
LIAB red	*mos* soft	*liab-mog* soft red	XX	V-V
	ncauj mouth	*liab-ncaug* (of a person who talks a lot)	XX	V-N
LIAJ paddy field	*iav* mud	*liaj-ia* land	B *iav, liaj*	N-N
	qhuav dry	*liaj-qhua* dry paddy field	H 113, 173, 451	N-Mod
LUJ heel/elbow	*taw* foot	*luj-taws* heel	B *luj, pob, taw* H 310, 453	N-Mod
LUJ to weigh	*nyiaj* silver	*luj-nyiag* to weigh silver	TC Thao	V-N
LUAJ ?	*daj* yellow	*luaj-dag* yellow earth	B *daj*	
LWJ bellows	*hlau* iron	*lwj-hlaus* blacksmith	B *hlau*	N-N

TRIGGER	Base	Compound	Source	Type
LWJ mushy	*plawv* heart	*lwj-plaw* to be upset	B *plawv, siab*	V-N
MAB strangers	*suav* others (Chinese)	*mab-sua* others	B *mab, suav*	N-N
MOB to be in pain	*laus* old	*mob-laug* to have a long illness	B *mob* H 449	V-V
	nqaij flesh	*mob-nqaig* to hurt the flesh	H 169, 249	V-N
MUAB to grasp	*qua* to give in marriage	*muab-quas* to take and give in marriage	Yaj (1987)	V-V
	siav life	*(sis)muab-sia* recp. wrestles with life (of dawn)	B *ntuj*	V-N
MUAJ to have	*caj* nose bridge	*muaj-cag* to have a good nose	B *caj*	V-N
	hmoov luck	*muaj-hmoo* to be lucky	B *hmoov* H 67, 451	V-N
	kwv younger brother	*muaj-kw* to have family	B *kwv, tij*	V-N
	nkees to be tired	*muaj-nkeeg* to be unwell	B *nkees*	V-V

TRIGGER	Base	Compound	Source	Type
	nyiaj silver	*muaj-nyiag* to be rich	B *nyiaj*	V-N
	plhu cheek	*muaj-plhus* to have face	B *plhu* H 254	V-N
	tij older brother	*muaj-tig* to have family	B *kwv, tij*	V-N
	txiv father	*muaj-txi* to have parents		V-N
	txiaj money	*muaj-txiag* to be rich	B *txiaj*	V-N
	zes nest	*muaj-zeg* to be nesting	B *zes*	V-N
NAB snake	*qav* frog	*nab-qa* lizard	B *nab*	N-Mod
NEEJ household, existence, humanity, person	*ntuj* sky (expanse)	*neej-ntug* judge	XX	N-Mod
	seev to com- plain	*neej-see* unhappy life	B *seev*	N-Mod
	tsav ?	*neej-tsa* wife's family	B *tsav*	
NOJ to eat	*hli* moon	(dab) *noj-hlis* spirit eclipse	B *noj*	V-N
	hno rice	*noj-hnos* (of a feast)	H 70, 452	V-N

TRIGGER	Base	Compound	Source	Type
	nqaij meat	*noj-nqaig* (of a feast)	H 70	V-N
	nyoos raw	*(dab) noj-nyoo* spirit (savage spirits)	B *nyoos*	V-V
	su lunch	*noj-sus* eat lunch	Dial #11[3]	V-N
NOOB seed	*maj* hemp	*noob-mag* hemp seed	B *maj*	N-Mod
	nplej rice	*noob-npleg* seed rice	B *noob* H 447	N-Mod
	nroj plant	*noob-nrog* plant seed	B *nroj*	N-Mod
	qe egg	*noob-qes* testicle	B *qes!* H 73, 142, 261	Mod-N
NCAB straighten	*duav* back	*ncab-dua* stretch oneself	B *duav* H 144	V-N
NCAJ straight	*kev* trail	*ncaj-ke* on the trail	B *ncaj*	V-N
NCAUJ mouth	*kev* trail	*ncauj-ke* mouth of a road	B *kev, ncauj* H 145, 451	N-Mod
	ntev long	*ncauj-nte* (of person who talks too much)	B *ntev*	N-Mod

---

[3] Dialogue #11, Hmong language materials SEASSI 1985 (available through Southeast Asian Refugee Studies Project, University of Minnesota).

175

TRIGGER	Base	Compound	Source	Type
	raj tube	*ncauj-rag* mouth of a tube	B *ncauj, raj*	N-Mod
	tes hand	*ncauj-teg (tsho)* end of sleeve	B *tes*	N-Mod
	yoov insect	*ncauj-yoo* insect bite bumps	B *ncauj, yoov*	N-Mod
	zaj dragon	*ncauj-zag* soldered point in a chain	B *ncauj, zaj*	N-Mod
NCEJ post	*cos* treadmill	*ncej-cog* post of mill	B *cos, ncej* H 16, 448	N-Mod
	ruv roof ridge	*ncej-ru* center posts (upright)	B *ruv* H 147, 281	N-Mod
	tas house center	*ncej-tag* column in foyer	B *ncej, tas*	N-Mod
	tsev house	*ncej-tse* column in house	B *ncej, tsev*	N-Mod
	txaj bed	*ncej-txag* bed legs	B *ncej, txaj*	N-Mod
	txee etagère	*ncej-txees* etagère legs	B *txee*	N-Mod
	vaj garden	*ncej-vag* posts of garden enclosure	B *ncej, vaj*	N-Mod
NKAJ ?	*zoov* forest	*nkaj-zoo* small red plant in forest	B *zoov*	

TRIGGER	Base	Compound	Source	Type
NKAUB yolk	*qe* egg	*nkaub-qes* egg yolk	B *qe*	N-Mod
NKAUJ girl	*laus* old	*nkauj-laug* an "old girl"	B *nkauj*	N-Mod
	mos soft	*nkauj-mog* a young girl	B *mos*	N-Mod
	npua pig	*nkauj-npuas* young female pig	B *npua* H 152, 161, 452	Mod-N
	qhev servant	*nkauj-qhe* female servant	H 270	Mod-N
	zaj dragon	*nkauj-zag* coquette	B *zaj*	N-Mod
	zam attire	*nkauj-zag* (of fancy dress)	B *ntxheb*	
NKAUJ song	*qeej* *keng*	*nkauj-qeeg* *keng* song	B *nkauj, qeej*	N-Mod
NKAUJ sty, pen	*npua* pig	*nkauj-npuas* pigsty	B *nkauj, npua*	N-Mod
NKOJ carrier	*dej* water	*nkoj-deg* boat	H 34, 154, 447	N-Mod
NKUAJ sty, pen	*npua* pig	*nkuaj-npuas* pigsty	B *nkuaj*	N-Mod
	nyuj cow	*nkuaj-nyug* cow pen	B *nkuaj, nyuj* H 447	N-Mod

TRIGGER	Base	Compound	Source	Type
NKHIB crotch	*ntoo* tree	*nkhib-ntoos* crotch in tree	XX	N-Mod
	tes hand	*nkhib-teg* crotch between 2 fingers	B *tes* H 156, 449	N-Mod
NPAUJ jewelry	*ntsej* ear	*npauj-ntseg* earring	XX	N-Mod
	nyiaj silver	*npauj-nyiag* silver jewelry	*Txiv Nraug Ntsuag*[4]	N-Mod
NPAUJ moth	*nplej* rice	*npauj-npleg* rice moth	B *npauj*	N-Mod
NPUAB to adhere	*txaj* bed	*npuab-txag* (of wood on side of bed)	XX	V-N
NPUAJ to clap	*tes* hand	*npuab-teg* to clap hands	B *npuaj, tes* H 162, 449	V-N
NPLEJ rice	*cauj* early	*nplej-caug* early-bearing rice	B *cauj, nplej*	N-Mod
	daj yellow	*nplej-dag* yellow rice	XX	N-Mod
	laus old	*nplej-laug* old rice	H 449	N-Mod

---

[4] *"Txiv Nraug Ntsuag thiab Ntxawm Qaum Ntuj"* as told by Yaj Txooj Tsawb, *Dab Neeg* [Folk tales] (Vientiane, 1974), 1.

TRIGGER	Base	Compound	Source	Type
	liaj paddy field	*nplej-liag* paddy field rice	B *liaj, nplej*	N-Mod
	taj late	*nplej-tag* late rice	B *taj*	N-Mod
NPLOOJ leaf	*nplej* rice	*nplooj-npleg* rice leaves	B *nplej*	N-Mod
	ntoo tree	*nplooj-ntoos* tree leaves	B *nplooj* H 191	N-Mod
	ntsej ear	*nplooj-ntseg* the outer ear	B *nplooj*	N-Mod
	qhuav dry	*nplooj-qhua* dry leaves	B *nplooj*	N-Mod
NPLHAIB finger ring	*tooj* copper	*nplhaib-toog* brass ring	B *nplhaib, tooj*	N-Mod
NQAJ bar, beam length	*hlau* iron	*nqaj-hlaus* bar of iron	B *hlau, nqaj*	N-Mod
	ruv roof ridge	*nqaj-ru* ridge pole	B *ruv* H 281	N-Mod
	toj hill	*nqaj-tog* chain of hills	B *nqaj*	N-Mod
NQAIJ meat	*npua* pig	*nqaij-npuas* pork	B *nqaij* H 452	N-Mod
	nyuj cow	*nqaij-nyug* beef	B *nqaij* H 447	N-Mod

179

TRIGGER	Base	Compound	Source	Type
	qeej *keng*	*nqaij-qeeg* meat offered to the *keng* (funeral)	B *qeej*	N-Mod
	qhuav dry	*nqaij-qhua* dried meat	XX	N-Mod
NQOB upper stalk	*nplej* rice	*nqob-npleg* upper part of rice stalk	H 171	N-Mod
NRAB middle	*hmo* night	*nrab-hmos* 1/2-way through the night	B *nrab*	N-Mod
	kev trail	*nrab-ke* 1/2-way point on journey	B *nrab*	N-Mod
	ntuj sky	*nrab-ntug* noon	XX	N-Mod
NRAJ (kind of bird)	*yij* (kind of bird)	*nraj-yig* (kind of bird)	B *yij*	N-N
NRAUJ to separate	*zoov* forest	*nrauj-zoo* to send (someone) off; to suppress	B *nrauj, zoov*	V-N
NREEB facile	*tes* hand	*nreeb-teg* a "good shot"	B *nreeb, tes*	V-N
NREEJ ?	*ntoo* tree	*nreej-ntoos* flanging tree root	H 176, 453	

TRIGGER	Base	Compound	Source	Type
NROJ				
weed, plant	*qhuav* dry	*nroj-qhua* dried weeds	XX	N-Mod
NRUAB				
middle	*dej* water	*nruab-deg* in the water	H 34, 447	N-Mod
	hli moon	*nruab-hlis* in the month after confinement	B *hli, nruab* H 62	N-Mod
	nras plain	*nruab-nrag* (of game)	H 180	N-Mod
	ntawv letter	*nruab-ntaw* in books; on paper	H 187	N-Mod
	ntuj sky	*nruab-ntug* in the heavens	H 28, 447	N-Mod
	qaim moonlight	*nruab-qaig* in the moonlight	B *qaim*	N-Mod
	qhov hole	*nruab-qho* in the hole	B *qhov*	N-Mod
	tsev house	*nruab-tse* in the house	H 349, 452	N-Mod
	zos village	*nruab-zog* in the village	B *nruab, zos* H 180	N-Mod
	zoov forest	*nruab-zoo* in the forest	B *nruab, zoov* H 452	N-Mod
NRUAB				
flat bamboo	*txaj* bed	*nruab-txag* bed covered with bamboo	B *nruab*	Mod-N

TRIGGER	Base	Compound	Source	Type
NTAB				
bee	*ntoo* tree	*ntab-ntoos* tree bees	B *ntab*	N-Mod
	nyuj cow	*ntab-nyug* wattles (look like bees' nests)	XX	N-Mod
	tsua rock	*ntab-tsuas* rock bees	B *ntab*	N-Mod
NTAJ				
sabre	*tes* hand	*ntaj-teg* open vertical hand	B *ntaj, tes*	N-Mod
NTAUB				
cloth	*mos* soft	*ntaub-mog* soft cloth	B *mos*	N-Mod
	paj flower	*ntaub-pag* designed cloth	B *paj*	N-Mod
	paj cotton	*ntaub-pag* cotton cloth	B *ntaub, paj*	N-Mod
	xiav blue	*ntaub-xia* blue cloth	B *xiav*	N-Mod
NTAUJ/NTOJ				
?	*kev* trail	*ntauj-ke* to be forever on the road	B *ntauj*	
NTIAJ				
stratum, surface	*ntuj* sky, layer	*ntiaj-ntug* the middle stratum (the surface of earth)	XX	N-Mod
NTUJ				
sky, expanse	*kaj* clear	*ntuj-kag* clear sky	B *kaj*	N-Mod

182

TRIGGER	Base	Compound	Source	Type
	nras plain	*ntuj-nrag* beneath the sky	LLCT[5]	N-Mod
	nrau beyond	*ntuj-nraus* the regions beyond	H 175	N-Mod
	qhuav dry	*ntuj-qhua* of the dry season	H 8	N-Mod
	siav life	*(tu) ntuj-sia* break (of the beginning of night)	B *ntuj*	Mod-N
	sov warm	*ntuj-so* of the hot season	B *ntuj, sov*	N-Mod
	taws fire	*ntuj-tawg* an expanse of fire	H 193	N-Mod
NTHAB storage platform	*tsev* house	*nthab-tse* storage platform	XX	N-Mod
NTSAJ trap	*ntses* fish	*ntsaj-ntseg* fish trap	H 197, 449	N-Mod
NTSEJ ear	*hneev* crossbow	*ntsej-hnee* crossbow "ears"	B *hneev, ntsej*	N-Mod
	ntev long	*ntsej-nte* (of person slow to decide)	B *ntev, ntsej*	N-Mod
	raj tube	*ntsej-rag* the middle ear	B *ntsej* H 199	N-Mod

5 *Liaj Luv Chaw Tsaws* (1986) no. 2, 16.

TRIGGER	Base	Compound	Source	Type
NTSIAB kernel	*ntsej* ear	*ntsiab-ntseg* (of very small person)	XX	Mod-N
NTXUB to hate	*ncauj* mouth	*ntxhub-ncaug* (of a critical person)	H 145, 210 213, 447	V-N
NTXUAJ to wave	*tes* hand	*ntxuaj-teg* to wave the hand	H 213, 449	V-N
NTXHEB ?	*zam* attire	*ntxheb-zag* to primp	B *npaub, ntxheb, zam*	
NTXHIB coarse	*nplej* rice	*ntxhib-npleg* coarse rice	XX	V-N
	txhuv hulled rice	*ntxhib-txhu* coarse hulled rice	B *ntxhib, txhuv, zig*	V-N
NTXHUAB moss	*dej* water	*ntxhuab-deg* algae	B *ntxhuab*	N-Mod
	ntoo tree	*ntxhuab-ntoos* tree moss	B *ntxhuab*	N-Mod
	taw foot	*ntxhuab-taws* (of a mossy trail)	B *ntxhuab*	N-Mod
NYAB ?	*nplej* rice	*nyab-npleg* rice straw	H 165, 267	

TRIGGER	Base	Compound	Source	Type
NYIAJ silver	*txiaj* money	*nyiaj-txiag* money	B *nyiaj, txiaj* H 380, 448	N-N
NYUJ cow	*daj* yellow	*nyuj-dag* yellow cow	XX	N-Mod
	laus old	*nyuj-laug* mature cow	P 68	N-Mod
	liaj paddy field	*nyuj-liag* paddy field cow	XX	N-Mod
	qhuav dry	*nyuj-qhua* strong cow	XX	N-Mod
OB ?	*ncauj* mouth	*ob-ncaug* saliva	B *ncauj*	
PAB group	*npua* pig	*pab-npuas* group of pigs	XX	N-Mod
	qeej keng	*pab-qeeg* group of *keng*s	XX	N-Mod
PAJ flower	*daj* yellow	*paj-dag* (flower from *hmab-dag*)	XX	N-Mod
	dej water	*paj-deg* bubbles	XX	N-Mod
	lus speech	*paj-lug* flowery speech	B *lug!, paj* H 119, 223, 449	N-Mod
	maj hemp	*paj-mag* poppy's 3rd leaf	B *maj*	N-Mod

185

TRIGGER	Base	Compound	Source	Type
	mos soft	*paj-mog* soft flower	XX	N-Mod
	nplej rice	*paj-npleg* puffed rice	B *paj* H 447	N-Mod
	ntawv letter	*paj-ntaw* literature ?		N-Mod
	ntoo tree	*paj-ntoos* tree flowers	B *paj* H 223	N-Mod
	tshauv ash	*paj-tshau* fine ash	B *tshau*	N-Mod
PAWJ ?	*dej* water	*pawj-deg* plant that grows in water, on rocks	XX	
PEEB male sex organ	*nyuj* cow	*peeb-nyug* bull's sex organ	XX	N-Mod
PIB to begin	*zaj* story	*pib-zag* tell stories (one after another)	B *pib*	V-N
POB clump, blob	*a v* earth	*pob-a* clod of earth	B *av*	N-Mod
	ncauj mouth	*pob-ncaug* sores on mouth	XX	N-Mod
	ntoo tree	*pob-ntoos* stump	H 191, 453	N-Mod
	ntsej ear	*pob-ntseg* ear	B *ntsej, pob*	N-Mod

186

TRIGGER	Base	Compound	Source	Type
	sov warm	*pob-so* fever blister	XX	N-Mod
	taw foot	*pob-taws* ankle bone	B *taw* H 231, 453	N-Mod
	tes hand	*pob-teg* wrist bone	H 231	N-Mod
	tsua rock	*pob-tsuas* rock mass	B *roob, tsua* H 357, 453	N-Mod
POJ woman	*cuas* (kin term)	*poj-cuag* child's mother-in-law	B *cuag!, poj* H 20	N-Mod
	suav others (Chinese)	*poj-sua* non-Hmong woman	B *suav*	N-Mod
POOB to fall	*dej* water	*poob-deg* to drown	B *poob* H 447	V-N
	ntoo tree	*poob-ntoos* to fall out of a tree	B *poob*	V-N
	nyiaj money	*poob-nyiag* to lose money	B *poob* H 219	V-N
	plhu cheek	*poob-plhus* to lose face	B *poob*	V-N
	qhov hole	*poob-qho* (of the sun setting)	B *poob, qhov*	V-N
	txaj bed	*poob-txag* to fall out of bed	B *poob*	V-N

TRIGGER	Base	Compound	Source	Type
	zoov forest	*poob-zoo* to get lost in the woods	B *poob, zoov* H 234, 440, 441, 452	V-N
PUAB ?	*tsaim* jaw	*puab-tsaig* jaw	B *puab, tsaim*	
PWJ ?	*nyuj* cow	*pwj-nyug* adolescent steer	B *nyuj*	
PHAB side; wall	*lauj* left	*phab-laug* left side	B *phab*	N-Mod
	tsua rock	*phab-tsuas* rock surface	H 357	N-Mod
	vaj garden	*phab-vag* garden wall	XX	N-Mod
PHAUJ (kin term)	*laus* old	*phauj-laug* grandfather's sisters	B *laus, phauj*	N-Mod
PHOB line	*tsi* snare	*phob-tsis* line of snares	B *phob*	N-Mod
PLAB stomach	*laus* ?	*plab-laug* stomach region	H 247	
	mòs soft	*plab-mog* lower abdominal region	B *mos* H 129, 247	N-Mod
	nplej rice	*plab-npleg* rice before it opens	XX	N-Mod

TRIGGER	Base	Compound	Source	Type
	nyuj cow	*(txiv)plab-nyug* fruit jackfruit	H 447	N-Mod
	plawv heart	*plab-plaw* intelligence; character	B *plab, plawv* H 451	N-N
	zaj dragon	*plab-zag* an acidic stomach	B *plab, zaj*	N-Mod
PLAUB hair	*npua* pig	*plaub-npuas* pig hair	XX	N-Mod
	nyuj cow	*plaub-nyug* cow hair	XX	N-Mod
PLIAB flat	*ncauj* mouth	*pliab-ncaug* flat mouth	XX	V-N
PLIAJ ?	*dej* water	*pliaj-deg* clam	XX	
PLUAJ ?	*cev* body	*pluaj-ce* (of a snake with a flat body)	B *cev*	
PLHAUB outer covering	*maj* hemp	*plhaub-mag* hemp stalk	B *maj*	N-Mod
	qe egg	*plhaub-qes* eggshell	B *qe*	N-Mod
QAB behind, beneath, the underside of	*cav* log	*qab-ca* under the log	H 8, 451	N-Mod
	dej water	*qab-deg* downstream	B *qab* H 34, 447	N-Mod

189

TRIGGER	Base	Compound	Source	Type
	kawm basket	*qab-kawg* bottom of the basket	B *qab* H 450	N-Mod
	kev trail	*qab-ke* downhill side of the trail	B *qab* H 451	N-Mod
	khav ?	*qab-kha* under roof on uphill side of house	B *qab*	N-Mod
	ntoo tree	*qab-ntoos* base of tree	H 256, 453	N-Mod
	ntuj sky	*qab-ntug* base of heaven (of sunset)	H 193, 256	N-Mod
	pas lake	*qab-pag* bottom of the lake	B *pas*	N-Mod
	raj tube	*qab-rag* bottom of the tube	B *qab, raj*	N-Mod
	rooj table	*qab-roog* under/downhill side of table	H 256, 448	N-Mod
	ruv roof ridge	*qab-ru* under the roof ridge	H 281	N-Mod
	tsev house	*qab-tse* downhill side of house	XX	N-Mod
	tsua rock	*qab-tsuas* base of cliff	B *qab, tsua* H 256, 357, 453	N-Mod
	tsho jacket	*qab-tshos* lower edge of jacket	H 453	N-Mod
	txaj bed	*qab-txag* under the bed	B *txaj* H 373, 448	N-Mod

190

TRIGGER	Base	Compound	Source	Type
	vaj garden	*qab-vag* downhill side of garden	XX	N-Mod
	xov thread	*qab-xo* end of the thread	B *pob, qab, xov*	N-Mod
	yias wok	*qab-yiag* bottom of wok	B *yias*	N-Mod
QAIB chicken	*tshauv* ash	*qaib-tshau* ashy-colored chicken	B *tshauv*	N-Mod
QAIJ to lean	*kev* trail	*qaij-ke* move to one side of trail	B *kev*	V-N
QAUB sour	*ncauj* mouth	*qaub-ncaug* spittle	B *ncauj, qaub* H 145, 447	V-N
QAUB ?	*npua* pig	*qaub-npuas* pig food	H 452	
QEJ ?	*tsua* rock	*qej-tsuas* (of tree with no branches)	XX	
QEEJ *keng*	*nruas* drum	*qeej-nruag* pipe and drums [funeral]	H 180	N-N
QIB/QEB trigger	*hneev* crossbow	*qib-hnee* crossbow trigger	B *hneev, qib* H 69, 261	N-Mod
QIB step	*ntaiv* ladder	*qib-ntai* ladder step	B *ntaiv, qib*	N-Mod

TRIGGER	Base	Compound	Source	Type
QOOB crops	*loo* crops	*qoob-loos* crops	B *loos!, qoob*	N-N
QUB of old	*chaw* place	*qub-chaws* original place	H 265	V-N
	kev trail, way	*qub-ke* the old way	H 265	V-N
	tes hand	*qub-teg* inherited things	H 265	V-N
	zos village	*qub-zog* old village	B *zos*	V-N
QUAB ?	*npua* pig	*quab-npuas* young pig	B *npua* H 161	
QUAB yoke	*nyuj* cow	*quab-nyug* yoke	B *nyuj, quab*	N-Mod
QUAJ to cry	*ntuj* sky	*quaj-ntug* to cry to heaven	*Haiv Hmoob* 1 #2	V-N
	taus able	*quaj-taug* crybaby	B *taus*	V-V
QWB back of instrument	*riam* knife	*qwb-riag* back of knife blade	B *qwb, riam*	N-Mod
QWJ snail	*dej* water	*qwj-deg* snail	XX	N-Mod

192

TRIGGER	Base	Compound	Source	Type
QHAB rafter	*ruv* roof ridge	*qhab-ru* anchor of beams on rooftop	XX	N-Mod
	tsev house	*qhab-tse* rafter	B *qhab*	N-Mod
QHEB to open	*tshav* bright	*qheb-tsha* to clear (of sky)	H 452	V-V
QHUAB to show	*kev* trail, way	*qhuab-ke* to show the way (to the spirit in funeral ritual)	H 81, 272	V-N
RAJ tube	*npua* pig	*raj-npuas* storage tube for pig food	XX	N-Mod
RIAB ?	*ntshauv* head louse	*riab-ntshau* small head louse	H 278, 451	
ROJ fat, oil	*av* earth	*roj-a* gasoline	B *av, roj*	N-Mod
	npua pig	*roj-npuas* pig fat	B *roj*	N-Mod
	nyuj cow	*roj-nyug* cow fat	B *roj* H 447	N-Mod
ROOB mountain	*qhuav* dry	*roob-qhua* mtn with no water source	B *roob*	N-Mod

TRIGGER	Base	Compound	Source	Type
	riam knife	*roob-riag* back of knife	B *riam* H 278, 280, 450	N-Mod
	thuv pine	*roob-thu* mtn covered with pines	B *thuv*	N-Mod
	tsua rock	*roob-tsuas* mtn of rock	B *roob, tsua*	N-Mod
	zoov forest	*roob-zoo* mtn of forest	B *roob, zoov*	N-Mod
ROOJ furniture	*ntawv* letter	*rooj-ntaw* desk	B *ntawv*	N-Mod
	tiaj level	*rooj-tiag (taw)* footstool foot	H 280	N-Mod
ROOJ ?	*ntej* earlier	*rooj-nteg* long ago	H 187, 281	
ROOJ door	*cooj* coop	*rooj-coog* door of the coop	B *rooj*	N-Mod
	loom courtyard	*rooj-loog* gate of the courtyard	B *rooj* H 117	N-Mod
	nkuaj stable	*rooj-nkuag* stable door	B *nkuaj, rooj* H 447	N-Mod
	ntuj sky	*rooj-ntug* gate of heaven	B *ntuj, rooj* H 280	N-Mod
	ntxa grave	*rooj-ntxas* opening of grave	B *ntxa* H 453	N-Mod

TRIGGER	Base	Compound	Source	Type
	txaj bed(room)	*rooj-txag* bedroom door	B *txaj* H 448	N-Mod
	vaj garden	*rooj-vag* garden gate	B *rooj, vaj* H 398, 448	N-Mod
SAB side	*lauj* left	*sab-laug* left side	B *lauj* H 285, 447	N-Mod
	ntiaj front	*sab-ntiag* front surface	H 189	N-Mod
	ntsej ear	*sab-ntseg* 1 (side of) ear	B *ntsej*	N-Mod
SAB ?	*nkees* to be tired	*sab-nkeeg* to be unwell	B *nkees, sab*	
SAB ?	*qhuav* dry	*sab-qhua* dry area	H 451	
SAJ to bend	*duav* back	*saj-dua* swayback	B *duav*	V-N
SIB/SIS (reciprocal)	*cem* scold	*sib-ceg* scold each other	B *cem* H 11, 292	R-V
	coj lead	*sib-cog* lead e.o.	B *coj*	R-V
	deev make love	*sib-dee* make love with e.o.	Yaj, 1987	R-V
	luaj same	*sib-luag* same as e.o.	H 120, 293	R-V

195

TRIGGER	Base	Compound	Source	Type
	ncaj straight	*sis-ncag* straight as e.o.	B *ncaj*	R-V
	npaum same	*sib-npaug* same as e.o.	B *npaum* H 450	R-V
	npuj collide	*sib-npug* collide with e.o.	H 161	R-V
	npua wrap around	*sib-npuas* wrap around e.o.	H 162	R-V
	nrau butt	*sib-nraus* butt e.o.	B *nrau* H 452	R-V
	nrawm quickly	*sis-nrawg* as quickly as e.o.	B *ncauj, nrawm*	R-V
	ntev long	*sib-nte* as long as e.o.	B *ntev*	R-V
	ntswj wrestle	*sib-ntswg* wrestle with e.o.	H 206	R-V
	ntxias braid	*sib-ntxiag* woven around e.o.	B *ntaub*	R-V
	qawm show affection	*sib-qawg* show affection for e.o.	B *qawm, quaj* H 260, 450	R-V
	tom bite	*sib-tog* bite e.o.	B *tom* H 450	R-V
	tua kill	*sis-tuas* kill e.o.	B *sab, sis, swb, tua*	R-V
	tuam kick	*sis-tuag* kick e.o.	B *tuam*	R-V

TRIGGER	Base	Compound	Source	Type
	twv compete	*sib-tw* compete with e.o.	P 93	R-V
	tsoo collide	*sib-tsoos* collide with e.o.	B *tsoo*	R-V
	txij tall	*sib-txig* as tall as e.o.	B *siab, txij*	R-V
	xyaw mix	*sib-xyaws* mix together	B *xyaw* H 293, 415, 453	R-V
	zes tease	*sib-zeg* tease e.o.	B *zes* H 436, 449	R-V
SIAB high	*qis* low	*siab-qig* high and low	B *qis*	V-V
SIAB liver	*npua* pig	*siab-npuas* pig liver	XX	N-Mod
	qhuav dry	*siab-qhua* satisfied heart	B *qhuav, siab*	N-Mod
SUAB sound	*nyiav* to lament	*suab-nyia* sound of lamentation	B *nyiav, quaj*	N-Mod
	nruas drum	*suab-nruag* sound of the drum	B *qeej*	N-Mod
	qeej *keng*	*suab-qeeg* sound of the *keng*	B *qeej*	N-Mod
	quaj to cry	*suab-quag* sound of crying	B *quaj*	N-Mod
TAB bar, slat	*txaj* bed	*tab-txag* bed slats	B *tab*	N-Mod

TRIGGER	Base	Compound	Source	Type
	txee etagère	*tab-txees* shelves of etagère	B *txee*	N-Mod
TAUB gourd	*daj* yellow	*taub-dag* pumpkin	B *taub* H 30, 307, 447	N-Mod
	hneev crossbow	*taub-hnee* body of crossbow	B *taub* H 308, 451	N-Mod
	nkawj hornet	*taub-nkawg* hornet swarm or nest	B *nkawj, taub*	N-Mod
	ntoo tree	*(txiv) taub-ntoos* (fruit) papaya	B *taub*	N-Mod
	ntsej ear	*taub-ntseg* earlobe	B *ntsej, taub* H 308	N-Mod
	qeej *keng*	*taub-qeeg* body of *keng*	B *qeej*	N-Mod
	taw foot	*taub-taws* toetip	B *taub, taw*	N-Mod
	tes hand	*taub-teg* fingertip	B *taub, tes* H 308, 449	N-Mod
	twm buffalo	*taub-twg* marrow (var. of gourd)	B *taub, twm* H 307	N-Mod
TEB land, field	*chaw* place	*teb-chaws* country	B *chaw, teb* H 452	N-N
	nplej rice	*teb-npleg* rice field	B *teb* H 313, 447	N-Mod
	nras plain	*teb-nrag* land	B *nras*	N-N

TRIGGER	Base	Compound	Source	Type
	qhuav dry	*teb-qhua* dry field	XX	N-Mod
TEJ other	*zaus/zaum* time, occasion	*tej-zaug* other occasion	H 313, 435	Mod-N
TEEJ utensils?	*qav* ?	*teej-qa* utensils	H 314	
TIB sole, alone;	*leej* person	*tib-leeg* 1 person alone	B *leej*	"Num"-N
	qhov place	*tib-qho* 1 place	H 315	"Num"-N
	tus (clf for animate, long things)	*tib-tug* sole person, thing	B *tib* H 315, 325	"Num"-Clf
single blow of	*plhaw* jump	*tib-plhaws* a single jump	B *plhaw*	"Num"-N
	riam knife	*tib-riag* a single stroke	H 450	"Num"-N
	tes hand	*tib-teg* a single blow	H 316	"Num"-N
TIJ elder brother	*laus* N-Mod old	*tij-laug* elder brother	B *laus, tij* H 316	
TIAB skirt	*nre* to pleat	*tiab-nres* pleated skirt	B *tiab*	N-Mod

TRIGGER	Base	Compound	Source	Type
TIAJ level	*nras* plain	*tiaj-nrag* plain	B *nras, tiaj*	V-N
	zoov forest	*tiaj-zoo* forested plain	B *zoov*	V-N
TOJ hill	*ntxa* grave	*toj-ntxas* hillside cemetery	B *ntxa* H 453	N-Mod
TOOJ copper	*daj* yellow	*tooj-dag* yellow copper	B *tooj*	N-Mod
	tshauv ash	*tooj-tshau* mix of copper and aluminum	B *tshauv*	N-Mod
TUB son; boy	*nkees* to be tired	*tub-nkeeg* lazy person	B *nkees, tub* H 154, 325, 449	N-Mod
	ntsoj ?	*tub-ntsog* orphan	H 202	N-Mod
	qhev servant	*tub-qhe* male servant	H 325, 451	N-Mod
	sev wife	*tub-se* wife and children	B *sev, tub*	N-N
	txawj able	*tub-txawg* an able person	H 377, 448	N-Mod
TUAB thick	*ncauj* mouth	*tuab-ncaug* thick mouth	XX	V-N
TWJ utensils	*tais* bowl	*twj-taig* dishes	B *tais*	N-N

TRIGGER	Base	Compound	Source	Type
THAUJ balance	*teev* scale	*thauj-tee* balance of scale	B *teev*	N-Mod
THAWJ first, head	*cawv* alcohol	*thawj-caw* head of the alcohol	B *cawv*	"Num"-N
	zaus/zaum time	*thawj-zaug* first time	B *thawj* H 335	"Num"-N
THOOB bucket	*npua* pig	*thoob-npuas* pig bucket	XX	N-Mod
	tes hand	*thoob-teg* hand pail	B *tes, thoob*	N-Mod
TSAB ?	*ntoo* tree	*tsab-ntoos* tree standing dead	B *tsab*	
TSAWB banana	*qis* short	*tsawb-qig* small banana	B *qis*	N-Mod
TSAWJ pad	*tes* hand	*tsawj-teg* part of palm close to fingers	B *tes, tsawj*	N-Mod
TSOJ net	*ntses* fish	*tsoj-ntseg* landing net	B *ntses, txiaj*	N-Mod
TSUJ reconnoiter	*kev* trail	*tsuj-ke* inspect the trail	XX	V-N
TSWB bell	*tsaim* jaw	*tswb-tsaig* jowl	B *tsaim, tswb* H 346	N-Mod

TRIGGER	Base	Compound	Source	Type
TSHAB send	*xov* message	*tshab-xo* send message to warn parents about impending kidnap	B *tshab*	V-N
TSHAJ spread	*xov* message	*tshaj-xo* spread news	B *tshaj*	V-N
TSHEB engine	*taws* wood	*tsheb-tawg* wood-burning engine	H 312, 449	N-Mod
TSHEEJ ?	*nqaij* meat	*tsheej-nqaig* as tasty as meat	H 447	
TSHEEJ ?	*zaj* ?	*tsheej-zag* long blasts (of a gun)	B *zaj*	
TSHOOJ levels	*ntuj* sky	*tshooj-ntug* levels of heaven	H 369	N-Mod
TXAJ trap	*ntses* fish	*txaj-ntseg* large fish trap	H 373	N-Mod
TXAJ bed	*qhua* guest	*txaj-qhuas* guest bed	B *qhua* , *txaj*	N-Mod
TXAIJ varicolored	*pliaj* forehead	*txaij-pliag* marks on forehead (of animal)	B *pliaj, txaij*	Mod-N
TXAWJ able	*dej* water	*txawj-deg* able swimmer	XX	V-N

TRIGGER	Base	Compound	Source	Type
	qeej *keng*	*txawj-qeeg* able *keng* player	B *qeej*	V-N
	txaj embar- rassed	*txawj-txag* easily embarrassed	H 373	V-N
TXEEB ?	*zis* urine	*(mob) txeeb-zig* (pain) difficulty in urinating	B *txeeb*, *zis* H 128, 376, 438, 449	
TXIAJ net	*ntses* fish	*txiaj-ntseg* landing net	B *tsoj*, *txiaj*	N-Mod
TXIAJ ?	*ntsim* ?	*txiaj-ntsig* gracious gift; kind act	H 200	
TXOJ length	*hmoov* fortune	*txoj-hmoo* fortune	H 67, 451	N-Mod
	kev trail	*txoj-ke* trail	B *kev*	N-Mod
	siav life	*txoj-sia* life	B *txoj* H 298, 382	N-Mod
TXOOB mane	*npua* pig	*txoob-npuas* pig mane	XX	N-Mod
TXHAB sore	*ncauj* mouth	*txhab-ncaug* sore in mouth	B *ncauj*, *txhab*	N-Mod
	sov warm	*txhab-so* fever sore	B *sov*, *txhab*	N-Mod

TRIGGER	Base	Compound	Source	Type
TXHEEJ previous	zaus/zaum time	txheej-zaug previous time	B txheej H 391	
TXHIB to split	taws wood	txhib-tawg length of wood split off	B txhib	V-N
TXHOJ shallow	hav valley	txhoj-ha shallow valley	H 395, 451	V-N
VAB tray	tshau to sift	vab-tshaus sieve	B tshau, vab H 364, 397, 453	N-Mod
VAJ garden	loom basin	vaj-loog closed-in park	B loom, vaj	N-Mod
	tsev house	vaj-tse house and grounds	B vaj	N-N
VIJ to surround	voj circle	vij-vog surrounding	B vij H 399	V-N
VOJ circle	hlua rope	voj-hluas lasso	B voj	N-Mod
	tes hand	voj-teg circle made with 2 hands	B tes, voj	N-Mod
XIB sole/palm	taw foot	xib-taws sole of foot	B taw H 310, 408, 453	N-Mod
	tes hand	xib-teg palm of hand	B xib H 313, 408, 449	N-Mod

TRIGGER	Base	Compound	Source	Type
XIAB to wax (of moon)	*rau* 6	*xiab-raus* 6th day of month	B *rau, xiab*	V-Num
	xya 7	*xiab-xyas* 7th day of month	B *xiab*	V-Num
	yim 8	*xiab-yig* 8th day of month	B *xiab* H 450	V-Num
	cuaj 9	*xiab-cuag* 9th day of month	B *xiab* H 447	V-Num
	kaum 10	*xiab-kaug* 10th day of month	B *xiab* H 450	V-Num
XOB ?	*hno* rice	*xob-hnos* (of eating without working for it)	B *hno*	
XOB mature male	*nyuj* cow	*xob-nyug* mature bull	H 447	N-Mod
XUB arrow	*hneev* crossbow	*xub-hnee* crossbow arrow	XX	N-Mod
	kev trail	*xub-ke* straight trail?	B *kev, qab, xub*	
XUB ?	*ntiaj* front	*xub-ntiag* front surface	H 189, 412	
XYAB incense	*ntawv* paper	*xyab-ntaw* offerings	B *ntawv, xyab*	N-N

205

TRIGGER	Base	Compound	Source	Type
XYOOB bamboo	*qeej* *keng*	*xyoob-qeeg* bamboo for making *keng*	B *qeej, xyoob*	N-Mod
	txaij vari- colored	*xyoob-txaig* varicolored bamboo	H 448	N-Mod
	txhiav ?	*xyoob-txhia* kind of small bamboo	B *txhiav, xyoob*	N-Mod
	yas length between knots	*xyoob-yag* length of bamboo between knots	B *xyoob*	N-Mod
YAJ sheep	*laus* old	*yaj-laug* old sheep	XX	N-Mod
	mos soft	*yaj-mog* soft sheep (wool)	B *yaj*	N-Mod
YEEB opium	*laus* old	*yeeb-laug* opium of previous year	B *yeeb* H 449	N-Mod
YEEB ?	*ntxhuav* to dry off	*yeeb-ntxhua* the silk is drying off	H 232	
YIJ (kin term)	*laus* old	*yij-laug* aunt's husband	B *laus, yij*	N-Mod
YOJ to agitate	*tes* hand	*yoj-teg* wave the hand	B *tes, yoj*	V-N

206

TRIGGER	Base	Compound	Source	Type
YUB sprout	*liaj* paddy field	*yub-liag* paddy rice sprout	B *yub* H 447	N-Mod
ZAJ dragon	*laus* old	*zaj-laug* old dragon	*Zaj-Laug Sau Se* [6]	N-Mod
ZAJ litter	*npua* pig	*zaj-npuas* litter of pigs	H 433	N-Mod
ZAJ ?	*npua* pig	*zaj-npuas* badger	B *zaj* H 161	
ZAJ ?	*qeej* keng	*zaj-qeeg* pieces for *keng*	B *qeej*	
ZAUB vegetable	*npua* pig	*zaub-npuas* pig food	B *npua, zaub* H 452	N-Mod
	ntsim peppery	*zaub-ntsig* a kind of peppery vegetable	B *zaub* H 200	N-Mod
	qhuav dry	*zaub-qhua* dried vegetables	XX	N-Mod
ZEB stone	*hov* to sharpen	*zeb-ho* whetstone	B *zeb* H 451	N-Mod
	tsua rock	*zeb-tsuas* rocky	B *tsua, zeb*	N-N

---

[6] *"Zaj Laug Sau Se," Dab Neeg* [Folk tales] (Vientiane, 1974), 192.

TRIGGER	Base	Compound	Source	Type
ZEJ				
?	*zos* village	*zej-zog* our village	B *zej, zos* H 436, 449	
ZIAB to dry in sun	*paj* flower	*ziab-pag* to dry into flower	B *paj, ziab* H 166, 438	V-N
ZIAJ				
?	*tsua* rock	*ziaj-tsuas* (of tree growing on rock)	XX	
ZIB honey	*muv* bee	*zib-mu* honey	B *zib*	N-Mod
ZIJ				
?	*ncauj* mouth	*zij-ncaug* grim mouth	B *ncauj, zij*	

APPENDIX B

Tone Sandhi Compounds Arranged by
High Frequency Second Word

Nature

KEV road, trail; way

1. *cab-ke*   to lead forcibly (*cab* to lead)
2. *coj-ke*   to observe (*coj* to follow)
3. *faib-ke*   a split in the trail (*faib* to divide)
4. *kab-ke*   ceremony (*kab* way)
5. *ncaj-ke*   on the trail (*ncaj* straight)
6. *ncauj-ke*   mouth of the road (*ncauj* mouth)
7. *nrab-ke*   1/2-way point on journey (*nrab* middle)
8. *ntauj-ke*   forever on the trail (*ntauj* ?)
9. *qab-ke*   downhill side of trail (*qab* beneath)
10. *qaij-ke*   move to one side of trail (*qaij* to lean)
11. *qub-ke*   the old way (*qub* of old)
12. *qhuab-ke*   to show the way (*qhuab* to show)
13. *tsuj-ke*   to scout out the trail (*tsuj* to reconnoiter)
14. *txoj-ke*   the trail (*txoj* length)
15. *xub-ke*   straight trail (*xub* arrow)

DEJ water; river

1. *vaubkib-deg*   turtle (*vaubkib* turtle)
2. *kwj-deg*   gulley (*kwj* gulley)
3. *nkoj-deg*   boat (*nkoj* carrier)
4. *nruab-deg*   in the water (*nruab* middle)
5. *ntxhuab-deg*   algae (*ntxhuab* moss)
6. *paj-deg*   bubbles (*paj* flower)
7. *pawj-deg*   aquatic plant (*pawj* ?)
8. *poob-deg*   to drown (*poob* to fall)
9. *pliaj-deg*   clam (*pliaj* ?)

209

10. *qab-deg*	downstream (*qab* behind, underneath)
11. *qwj-deg*	water snail (*qwj* snail)
12. *txawj-deg*	able swimmer (*txawj* able)

NTOO tree

1. *hleb-ntoos*	wood coffin (*hleb* coffin)
2. *nkhib-ntoos*	crotch between two branches (*nkhib* crotch)
3. *nplooj-ntoos*	tree leaves (*nplooj* leaf)
4. *nreej-ntoos*	flanging tree root (*nreej* ?)
5. *ntab-ntoos*	tree bees (*ntab* bee)
6. *ntxhuab-ntoos*	tree moss (*ntxhuab* moss)
7. *paj-ntoos*	tree flowers (*paj* flower)
8. *pob-ntoos*	tree stump (*pob* blob, clump)
9. *poob-ntoos*	to fall out of a tree (*poob* to fall)
10. *qab-ntoos*	base of the tree (*qab* beneath, under)
11. *taub-ntoos*	(w/*txiv* fruit:) papaya (*taub* gourd)
12. *tsab-ntoos*	tree standing dead (*tsab* ?)

NPLEJ rice (growing)

1. *hnab-npleg*	rice hull (*hnab* bag)
2. *noob-npleg*	seed rice (*noob* seed)
3. *npauj-npleg*	rice moth (*npauj* moth)
4. *nplooj-npleg*	rice leaves (*nplooj* leaf)
5. *nqob-npleg*	upper part of rice stalk (*nqob* upper stalk)
7. *nyab-npleg*	rice straw (*nyab* ?)
8. *paj-npleg*	puffed rice (*paj* flower)
9. *plab-npleg*	rice head before it opens (*plab* stomach)
10. *teb-npleg*	dry rice field (*teb* field)

NTUJ sky, heaven; expanse

| 1. *dab-ntug* | spirits that live inside the earth (*dab* spirit) |
| 2. *kaj-ntug* | morning (*kaj* bright) |

3.	*neej-ntug*	judge (*neej* person)
4.	*nrab-ntug*	noon (*nrab* middle)
5.	*nruab-ntug*	in the heavens (*nruab* middle)
6.	*ntiaj-ntug*	the middle level, earth
		(*ntiaj* stratum, surface)
7.	*qab-ntug*	base of heaven; horizon
		(*qab* beneath)
8.	*quaj-ntug*	cry to heaven (*quaj* to cry)
9.	*rooj-ntug*	gate of heaven (*rooj* door)
10.	*tshooj-ntug*	levels of heaven (*tshooj* level)

TSUA rock

1.	*ntab-tsuas*	rock bees (*ntab* bee)
2.	*pob-tsuas*	rock mass (*pob* blob, clump)
3.	*phab-tsuas*	wall of rock (*phab* wall)
4.	*qab-tsuas*	base of the cliff
		(*qab* underneath)
5.	*qej-tsuas*	of tree with no branches (*qej* ?)
6.	*roob-tsuas*	rocky mountain (*roob* mountain)
7.	*zeb-tsuas*	rocky (*zeb* stone)
8.	*ziaj-tsuas*	of tree growing in rock (*ziaj* ?)

ZOOV forest

1.	*kaj-zoo*	bright forest (*kaj* bright)
2.	*laj-zoo*	forest ridge (*laj* ridge)
3.	*nkaj-zoo*	small red plant in forest (*nkaj* ?)
4.	*nrauj-zoo*	to send someone away; suppress
		(*nrauj* to separate)
5.	*nruab-zoo*	in the forest (*nruab* middle)
6.	*poob-zoo*	lost in the woods (*poob* to fall)
7.	*roob-zoo*	forested mountain
		(*roob* mountain)
8.	*tiaj-zoo*	forested plateau (*tiaj* level)

LIAJ paddy field

1.	*dej-liag*	paddy canal water (*dej* water)
2.	*kwj-liag*	canal (*kwj* gulley)

3. *laij-liag* to plow paddy fields
        (*laij* to plow)
4. *nplej-liag* paddy field rice (*nplej* rice)
5. *nyuj-liag* paddy field cow (*nyuj* cow)
6. *yub-liag* paddy rice sprout (*yub* sprout)

Man-Made Artifacts

QEEJ keng (Hmong pipes)

1. *nkauj-qeeg* keng songs (*nkauj* song)
2. *nqaij-qeeg* offerings to the keng (*nqaij* meat)
3. *pab-qeeg* group of kengs (*pab* group)
4. *suab-qeeg* sound of the keng (*suab* sound)
5. *taub-qeeg* body of the keng (*taub* gourd)
6. *txawj-qeeg* able keng player (*txawj* able)
7. *xyoob-qeeg* bamboo used for keng tubes
        (*xyoob* bamboo)
8. *zaj-qeeg* pieces of the keng (*zaj* ?)

TSEV house

1. *dej-tse* water in eaves (*dej* water)
2. *kwj-tse* house drainage ditch (*kwj* gulley)
3. *ncej-tse* column in house (*ncej* post)
4. *nruab-tse* in the house (*nruab* middle)
5. *nthab-tse* storage platform
        (*nthab* storage platform)
6. *qab-tse* downhill side of the house
        (*qab* underneath)
7. *qhab-tse* rafter (*qhab* rafter)
8. *vaj-tse* house and grounds (*vaj* garden)

TXAJ bed

1. *ncej-txag* legs of the bed (*ncej* post)
2. *npuab-txag* of wood on side of bed
        (*npuab* to adhere)
3. *nruab-txag* bed covered with bamboo
        (*nruab* flat bamboo)

212

4.	*poob-txag*	to fall out of bed (*poob* to fall)
5.	*qab-txag*	under the bed (*qab* underneath)
6.	*rooj-txag*	bedroom door (*rooj* door)
7.	*tab-txag*	bed slats (*tab* slat)

Body Parts

TES hand

1.	*dab-teg*	wrist (*dab* narrowing)
2.	*daj-teg*	outstretched arms (*daj* unit of measurement)
3.	*hwb-teg*	of whistling through hands (*hwb* ?)
4.	*hnoob-teg*	sunrays (*hnoob* sun)
5.	*kab-teg*	line of the hand (*kab* line)
6.	*ncauj-teg*	of end of the sleeve (*ncauj* mouth)
7.	*nkhib-teg*	crotch between two fingers (*nkhib* crotch)
8.	*npuaj-teg*	to clap hands (*npuaj* to clap)
9.	*nreeb-teg*	a "good shot" (*nreeb* facile)
10.	*ntaj-teg*	open vertical hand (*ntaj* sabre)
11.	*ntxuaj-teg*	to wave the hand (*ntxuaj* to wave)
12.	*pob-teg*	wrist bone (*pob* blob)
13.	*qub-teg*	inherited things (*qub* of old)
14.	*taub-teg*	fingertips (*taub* gourd)
15.	*tib-teg*	a single blow of the hand (*tib* single blow)
16.	*thoob-teg*	hand pail (*thoob* bucket)
17.	*tsawj-teg*	part of palm close to fingers (*tsawj* pad)
18.	*voj-teg*	circle made with 2 hands (*voj* circle)
19.	*xib-teg*	palm of the hand (*xib* sole/palm)
20.	*yoj-teg*	to wave the hand (*yoj* to agitate)

NCAUJ mouth

1.	*aub-ncaug*	saliva (*aub* ?)
2.	*dub-ncaug*	of an enemy; one who doesn't talk (*dub* black)
3.	*liab-ncaug*	of a person who talks a lot

(*liab* red? monkey?)

4. *ntxub-ncaug*   of a critical person (*ntxub* to hate)
5. *ob-ncaug*   saliva (*ob* ?)
6. *pob-ncaug*   sores on the mouth (*pob* bump)
7. *pliab-ncaug*   flat mouth (*pliab* flat)
8. *qaub-ncaug*   spittle (*qaub* sour) = *aub-ncaug* ?
9. *tuab-ncaug*   thick mouth (*tuab* thick)
10. *txhab-ncaug*   sores on the mouth (*txhab* sore)
11. *zij-ncaug*   grim mouth (*zij* ?)

NTSEJ ear (by extension, face)

1. *daj-ntseg*   yellow face (sick) (*daj* yellow)
2. *kauj-ntseg*   earring (*kauj* ring)
3. *npauj-ntseg*   earring (*npauj* jewelry)
4. *nplooj-ntseg*   outer ear (*nplooj* leaf)
5. *ntsiab-ntseg*   descriptive of small person
                          (*ntsiab* kernel)
6. *pob-ntseg*   ear (*pob* blob, clump)
7. *sab-ntseg*   1 ear (*sab* side)
8. *taub-ntseg*   earlobe (*taub* gourd)

TAW foot

1. *dab-taws*   ankle (*dab* narrowing)
2. *luj-taws*   heel (*luj* heel/elbow)
3. *ntxhuab-taws*   a mossy trail (*ntxhuab* moss)
4. *pob-taws*   ankle bone (*pob* blob)
5. *taub-taws*   toetips (*taub* gourd)
6. *xib-taws*   sole of the foot (*xib* sole/palm)

Animals

NPUA pig

1. *dab-npuas*   pig trough (*dab* trough)
2. *dej-npuas*   pig water (*dej* water)
3. *nkauj-npuas*   young female pig (*nkauj* girl)
4. *nkauj-npuas*   pigsty (*nkauj* sty, pen)
5. *nkuaj-npuas*   pigsty (*nkuaj* sty, pen)
6. *nqaij-npuas*   pork (*nqaij* meat)

214

7.	*pab-npuas*	group of pigs (*pab* group)
8.	*plaub-npuas*	pig hair (*plaub* hair)
9.	*qaub-npuas*	pig food (*qaub* ?)
10.	*quab-npuas*	young pig (*quab* ?)
11.	*raj-npuas*	storage tube for pig food (*raj* tube)
12.	*roj-npuas*	pig fat (*roj* fat)
13.	*siab-npuas*	pig liver (*siab* liver)
14.	*thoob-npuas*	pig bucket (*thoob* bucket)
15.	*txoob-npuas*	mane of a pig (*txoob* mane)
16.	*zaj-npuas*	litter of pigs (*zaj* litter)
17.	*zaj-npuas*	badger (*zaj* ?)
18.	*zaub-npuas*	pig food (*zaub* vegetable)

NYUJ cow

1.	*dab-nyug*	cow trough (*dab* trough)
2.	*kub-nyug*	variety of large peach (*kub* ?)
3.	*laij-nyug*	to plow with a cow (*laij* to plow)
4.	*nkuaj-nyug*	cow pen (*nkuaj* pen)
5.	*nqaij-nyug*	beef (*nqaij* meat)
6.	*ntab-nyug*	wattles (look like bees' nests) (*ntab* bee)
7.	*peeb-nyug*	bull's sex organ (*peeb* male sex organ)
8.	*pwj-nyug*	adolescent steer (*pwj* ?)
9.	*plab-nyug*	(w/*txiv* fruit:) jackfruit (*plab* stomach)
10.	*plaub-nyug*	cow hair (*plaub* hair)
11.	*quab-nyug*	yoke (*quab* yoke)
12.	*roj-nyug*	cow fat (*roj* fat)
13.	*xob-nyug*	mature bull (*xob* mature male)

Verbs

QHUAV dry

1.	*caj-qhua*	serpent (*caj* vine)
2.	*liaj-qhua*	dry paddy field (*liaj* paddy field)
3.	*nplooj-qhua*	dry leaves (*nplooj* leaf)
4.	*nqaij-qhua*	dried meat (*nqaij* meat)
5.	*nroj-qhua*	dried weeds (*nroj* weed)

6.	*ntuj-qhua*	(w/*caij* season:) the dry season (*ntuj* sky)
7.	*nyuj-qhua*	strong cow (*nyuj* cow)
8.	*roob-qhua*	mountain without water source (*roob* mountain)
9.	*sab-qhua*	dry area (*sab* ?)
10.	*siab-qhua*	satisfied heart (*siab* liver)
11.	*teb-qhua*	dry field (*teb* field)
12.	*zaub-qhua*	dried vegetables (*zaub* vegetable)

LAUS old

1.	*dab-laug*	mother's brothers (*dab* kin term)
2.	*mob-laug*	old illness (*mob* to be ill)
3.	*nkauj-laug*	an "old girl" (*nkauj* girl)
4.	*nplej-laug*	old rice (*nplej* rice)
5.	*nyuj-laug*	mature cow (*nyuj* cow)
6.	*phauj-laug*	grandfather's sisters (*phauj* kin term)
7.	*tij-laug*	elder brother (*tij* elder brother)
8.	*yaj-laug*	old sheep (*yaj* sheep)
9.	*yeeb-laug*	opium of previous year (*yeeb* opium)
10.	*yij-laug*	aunt's husband (*yij* kin term)
11.	*zaj-laug*	old dragon (*zaj* dragon)

DAJ yellow

1.	*dej-dag*	turbulent water (*dej* water)
2.	*hmab-dag*	tree with white(!) flowers (*hmab* vine)
3.	*luaj-dag*	yellow earth (*luaj* ?)
4.	*nplej-dag*	yellow rice (*nplej* rice)
5.	*nyuj-dag*	yellow cow (*nyuj* cow)
6.	*paj-dag*	white(!) flowers of *hmab-dag* (*paj* flower)
7.	*taub-dag*	pumpkin (*taub* gourd)
8.	*tooj-dag*	yellow copper (*tooj* copper)

MOS soft, tender

1. *daj-mog* — light yellow (*daj* yellow)
2. *dawb-mog* — soft white (*dawb* white)
3. *liab-mog* — light red (*liab* red)
4. *nkauj-mog* — young girl (*nkauj* girl)
5. *ntaub-mog* — soft material (*ntaub* cloth)
6. *paj-mog* — soft flower (*paj* flower)
7. *plab-mog* — lower abdominal region
   (*plab* stomach)
8. *yaj-mog* — soft sheep (wool) (*yaj* sheep)

APPENDIX C

Some White Hmong Two-Word Expressives
Arranged by Tone Pattern[1]

/-ib   -b /

nplhib   nplheeb
—silverware or other metal rattling
—pin coming out of hand grenade

nplhib   nplhob
ntses nti nplhib nplhob   (H 168)
fish writhe
the fish writhed (manner) (on the hook)

plib   pleb
wood crackling

plib   plob
—*hlawv xyoob, xyoob tawg nrov plib plob*   (B *plib*)
burn bamboo bamboo explode sound
when bamboo burns, it makes the sound...

zib   zeb
a big pig fighting   (XX)

---

[1] In the right hand column are illustrative examples, associations, and abstractions; expressives do not have "definitions." Sources: H (Heimbach), B (Bertrais-Charrier), P (Vwj et al., *Primer*), XX (Xab Xyooj), KY (Kuam Yaj). Those associations for which no source is listed came from either Xab Xyooj or Kuam Yaj in one of a number of joint sessions.

/-ig -g/
Low-Pitched, Echoic, Hollow, Airy Sounds; (Big)

dig dug

boiling of thick liquid like corn mash (thick, ponderous bubbles) (XX, KY)

ig awg

wild pigs fighting: open-mouthed gobbling and growling (XX, KY)

kig kuag

—mouse's feet on an empty box (KY)
—*wb ua kig kuag lawv kooj qab* (P 30)
  we-2 make   follow locust behind
  we went after the locust making the sound...

mig mog

—*nyuj quaj mig mog* (B *mig*)
  cow cry
  the cow calls...
—*miv mos mab mig mog* (P 33)
  cat roll civet
  the cats roll around and jump on top of each other

mlig mlog

tsov quaj mlig mlog tim roob (P 112)
tiger cry   across on mountain
the tiger calls ... over on the mountain

ntig ntwg

—thunder
—*noog ya ntig ntwg* (B *ya*)
  bird fly
  the birds fly by making a great flapping

nyig nyeg
  ~*nyiag*

huas nyig nyiag (B *nyiag*)
go around

219

(of dogs growling and snarling over something)

pig poog
        —bomb impact
        —*khiav nrov pig poog*   (B *poog*)
          run sound
          run with the sound... (of feet hitting earth)
        —*neeg peem las qaug pig poog*   (P 29, modified XX)
          person fat totter
          the fat person totters by...

plig plawg
        —bird rising from a nest on the ground
        —*ib pab noog ya plig plawg*
          1 group bird fly
          a flock of birds fly by making a great flapping

plig plog
        body jumping into water

qig qug
        plab npau qig qug   (B *plab*)
        stomach boil
        the stomach is growling...

rig reg
        Riam dua Riam lub ris ruaj ruaj rig reg   (P 49)
        Riam tear Riam clf pants firm firm
        Riam tore his pants firmly, with sound...

sig suag[2]
        rain on thatch roof   (KY)

tig toog
        heavy footsteps

---

[2] Expressive phonology: in prosaic words, there is a co-occurrence block between s- [ʃ] and the -g (breathy) tone (see chapter two, section 2.2.2).

tsig tsuag

      —a downpour

      —monkeys making abrupt jumps

vig vag

      —a tree falling...the sound it makes hitting other
        growth on its way down

      —*cov vuas vau vig vag*   (P 52)
        clf tile fall
        the tiles fell making the sound...

vig voog

      a herd stampeding

vig vwg

      —strong wind

      —fast traffic

      —small airplane motor

zig zawg

      —*hawb oob zig zawg*   (B *oob*)
        strong-breathe
        (of asthmatic breathing; heavy breathing while
        exercising)

      —of snoring

zig ziag

     kab quaj zig zuag   (P 35)
     insect cry
     the insect makes the sound... (of legs rubbing
     together)

zig zuag

      —walking through high grass   (XX)

     —*pem toj siab huab ntsauv ntsawv nag*
       up hill high cloud surround multiply rain
       tshauv poob zig zuag
       drizzle fall
       up on the high hill, the clouds gather and grow
       and the drizzling rain falls...

—monkeys jumping from branch to branch

zawg ziag[3]
> *nag tshauv zawg ziag*   (H 135)
> rain drizzle
> the drizzling rain makes the sound...

zawg zog[4]
> —*saj zawg zog*   (H 286)
>   bend
>   flexible (manner)
> —*rooj zaum zooj zawg zog*   (B *zooj*)
>   chair malleable
>   (of chair with good support, flexibility)

/-ij -j/
Energetic, Fast, Short Sounds; (Many, High, Close)

cij coj
> *menyuam qaib quaj cij coj*   (B *qaib*)
> young chicken cry
> the chicks chirp (cheep)

dhij dhuj
> breathing with a full nose

fij fwj
> —bird or plane whizzing by
> —*cua mas tuaj fij fwj*   (P 43)
>   wind topic come
>   the wind comes out... (of air in a bellows)

gij gaj[5]
> babies crying

---

[3] In a minor pattern, the vowel of the first word is *-aw-* instead of *-i-*.

[4] See above.

[5] Expressive phonology: [ŋ] is an extremely restricted initial in prosaic words.

hij haj

> —laughter
> —fighting

ij aj

> babies (baby animals?) crying

ij awj

> hiccups   (XX, KY)

khij khuaj

> *qaib qus khiav nrov khij khuaj*   (B *khij*)
> chicken wild run sound
> the wild chicken runs with the sound...

mij mej

> —mosquitos or other insects flying around your ear
> —*nees sis tuam quaj mij mej*   (B *mij*)
>   horse recip kick cry
>   the horses kick each other, whinneying

mij mẽw̃j[6]

> bullet whizzing past   (KY)

nkij nkuaj

> *ntoo dam nrov nkij nkuaj*   (B *nkij*)
> tree break sound
> the tree breaks in two making a dry, resounding
> noise

bhij bhooj[7]
  ~nphij nphooj

> —pop of bamboo in fire
> —sound of a lot of popcorn popping
>   (full pan)   (KY)

---

[6] Expressive phonology: the nasalized vowel of the second word does not occur in prosaic words.

[7] Expressive phonology: the initial *bh-* does not occur in prosaic words.

nplij nplaj
>*txoj hlua tuj lub nplawm nrov nplij nplaj* (B *nplaj*)
>clf cord   top   whip sound
>the cord of the top (a toy) makes the whipping
>sound...

nplij nploj
  ~nplooj
>—foot pulling out of tar
>—pop of chewing gum
>—clap of bamboo

nplij npluaj
>*lawv ua peb cov nqaij sawb poob nrov*
>they make we clf meat rib   fall sound
>*nplij npluaj rau hauv av* (P118)
>>to in earth
>they threw our ribs to the earth, making the
>sound...

nplhij nplhawj
>*ntses nti nplhij nplhawj* (B *nplhij*)
>fish writhe
>the fish are frisky, wriggling

nrij nrawj
  ~ntij ntawj
>typewriter (fast, sharp: paper tight against
>platen) (XX)

nrhij nrhawj
>—*tu nrov nrhij nrhawj* (B *nrhij* , H 178)
>>break sound
>>(of fibers, strands tearing apart)
>—*leeg tu nrhij nrhawj* (B *nrhij*)
>>nerve break
>>(of sensation of cracking nerves)

ntij ntoj
>—low impact sound

224

—cut lengths of bamboo rolling, hitting each other
—sound of toy gun made from bamboo with string
  inside

nthij nthooj
> heads butting (cows, children...)

ntsij ntsiaj
> pushing-pulling bolt on an M-16

pij pauj
> —hail falling
> —fruit falling

plij plej
> just a little popcorn popping (pan not full)   (KY)

plij ploj
> —bullet impact
> —bamboo bursting
> —*hais lus plij ploj plij ploj*   (H 49)
>   speak word
>   to speak queerly, like the sound of bamboo
>   bursting

plhij plhawj
> —sound of helicopter propellers
> —birds making short flights (such as, pigeons
>   flying from one roof roost to another)

rhij rhej
> —light and sound combination: lightning (light
>   and crack) or small amount of water on hot
>   grease
> —*kuv kib zaub tawg rhij rhej*   (P 75)
>   I fry vegetable explode
>   when I fry vegetables, they make the sound...

rhij rhuaj
> —sound of dry leaves crackling, rustling   (H 178)

—wb hnov tus nraj khiav rhij rhuaj   (P 105)
   we-2 hear clf pheasant run
   we heard the pheasant running...
—qaib rheeb kab rhij rhuaj   (P 75)
   chicken scratch insect
   the chicken scratches for worms...

tij tauj

   raindrops

tsij tsuaj

   lwg zeeg nrov tsij tsuaj   (B *tsij*)
     dew falls sound
     the dew is shaken off...

txij txej

   —nrov txij txej   (H 178)
   (of sucking sounds)
   —rat crying out in a snake's mouth
   —foot pulling out of mud

vij vawj

   —dogs barking at something   (XX, KY)
   —dev tsem vij vawj   (H 400)
     dog bark
     the dog whimpered and cried

zij zej

   the sound a pig makes when you pick it up   (KY)

/-is -s/
Continuous Sights and Sounds

   chis chaus
     nws tham chis chaus   (P 84)
     s/he chat
     s/he talks...

dis daws

>—a continuous mixed sound: such as, a group of mon-
>keys chattering and jumping around, heard at a
>distance; many people walking on a surface of
>twigs, rocks, soil   (XX, KY)
>—the appearance of a long line of people   (KY)

his huas

>*peb luag his huas los*
>we laugh   come
>we come joking and laughing

is as

>*tus neeg ruam ua is as*   (P 50)
>clf person mute make
>the mute person goes...

is ws

>—speaking in a monotone
>—little pig running after its mother   (XX)
>—everyone saying *"ws"* (babytalk "yes")   (KY)

lis lais

>*hais phis lis phais lais*   (H 241)
>speak
>to talk nonsense

lis loos

>—bees buzzing
>—*ntaub lis loos*[8]
> cloth
> synthetic material (with reference to smooth-
> ness)
>—loud droning   (H 178)

mlis mlas
~mlos

>*miv quaj mlis mlas/mlos*   (B *miv, mlis*)

---

[8] This phrase contains the very unusual combination *noun*-expressive.

cat cry
(of a cat's growl)

nkhis nkhas
 ~nkhoos

    tso cuav hlau poob nrov nkhis
    let waste iron fall sound
    nkhas/nkhoos
    when one throws down scrap iron, it makes the
    sound...

nkhis nkhoos

    —sound of hollow things   (H 156)
    —*tsoo taub hau nrov nkhis nkhoos*   (B *nkhis*)
      collide head sound
      (of sound of head bumping against something)
    —*xo pob txha nrov nkhis nkhoos*   (B *nkhis*)
      bite bone sound
      (of sound of chewing bones)

nris nraws

    kauv mus kev nrov nris nraws   (B *nris*)
    deer go trail sound
    when the deer walks, he makes the sound...

phis phais

    hais phis lis phais lais   (H 241)
    speak
    to talk nonsense

qhis qhaws

    pob txha ntsoog tas nrov qhis qhaws   (B *qhis*)
      bone broken all sound
    the bones are all broken and make the sound...

nraws nris[9]

    mus nraws nris (B *nris*)
    go; to walk right along, with application

---

[9] In a minor pattern, the vowel of the first word is *-aw-* instead of *-i-*.

228

vaws vos

> *nws quaj vaws vos los*   (P 52)
> s/he cry   come
> s/he comes crying...

/-iv -v/, /-awv -v/[10]
Slow

iv awv

> —*dev raws kauv dev tsem iv awv los*   (P 58)
> dog pursue deer dog bark   come
> when the dog chases the deer, it barks...
> —hiccups (XX)

nphiv nphav

> —sound of chopping a tree   (H 178)
> —*ntaus nruas nrov nphiv nphav*   (B *nruas*)
> hit drum sound
> when one hits the drum, it sounds...

nphiv nphoov

> *tua phom nrov nphiv nphoov*   (B *nphoov*)
> shoot gun sound
> when one shoots a gun, it sounds...

nthiv nthav

> *nag poob nthiv nthav*   (B *nthiv*)
> rain fall
> the rain falls in large, distinct drops

pliv ploov

> —ducks diving underwater (XX)
> —the sound of an empty bottle submerged in water
>   filling up (XX)
> —*lub plab nrov pliv ploov*   (B *pliv*)
>   clf stomach sound

---

[10] With the tone pattern *-v -v*, the vowel of the first word is *-aw-* as often as
it is *-i-*.

229

the sound of one's stomach after one has had a
lot to drink and then goes running

qiv qawv

> *zom hniav qiv qawv* (B *qawv*)
> grind teeth
> (manner of grinding teeth, as of a sleeping child)

txiv txev

> rats or birds chirping

txhiv txhev

> —sound of grease spattering (XX)
> —rodent cry

ziv zev

> *quaj ziv zev* (H 438)
> cry
> (of pigs squealing)

dhawv dhev

> —*quaj nqus ntswg dhawv dhev* (H 266)
>   cry inhale nose
>   wept loudly and bitterly
> —of whimpering, 2 distinct sounds (XX)

hawv huav

> —sound of animals growling and ready to bite
>   (H 479)
> —human panting (XX)
> —nervous tense pacing (Cua Yaj)

hmlawv hmlav

> of a complaining cry:
>
> > *nws quaj hmlawv hmlav rau kuv niam tias,*
> > s/he cry   to   I mother that
> > "*ua cas...*" (P 153, B *quaj*)
> > why
> > s/he cried whining to my mother asking
> > "why"?

230

khawv khuav
> *tub nquag khiav khawv khuav* (P 100)
> son energetic run
> the boy ran energetically and steadily

nkawv nkuav[11]
> *nab taum nplaig nkawv nkuav* (B *nkuav*)
> snake move tongue
> the snake sticks out his tongue quickly

nphawv nphoov
> *xuas qws ntaus nphawv nphoov* (B *nphoov*)
> take club hit
> (manner of hitting)

nthawv nthav[12]
> —*nws mob nthawv nthav tuag* (B *nthav*)
>   s/he ill   die
>   s/he was stricken by a sudden illness and died

> —*nag poob nthawv nthav* (B *nthav*)
>   rain fall
>   drops of rain fall everywhere
> —*tua hneev nthawv nthav* (B *nthav*)
>   shoot crossbow
>   shoot the crossbow rapidly
> —*huaj cheej nti nthawv nthav tuag* (B *nthawv*)
>   have spasms writhe   die
>   (s/he) made several spasmodic movements and
>   suddenly died

---

[11] The meaning of this expressive is something like 'suddenly', which is the opposite of the general meaning I have associated with this tone pattern.
[12] See above.

rhawv   rhev

    qaib qus teb rhawv rhev   (B *rhawv*)

    chicken wild answer

    the wild hen responds... (to a bird-call)

/-uj   -ø/

duj de

    qaij duj de   (B *qaij*)

    lean

    to oscillate

hnyuj hnyo

    xawb hnyuj hnyo   (B *xawb*)

    search

    (manner of searching)

ncuj ncee

    tus ncej no ua ncuj ncee tsis ruaj li   (P 63)

    clf pillar this make   not firm at all

    this pillar goes...and is not steady at all

ncuj nco

    ncaws hau ncuj nco   (H 148)

    nod head

    nodding the head in sleep

nkuj nki

    slowly, easily:

        —*noj nkuj nki*   (B *nkuj*)

          eat

          to eat very slowly

        —*tham nkuj nki*   (B *nkuj*)

          talk

          to speak too slowly, in a mournful manner

nrhuj nrho

    hais lus tu nrhuj nrho   (B *nrho*)

    speak word break

    talking, making inopportune pauses

txhuj txhoo
>*ua txhuj txhoo*   (H 395)
>make
>to be weak in body

/-uj   -b/

chuj chiab
>—of a walk with swinging gait   (XX)
>—*majmam mus chuj chiab*   (H 26)
>slowly   go
>to absentmindedly or unconciously walk very slowly

hnyuj hnyiab
>*ua hnyuj hnyiab*   (XX)
>make
>to do something against one's own desires to please another

kuj kaub
>*Xwm xuav kuj kaub*   (P 41)
>Xwm whistle
>Xwm whistled slowly, to himself

mluj mlob
>—whining   (XX)
>—of a cat crying   (H 479)

nuj neb
>—*hais nuj neb*   (H 143)
>speak
>to speak in a whining voice
>—to mumble (as in prayer)   (B *nuj*)

ncuj nciab
>to do something grudgingly   (XX)

233

nruj nreeb
>—sound of tree popping right before it falls
>(several separated pops)   (XX)
>—sound of cutting wood   (H 478)

txhuj txheb
>sound of grease spattering   (XX)

zuj zeb
>—of a pig squealing   (H 441)
>—of little hungry pigs   (XX)

/-*uj -g*/

duj dig
>*maub duj dig*   (B *dig*)
>grope
>to grope along, tapping hands and feet like a blind
>person

duj dog
>*mus duj dog*   (B *duj*)
>go
>to walk at a good clip

nuj nuag
>*tus nqaij maub nuj nuag los*   (B *nuj*)
>clf game grope   come
>the wild animal comes...through the
>undergrowth

ntxuj ntxiag
>*kuv hnov cua tuaj ntxuj ntxiag*   (P 129)
>I hear wind come
>I hear the cool refreshing little wind coming

nyuj nyag
>*ua nyuj nyag*   (XX)
>make

(the happy sound of children hugging and nuzzling homecoming parent)

puj poog

>*neeg peem las qaug puj poog* (P 29)
>person fat totter
>the fat man comes tottering...

ruj rwg

>*ntshai ruj rwg* (B *ruj*)
>fear
>to be full of fear...

zuj ziag

>—of a cicada singing (H 438)
>—the sound of pulling a metal chain over something (XX)

/-uj -m/

duj duam

>—*mus duj duam* (H 39)
>go
>to walk with big steps
>—of young child walking awkwardly (toddling) (XX)
>—to walk at a good clip (B *duj*)

quj qaim

>*cev yiag quj qaim* (B *qaim*)
>body slim
>a svelte body (poetic)

qhuj qhem

>—*Qhua Xwm hnoos qhuj qhem* (P 108; B *qhuj*)
>Qhua Xwm cough
>Qhua Xwm coughed without ceasing
>—the sound of clearing the throat (H 270)

txuj txoom

> *noj txuj txoom*   (B *txuj*)
> eat
> to be always eating

uj iam

> *ntuav uj iam*   (B *uj*)
> vomit
> to vomit without ceasing

/-uj -s/

cuj coos

> of movement of a sick chicken or of a mad person
> (XX)

duj das

> *Foom ua tib tug fee duj das xwb*   (P 43)
> Foom make single clf turn   only
> Foom merely turned his head, shaking his head
> and shoulders, "I don't know"

luj laws

> —big, continuous humming sound, as of an electric
>   generator (XX)
> —*nroo luj laws*   (XX)
>   sound
>   (sound of continual complaining to oneself)
> —*ua luj laws*   (XX)
>   make
>   to do something without liking it
> —*hais luj laws*   (XX)
>   speak
>   to speak without expression (but not without
>   feeling)

luj les

> the sound of a vacuum cleaner, bees or an airplane
> (XX)

236

luj lias

> *tus npauj npaim ya dawb luj lias*   (P 60)
> clf   butterfly   fly freely
> the butterfly flies freely...

luj luas

> —*nws nkees nkees qaug zog luj luas*   (P 58)
>   s/he tired tired   weak
>   s/he is lethargic and unsteady...
> —*ua luj luas*   (H 119)
>   make
>   to be a wanderer, a person who seldom stays
>   home

mluj mlas
 ~mlos

> *miv quaj mluj mlas*   (B *mluj*)
>   cat cry
>   (of a cat's meow)

nuj nuas

> *liab ncav nuj nuas*   (B *nuj*)
> monkey extend
> the monkey extends his long arms this way and
> that

nkuj nkaus

> *nthos nkuj nkaus*   (XX)
> grasp
> to snatch and put back quickly

nkuj nkaws

> *no no tshee nkuj nkaws*   (B *nkuj*)
> cold cold shiver
> to be cold and tremble all over

nkuj nkoos

> —*peb yawg nkag nkuj nkoos tuaj*   (P 53)
>   we grandfather creep   come
>   our grandfather crept this way...

—laus laus ua nkuj nkoos   (B *nkuj*)
    old old make
    to be old and all broken

nkhuj nkhoos
    —sound of chopping on dead or hollow tree or log
    with an ax   (XX)
    —sound of a dog gnawing a bone (XX)
    —sound of chopping soft wood   (H 478)
    —appearance of an old person walking with a bent
    back   (XX)

nphuj nphoos
    —sound of a tiger crying   (H 479)
    —sound of a boar grunting   (XX)
    —of behavior: putting off duty, bad behavior,
    hurtful to others   (XX)

nruj nris
    —*nees taub hau ncaws nruj nris*   (B *nris*)
      horse head   dip
    the horse walks raising and lowering his head
    at each step
    —*tsaug zog nruj nris*   (H 179)
    sleep
    to nod while sleeping
    —*mus nruj nris*   (B *nris*)
    go
    to walk right along; with application

ntsuj ntsees
    tos ntsuj ntsees   (H 200)
    wait
    to wait...

nyuj nyas
  ~nyes
    lub siab ua nyuj nyas nyuj nyes   (B *siab*)
    clf liver make

to feel restless (for one who is absent, for
example)

nyuj nyos

>*tib leeg dob nyuj nyos* (B *nyuj*)
>single person weed
>for one alone to work (weed) without a let-up

pluj plaws

>—*txoj kev nrad nplua nplua mus kev npleem pluj*
>clf road down slippery   go road   slip
>*plaws* (P 118)
>the trail down there is very slippery; one goes
>slipping and sliding
>—*kuv siab yuj pluj plaws* (B *pluj*)
>I liver hover
>my heart dwells (on something) continually

quj qees

>slowly; steadily:
>>—*chim quj qees* (H 263)
>>anger
>>to gradually give rise to anger
>>—*tos quj qees* (H 263)
>>wait
>>to wait patiently
>>—*mus kev qoj quj qees* (B *qoj*)
>>go road balance
>>to walk slowly, balancing oneself

tuj taws

>*ntuas tuj taws* (B *tuj*)
>chant
>to chant (speak a song)

tshuj tshaws

>*tuaj tshuj tshaws* (B *tshuj*)
>come
>to keep on coming, so that one cannot see the end (of
>their coming)

vuj vias
>—of going back and forth on a swing   (KY)
>
>—of a toddler's or a drunk's walk   (KY)

yuj yees
>—*cov ntses ya ua yuj yees*   (P 120)
>clf fish fly make
>the fish flash circling through the water
>—*kiv kiv kuv qhov muag, kuv ua yuj yees*   (B *yuj*)
>spin spin I   eyes   I make
>when my head turns, I get dizzy

zuj zas
>—*nws mus faj zuj zas dua pem qaum kev*   (P 44)
>s/he go careful   again up back road
>he went cautiously back, on the uphill side of
>the trail
>—*roob ris mus kev faj zuj zas*   (B *roob ris*)
>crab go road careful
>the crab walks sideways

/*-uj   -v*/
Double Orientation: Back and Forth, Up and Down, In and Out
Movements, Attitudes, Sounds; Separate Sounds

cuj civ
>*menyuam qaib cuj civ*   (B *qaib*)
>young chicken
>the chicks chirp/cheep

dhuj dhev
>*quaj dhuj dhev*   (B *quaj*)
>cry
>to cry sniffling and snuffling

dhuj dheev
>—*nco dhuj dheev*   (H 148)
>remember
>to suddenly remember
>—to almost remember, then forget again

240

—of rising from and falling back into unconciousness
—sound of whimpering on and off

huj huav

    vaub kib ua pa hawb huj huav   (P 51)
    turtle make breathe
    (of open mouth panting/purring, from within throat)

hluj hluav

    xuab taw hluj hluav   (H 412)
    rub foot
    to drag the feet; delay in taking action

khuj khuav

    —*qaib rheeb kab khuj khuav*   (P 92)
      chicken scratch insect
      the chicken scratches for worms...
    —deliberate, slow manner

nruj nreev

    —sound of cutting wood   (H 478)
    —sound of tree popping right before it falls   (XX)
    —sound of tight string of bow reverberating
      ("twanging") after arrow is released (XX)

nrhuj nrhawv

    —*hais lus nrho nrhuj nrhawv*   (H 120)
      speak word all
      slow of speech
    —sound of hopping: rabbit or bird   (XX)

nrhuj nrheev

    sawv nrhuj nrheev   (H 182)
    arise
    to stand up with difficulty, to stand slowly (as of an infant just learning to walk)

ntuj ntiv

    sound of rats eating

nthuj nthav
>> —*ua ntos nthuj nthav*   (H 190)
>>> make loom
>>> the sound of weaving on a loom
>> —*Nplooj ua txiv tsawb poob nthuj nthav*   (P 126)
>>> Nplooj make banana fall
>>> Nplooj dropped the bananas with the sound...

ntsuj ntsoov
>> *tos ntsuj ntsoov*   (H 200)
>> wait
>> to wait...

ntshuj ntshiv
>> *quaj ntshuj ntshiv*   (B *ntshuj*)
>> cry
>> to cry gently

nyuj nyav
>> —*quaj nyuj nyav*   (XX)
>>> cry
>>> whining
>> —*mus kev nyuj nyav*   (XX)
>>> go road
>>> (of a turtle's walk)
>> —of an insincere smile (double entendre)   (XX)
>> —of the bittersweet feeling of missing someone (KY)

nyuj nyev
>> *quaj nyuj nyev*   (B *quaj*, P 69)
>> cry
>> to whimper, whine (of a misbehaving youngster)

nyuj nyov
>> *ua nyuj nyov*   (KY)
>> make
>> (of something indistinct in the dark, moving around; as an animal outside the house)

242

phuj phiv

  nti aub-ncaug phuj phiv (B *phuj*)
  spit saliva
  to spit without ceasing

pluj plawv

  the sound of heavy bubbles bursting (XX)

pluj pliv

  hluav ncaig liab pluj pliv (B *pliv*)
  burn coals red
  the coals which are going out make little red
  lights

pluj pliav

  ntsais muag pluj pliav (B *pliav*)
  squint eye
  to screw up the eyes at something

quj qev

  the sound of a creaky door

rhuj rhev

  lightning and thunder (light-pause-sound) (XX)

rhuj rhuav

  —sound of cutting vegetation (H 478)
  —the sound of a bird shuffling through leaves
   looking for insects (XX)

tuj tauv

  —*dej nrog tuj tauv* (B *teev*)
   water drip
   the water drips drop by drop
  —the sound of a flatterer's voice

tuj tev

  —*hais tuj tev* (H 479, modified XX)
   speak

to speak in a whining or whimpering voice
—*hais tuj tev*   (XX)
to mutter (but not necessarily low pitch)

tuj teev

dej nrog tuj teev   (B *teev*)
water drip
the water drips drop by drop

thuj thawv

ua neeb nchos thuj thawv   (B *thuj*)
make shaman shake
to perform a shamanistic rite by moving in a
regular, rhythmic way

tsuj tsawv

a little:
—*pa taws ncho tsuj tsawv*   (B *tsuj*)
air fire smoke
the fire smokes a little
—*mob tsuj tsawv*   (B *tsuj*)
ill
to be a little indisposed

tshuj tshuav

evasive:
—*tauv las tshuj tshuav*   (H 310)
?   ?
to avoid doing work; to get out of doing
things
—*tsiv tshuj tshuav*   (H 369)
?
to deliberately keep from someone's com-
pany

txuj txwv

—*menyuam dev quaj txuj txwv*   (B *txuj*, H 384)
young dog cry
the little dogs squall...

244

—*quaj txuj txwv*   (B *quaj*)
   cry
   to whine (of a misbehaving youngster)

txhuj txhoov

   ua npaws txhuj txhoov   (B *txhuj*)
   make fever
   to have chills and fever...

xuj xuav

   —*los nag xuj xuav*   (B *xuj*, H 412, KY)
     come rain
     the rain falls lightly, all day
   —*kauv maub xuj xuav*   (B *xuj*)
     deer grope
     the deer makes his way...
   —of the snake's slow wriggle   (XX)

yuj yeev

   —*qav taub ya ua yuj yeev*   (P 25)
     frog short fly make
     the little frog flies around
   —*piav yuj yeev*   (B *yuj*)
     dawdle
     to balance oneself lightly (as of movement while
     singing)
   —*kuv nyob yuj yeev*   (B *yuj*)
     I stay
     I'm fooling around

zuj zuav

   —*quaj zuj zuav*   (B *quaj*)
     cry
     to whine
   —*txav zuj zuav*   (H 373)
     move
     to move slowly and dilatorily

APPENDIX D

Sources and Map[1]

A. East Hmongic ("Mhu"): East Guizhou or Qiandong fangyan

DIALECT	Sub-fangyan	Village	Commune	District	Province
YANGHAO	—	Yanghao	—	Kaili (formerly Lushan)	Guizhou

Sources: Wang 1979 #1 ("Yanghao"), Wang 1985 ("Yanghao"), Hmub-Diel dictionary 1958 ("Hmub"), Chang 1976 ("Yang-hao"), Purnell 1970 (MKL: "K'ai-li"), Li 1984 ("Yanghao"), Cao 1981 ("Yanghao"), Chen and Li 1981 ("Yanghao"), Ying 1962 ("Yang hao"), INL 1962 ("Yanghao"), Li, Ch'en, and Ch'en 1959 ("Yang hao").

---

1 I am deeply indebted to David Strecker, who organized my sources according to village, commune, district, and province in the following source list. I also want to thank him at this point for giving me an explanation of the Chinese system of language subcategory reference and terminology, and many extremely useful hand-drawn maps.

DIALECT	Sub-fangyan	Village	Commune	District	Province
SHIDONGKOU	—	Shidongkou	—	Taijiang	Guizhou

Sources: Purnell 1970 (MTK: "Tai-kung"), Kwan 1966 ("Ch'ing Chiang Miao"), Chang 1947, 1953 ("Taikung"), 1972, 1976 ("Shih-tung-k'ou").

LUSHAN (that is, Ma and T'ai's Lushan group)	—	Zhouxi	—	Kaili (formerly Lushan)	Guizhou

Sources: Ma and T'ai 1956

KAILI	—	—	—	Kaili (formerly Lushan)	Guizhou

Sources: P'an and Ts'ao 1958 ("Lu shan").

KAITANG	—	—	Kaitang	Kaili (formerly Lushan)	Guizhou

Sources: Purnell 1970 (MLS: "Lu-shan"), Cao 1961 ("Kaitang"), Li, Ch'en, and Ch'en ("Kaitang") 1959.

DIALECT	Sub-fangyan	Village	Commune	District	Province
ZHENFENG	—	—	—	Zhenfeng	Guizhou

Sources: Purnell 1970 (MCF: "Cheng-feng"), Chang 1947, 1953 ("Chengfeng"), (Esquirol 'Ka˩ nao˄ dictionary 1931).[2]

RONGJIANG	—	Gaotongzhai	—	Rongjiang	Guizhou

Sources: Purnell 1970 (MJC: "Jung-chiang"), Chang 1947, 1953 ("Jungchiang"), 1972, 1976 ("Kao-t'ung-chai").

B. North Hmongic ("Qo-Xiong"): West Hunan or Xiangxi fangyan

JIWEI	—	Layiping	Jiwei	Huayuan	Hunan

Sources: Wang 1979 #2 ("Jiwei"), Wang 1985 ("Jiwei"), Purnell 1970 (MHY: "Hua-yuan"), Xiang 1983 ("Jiwei"), Chen and Li 1981 ("Layiping"), Ying 1962 ("Layiping") INL 1962 ("Layiping"), (I 1961 ("Jiwei"))[3], Li, Ch'en and Ch'en 1959 ("Jiwei").

---

2 Joseph Esquirol, *Dictionnaire 'Ka˩nao˄-Français et Français-'Ka˩nao˄* (Hong Kong: Imprimerie Société des Missions étrangères, 1931). This work was unavailable at the time of this study.

3 I Hsien-p'ei, [Noun categories in the Miao dialect of Jiwei, in the district of Hua-yuan, in western Hunan] ZGYW 102 (1961). This work was unavailable at the time of this study.

DIALECT	Sub-fangyan	Village	Commune	District	Province
DONGTOUZHAI	—	—	—	Luxi	Hunan

Sources: Chen 1984 ("Dongtou"), Li, Ch'en, and Ch'en 1959 ("Dongtouzhai").

C. West Hmongic ("Hmong" or "Bunu"): Sichuan-Guizhou-Yunnan or Chuanqiandian fangyan

DIALECT	Sub-fangyan	Village	Commune	District	Province
WHITE HMONG	S-G-Y	—	—	—	Petchabun Pitsanuloke (Thailand)

Sources: Heimbach 1979 ("White Hmong"), Mottin 1978 ("Hmong Blanc"), Purnell 1970 (MPT: "Petchabun").

	S-G-Y	—	—	—	Sam Neua, Xieng Khouang, Louang Prabang (Laos)

Sources: Bertrais-Charrier 1964 ("Hmong Blanc"), author's fieldnotes.

GREEN HMONG	S-G-Y	Baan Khun	—	—	Nan Sathaan; Kang Ho (Thailand)

Sources: Lyman 1974 ("Mong Njua").

DIALECT	Sub-fangyan	Village	Commune	District	Province
	S-G-Y	—	—	—	Tak (Thailand)
Sources:	Purnell 1970 (MTT: "Tak").				
	S-G-Y	Pha Hok	—	—	Sayaboury (Laos)
Sources:	Lemoine 1972 ("Hmong Vert").				
	S-G-Y	—	—	—	(Laos)
Sources:	Xiong, et al. 1983 ("Mong").				
MOSHICUN	S-G-Y	Moshicun	—	Eshan	Yunnan
Sources:	Gao 1982 ("Qing Miao").				
XUYONG	S-G-Y	Majiatun	—	Xuyong	Sichuan
Sources:	Ruey and Kuan 1962 ("Magpie Miao"), Purnell 1970 (MSY: "Su-yung"), Ruey 1958 ("Magpie Miao").				
XIANJIN	S-G-Y	Dananshan	Xianjin	Bijie (also called Huajie)	Guizhou
Sources:	Wang 1979 #3 ("Xianjin"), Wang 1985 ("Xianjin"), Hmongb-Shuad dictionary 1958 ("Hmongb"), Purnell 1970 (MHC:"Hua-chieh"), Chen and Li 1981 ("Dananshan"), Chang 1972, 1976 ("Hsien-chin"), Ying 1962 ("Dananshan"), INL 1962 ("Dananshan"), Li, Ch'en, and Ch'en 1959 ("Xianjin").				

DIALECT	Sub-fangyan	Village	Commune	District	Province
SHIMEN	NE Yunnan	Shimenkan	Jiahe	Weining	Guizhou

Sources: Wang 1979 #4 ("Shimen"), Purnell 1970 (MWN: "Wei-ning"), Wang and Wang (1984)[4], 1983, 1982 ("Weining"), Wang 1957 ("Weining"), Ying 1962 ("Shimenkan"), INL 1962 ("Shimenkan"), Li, Ch'en, and Ch'en 1959 ("Shimenkan").

QINGYAN	Guiyang	Baituo	Qingyan	Guiyang City	Guizhou

Sources: Wang 1979 #5 ("Qingyan"), Ying 1962 ("Baituo").

GAOPO	Huishui	Jiading	Jiading	Gaopo *qu* Guiyang City	Guizhou

Sources: Wang 1979 #6 ("Gaopo"), Purnell 1970 (MKC: "Kwei-chu"), Chang 1947, 1953, 1972, 1976 ("Kao-p'o"), Ying 1962 ("Jiading"), INL 1962 ("Jiading").

BAIJIN	Huishui	Baijin	—	Huishui	Guizhou

Sources: Li, Ch'en, and Ch'en 1959 ("Baijin")

ZONGDI	Mashan	Jiaotuozhai	Zongdi	Ziyun	Guizhou

Sources: Wang 1979 #7 ("Zongdi"), Ying 1962 ("Jiaoyi"), INL 1962 ("Jiaoyi"), Li, Ch'en, and Ch'en 1959 ("Zongdi").

---

[4] A translation of this work was unavailable at the time of this study.

DIALECT	Sub-fangyan	Village	Commune	District	Province
FUYUAN	Luobo River	Yejipo	Fuyuan	Fuquan	Guizhou
Sources:	Wang 1979 #8 ("Fuyuan"), Chen and Li 1981 ("Yejipo"), Ying 1962 ("Yejipo"), INL 1962 ("Yejipo").				
SHUIWEI	Luobo River	Shuiwei	—	Longli	Guizhou
Sources:	Purnell 1970 (MLL: "Lung-li"), Li, Ch'en, and Ch'en 1959 ("Shuiwei").				
FENGXIANG	Eastern	Fengxiang	—	Huangping	Guizhou
Sources:	Wang 1979 #9 ("Fengxiang"), Ying 1962 ("Fengxiang").				
GEZHENG	?	Gezhengzhai	—	Changshun (formerly Guangshun)	Guizhou
Sources:	Purnell 1970 (MKS: "Kwang-shun"), Chang 1958 ("Yi Miao"), Chang 1947, 1953, 1972, 1976 ("Ke-cheng").				
YAOLU	?	Yaolu	—	Libo	Guizhou
Sources:	Chang 1947, 1953, 1972, 1976 ("Yao-lu")				
MEIZHU	Tung-Nu	Meizhu	—	Du'an	Guangxi
Sources:	Mao, Meng, and Zheng 1982 ("Bunu"), Wang 1986a ("Meizhu"), Chen and Li 1988("Meizhu"), Moskalev 1978 ("Du'an Yao").				

DIALECT	Sub-fangyan	Village	Commune	District	Province
LONGMO	Tung Nu	Longmo	—	Du'an	Guangxi

Sources: Meng 1983 ("Longmo").

D. Pa Hng

WENJIE	—	Wenjie	—	Sanjiang	Guangxi

Sources: Mao, Meng, and Zheng 1982 ("Wenjie"), Wang 1986a ("Wenjie").

XISHANJIE	—	Xishanjie (near Yongcong)	—	—	Guizhou

Sources: Chang 1947, 1953 ('Tahua Yao'), 1972, 1976 ('Hsi-shan-chieh').

E. Na-e

BAO LAC	—	(near Bao Lac village)	—	—	(Vietnam)

Sources: Bonifacy 1905 ('Pa-teng' or 'Na-ê').

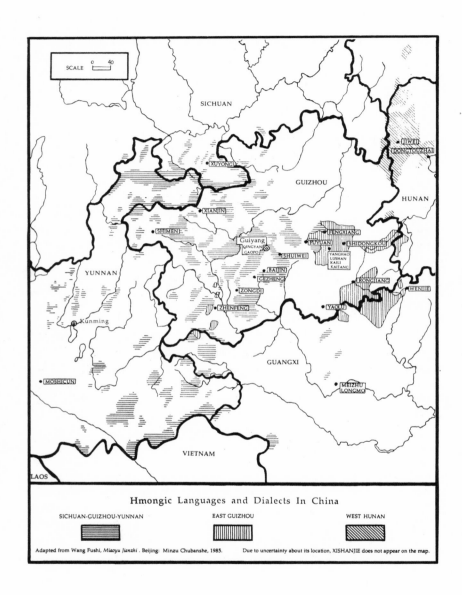

Hmongic Languages and Dialects In China

SICHUAN-GUIZHOU-YUNNAN   EAST GUIZHOU   WEST HUNAN

Adapted from Wang Fushi, *Miaoyu Jianzhi* . Beijing: Minzu Chubanshe, 1985.   Due to uncertainty about its location, XISHANJIE does not appear on the map.

254

REFERENCES

Serial Abbreviations

BEFEO   *Bulletin de l'Ecole Française d'Extrême-Orient*
BIHP   *Bulletin of the Institute of History and Philology*
BSOAS   *Bulletin of the School of Oriental and African Studies*
CAAAL   *Computational Analyses of Asian and African Languages*
JAOS   *Journal of the American Oriental Society*
LTBA   *Linguistics of the Tibeto-Burman Area*
MZYW   *Minzu Yuwen* [Languages of the Nationalities]
YYYJ   *Yuyan Yanjiu* [Languages of China]
ZGYW   *ZhongguoYuwen* [Languages of China]
ZYMZ   *Zhongyang Minzu Xueyan Xuebao*
           [Central Nationalities Institute Research Reports]

Conference Abbreviations

ICSTLL   International Conference of Sino-Tibetan Languages and Linguistics
SEASSI   Southeast Asian Studies Summer Institute

Ballard, W. L.
1985   "The Linguistic History of South China: Miao-Yao and Southern Dialects." In *Linguistics of the Sino-Tibetan Area: The State of the Art,* edited by Graham Thurgood, James A. Matisoff, and David Bradley, 58-84. Pacific Linguistics Series C, no. 87. Canberra: The Australian National University.

Barney, G. Linwood
1967   "The Meo of Xieng Khouang Province, Laos." In *Southeast Asian Tribes, Minorities, and Nations,* vol. 1, edited by Peter Kunstadter, 271-294. Princeton: Princeton University Press.

Benedict, Paul K.
1987   "Early MY/ST Loan Relationships." *LTBA* 10:2, 12-21.

1986   "Miao-Yao Enigma: The Na-e Language." *LTBA* 9:1, 89-90.

1975 ·   *Austro-Thai Language and Culture with a Glossary of Roots.* HRAF Press.

Bertrais-Charrier, Yves, R. P.
1964   *Dictionnaire Hmong (Mèo Blanc)-Français.* Vientiane: Mission Catholique.

Bolinger, Dwight
1950   "Rime Assonance and Morphemic Analysis," *Word* 6, 117-136.

Bonifacy, [Auguste Louis]
1905   "Etude sur les langues parlées par les populations de la haute Rivière Claire." *BEFEO* 5, 306-327.

Cao Cuiyun (Ts'ao Ts'ui-yün)
1961   "A Preliminary Study of Descriptive Words in the Miao Language of Eastern Kweichow." *Miao and Yao Linguistic Studies: Selected Articles in Chinese, Translated by Chang Yü-hung and Chu Kwo-ray* (Linguistic Series V, Data Paper no. 88, Southeast Asia Program Cornell University), edited by Herbert C. Purnell, Jr., 187-210. Ithaca: Cornell Southeast Asia Program, 1972. (Originally published in ZGYW 103, 36-42 [in Chinese].)

1981   "*Miaoyu Qiangdong fangyan de xici* ti^{13}" [*ti^{13}*, the copula of the Eastern Guizhou fangyan of Miao]. *MZYW* no. 3, 54-56. (Unpublished translation by Jiang Zixin.)

Catford, J. C.
1977   *Fundamental Problems in Phonetics.* Bloomington: Indiana University Press.

Chang Chou
1985   "*Hmoob txawj hloov raws caij raws nyoog*" [The Hmong are able to change according to the times]. *Haiv Hmoob* 1:1, 13-15.

Chang Kun

1947   "*Miao-Yao yu shengdiao wenti*" [On the tone system of the Miao-Yao languages]. *BIHP* 16, 93-110.

1953   "On the Tone System of the Miao-Yao Languages." *Language* 29, 374-378.

1958   "The Phonemic System of the Yi Miao Dialect." *BIHP* 29, 11-19.

1966   "A Comparative Study of the Yao Tone System." Language 42, 303-310.

1972   "The Reconstruction of Proto-Miao-Yao Tones." *BIHP* 44, 541-628.

1976   "Proto-Miao Initials." *BIHP* 47, 155-218.

Chen Qiguang

1984   "*Gu Miao-Yao yu bi guan bise yin shengmu zai xiandai fangyan zhong fanying xingshi de leixing*" [The reflected patterns of modern dialects of the pre-nasalized stop initials of Proto-Miao-Yao]. *MZYW* no. 5, 11-22. (Unpublished translation by Jiang Zixin.)

Chen Qiguang and Li Yongsui

1981   "*Hanyu Miao-Yaoyu tongyuan lizheng*" [Some examples of the genetic affinity between Han and Miao-Yao]. *MZYW* no. 2: 13-26. (Unpublished translation by Jiang Zixin.)

Clark, Marybeth

1979   "Coverbs: Evidence for the Derivation of Prepositions from Verbs—New Evidence from Hmong." In *University of Hawaii Working Papers in Linguistics* 11:2, 1-12.

Court, Christopher

1986   "Some Observations on Classifiers in Iu Mien (Yao)." Paper presented at the International Symposium on the Minority Nationalities of China, Santa Barbara, 27-29 January.

Diffloth, Gérard

1972   "Notes on Expressive Meaning." In *Papers from the 8th Regional Meeting*, 440-447. Chicago: Chicago Linguistic Society.

257

1976   "Expressives in Semai." *Austroasiatic Studies* (Oceanic Linguistics Special Publication no. 13), 249-64. Honolulu: University of Hawaii Press.

1979   "Expressive Phonology and Prosaic Phonology." In *Studies in Tai and Mon-Khmer Phonetics and Phonology, in Honor of Eugenie J. A. Henderson*, edited by Theraphan L. Thongkum, V. Panupong, P. Kullavanijaya, and M. R. K. Tingsabadh, 49-59. Bangkok: Chulalongkorn University Press.

Downer, Gordon B.
1967   "Tone-Change and Tone-Shift in White Miao." *BSOAS* 30, 589-599.

1973   "Strata of Chinese Loanwords in the Mien Dialect of Yao." *Asia Major* 18, 1-33.

1982   "Problems in the Reconstruction of Proto-Miao-Yao." Paper presented at the 15th ICSTLL, Beijing, 17-19 August.

Gao Hua-nian
1982   "The Phonology of Qing-miao." *Zhongshan Daxue Xuebao* [Sun Yat-sen University Journal] no. 4, 94-107.

Haudricourt, André G.
1954   "Introduction à la phonologie historique des langues miao-yao." *BEFEO* 44, 555-574. (Reprinted in André G. Haudricourt, *Problèmes de Phonologie Diachronique*, 183-208. Paris: Société pour l'Étude des Langues Africaines, Langues et Civilisations à Tradition Orale, 1972.)

1961   "Bipartition et tripartition des systèmes de tons dans quelques langues d'Extrême-Orient." *Bulletin de la Société de Linguistique de Paris* 56, 163-180. (Reprinted in [1] André G. Haudricourt, *Problèmes de Phonologie Diachronique*, 283-302. Paris: Société pour l'Étude des Langues Africaines, Langues et Civilizations à Tradition Orale 1, 1972; and [2] in *Tai Phonetics and Phonology*, edited by Jimmy G. Harris and Richard B. Noss, 58-86. Translated and developed by Christopher Court and reviewed by the author. Bangkok: Central Institute of English Language, 1972).

Heimbach, Ernest E.
1979   *White Hmong-English Dictionary.*   Revised edition.
(Linguistic Series IV, Data Paper no. 75, Southeast Asia
Program, Cornell University).   Ithaca: Southeast Asia
Program.

Henderson, Eugénie J. A.
1965a   "The Topography of Certain Phonetic and Morphological
Characteristics of South East Asian Languages." *Lingua* 15,
400-434.

1965b   *Tiddim   Chin/A   Descriptive   Analysis   of   Two   Texts.*
London: Oxford University Press.

1967   "Grammar and Tone in South East Asian Languages."
*Wissenschaftliche Zeitschrift der Karl-Marx-Universität
Leipzig* 16, 171-178.

*Hmongb-Shuad Jianming Cidian (Chugao):   Chuanqiandian
Fangyan* [Hmong-Chinese pocket dictionary: Sichuan-Guizhou
Yunnan fanygan]
1958   Guizhou: Guizhou Minzu Chubanshe [Guizhou Nationalities Press].

Hmub-Diel Jianming Cidian (Chugao):   Qiandong Fangyan [Mhu-
Chinese pocket dictionary: Eastern Guizhou fangyan]
1958   Guizhou: Guizhou Minzu Chubanshe [Guizhou Nationalities Press].

Huffman, Marie K.
1985   "Measures of Phonation Type in Hmong." *University of
California Working Papers in Phonetics* 61, 1-25.

Institute of Nationality Languages.
1962   "A Brief Description of the Miao Language." In *Miao and
Yao Linguistic Studies: Selected Articles in Chinese,
Translated by Chang Yü-hung and Chu Kwo-ray* (Linguistic
Series V, Data Paper no. 88, Southeast Asia Program
Cornell University), edited by Herbert C. Purnell, Jr., 1-25.
Ithaca: Cornell Southeast Asia Program, 1972. (Originally
published in ZGYW 111, 28-37 [in Chinese].)

Jarkey, Nerida.
1985a   "Consonant Phonemes of White Hmong" (unpublished
manuscript.)

1985b "Vowel Phonemes of White Hmong" (unpublished manuscript.)

1987 "An Investigation of Two Alveolar Stop Consonants in White Hmong." *LTBA* 10:2, 57-70.

Johns, Brenda and David Strecker.
1982 "Aesthetic Language in White Hmong." In *The Hmong in the West, Observations and Reports,* edited by Bruce T. Downing and Douglas P. Olney, 160-169. Minneapolis: Center for Urban and Regional Affairs.

Karlgren, Bernhard
1957 *Grammata Serica Recensa.* Bulletin no. 29. Stockholm: The Museum of Far Eastern Antiquities.

Kwan, Julia Chin
1966 "Phonology of a Black Miao Dialect." M.A. thesis, University of Washington.

Lemoine, Jacques
1972 *Un village Hmong vert du haut Laos.* Paris: Centre National de la Recherche Scientifique.

Li Rulong
1984 *"Min fangyan he Miao, Zhuang, Dai, Zang zhu yuyan de dongci te shi chongdie"* [The special reduplication of verbs in the Min fangyan and the Miao, Zhuang, Dai, and Tibetan languages]. *MZYW* no. 1, 17-25. (Unpublished translation of section on Miao by Jiang Zixin.)

Li Yung-sui, Ch'en K'o-chung and Ch'en Ch'i-kuang
1959 "Some Problems Concerning Initials and Tones in the Miao Language." In *Miao and Yao Linguistic Studies: Selected Articles in Chinese, Translated by Chang Yü-hung and Chu Kwo-ray* (Linguistic Series V, Data Paper no. 88, Southeast Asia Program Cornell University), edited by Herbert C. Purnell, Jr., 55-81. Ithaca: Cornell Southeast Asia Program, 1972. (Originally published in *YYYJ* 4, 65-80 [in Chinese].)

Lu Yichang
1985 *"Yaozu Mianyu Biaomin fangyan de gouci bian diao yu gouxing bian diao"* [The Tonal Change in Word-Formation

and the Tonal Change in Morphology in Biaomin Dialect of Mien Language] *MZYW* 6.

Lyman, Thomas Amis
1974   *Dictionary of Mong Njua, A Miao (Meo) Language of Southeast Asia.* The Hague: Mouton.

Ma Hsueh-liang and T'ai Ch'ang-hou
1956   "A Preliminary Comparison of the Phonology of the Miao Dialects in Southeastern Kweichow." In *Miao and Yao Linguistic Studies: Selected Articles in Chinese, Translated by Chang Yü-hung and Chu Kwo-ray* (Linguistic Series V, Data Paper no. 88, South Asia Program Cornell University), edited by Herbert C. Purnell, Jr., 27-54. Ithaca: Cornell Southeast Asia Program, 1972. (Originally published in *YYYJ* 1, 265-82 [in Chinese].)

Mao Zongwu, Meng Chaoji, and Zheng Zongze
1982   *Yaoyu yuyan jianzhi* [A sketch of the languages of the Yao people]. Beijing: *Minzu Chubanshe* [Nationalities Press]. (Unpublished translation of section on Bunu by Jiang Zixin.)

Matisoff, James A.
1986   "Tone, Intonation, and Sound Symbolism in Lahu." Paper presented at a Conference on Sound Symbolism, Berkeley, January 16-18.

Meng Chaoji
1983   "*Yaozu Bunuyu* 1' *zhi* 4' *diao de xingcheng he fazhan*" [The origin and development of tones 1'-4' in the Bunu language of the Yao people]. *MZYW* no. 2, 56-59. (Unpublished translation by Jiang Zixin.)

Moskalev, A. A.
1978   *Jazyk duan'skix jao (jazyk nu)* [The Yao language of Du'an (the Nu language)]. Moscow: "Nauka" Press.

Mottin, Jean
1978   *Eléments de grammaire Hmong Blanc.* Bangkok: Don Bosco Press.

Noss, Richard
1964   *Thai Reference Grammar.* Washington: Foreign Service Institute.

Olney, Douglas
1986   "The Hmong Resettlement Study: Population Trends." In
        The Hmong in Transition, edited by Glenn L. Hendricks,
        Bruce T. Downing, and Amos S. Deinard, 179-184. New
        York: Center for Migration Studies.

P'an Yuan-en and Ts'ao Ts'ui-yun
1958   "Four-Syllable Coordinative Constructions in the Miao
        Language of Eastern Kweichow."   In *Miao and Yao
        Linguistic Studies: Selected Articles in Chinese, Translated
        by Chang Yü-hung and Chu Kwo-ray* (Linguistic Series V,
        Data Paper no. 88, Southeast Asia Program Cornell
        University), edited by Herbert C. Purnell, Jr., 55-81.
        Ithaca: Cornell Southeast Asia Program, 1972. (Originally
        published in *Shao Shu Minzu Yuwen Lunji* 1: 91-109 [in
        Chinese].)

Pederson, Eric
1985   "Intensive and Expressive Language in White Hmong
        (*Hmoob dawb*)."   M.A. thesis, University of California—
        Berkeley.

Pike, Kenneth L.
1948   *Tone Languages*. Ann Arbor: University of Michigan Press.

Purnell, Herbert C., Jr.
1970   "Toward a Reconstruction of Proto-Miao-Yao."   Ph.D.
        dissertation, Cornell University.

1972   (editor) *Miao and Yao Linguistic Studies: Selected Articles
        in Chinese, Translated by Chang Yü-hung and Chu Kwo-
        ray* (Linguistic Series V, Data Paper no. 88, Southeast Asia
        Program Cornell University). Ithaca: Cornell Southeast
        Asia Program.

Ratliff, Martha
1986   "An Analysis of Some Tonally Differentiated Doublets in
        White Hmong (Miao)." *LTBA* 9:2, 1-35.

1986   "Two-Word Expressives in White Hmong." In *The Hmong
        in Transition*, edited by Glenn L. Hendricks, Bruce T.
        Downing, and Amos S. Deinard, 219-236. New York: Center
        for Migration Studies.

1988   "Archaisms in Hmong Traditional Literature."   Paper presented at the SEASSI Conference, University of Hawaii at Manoa, Honolulu.

1989   "On [Spread Glottis]."   Paper presented at the Annual Meeting of the Michigan Linguistics Society, October 13, Eastern Michigan University.

1990   "The Influence of Geographic Change on Grammar: The Case of Hmong Spatial Deictics." Paper presented at the 23rd ICSTLL, Arlington, Texas.

1991   *"Cov*, the Underspecified Noun and Syntactic Flexibility in Hmong." Paper presented at the 22nd ICSTLL, Honolulu. Forthcoming in *JAOS* 111:4 (October-December 1991).

1991   "The Development of Nominal/Non-nominal Class Marking by Tone in Shimen Hmong." In *Proceedings of the 17th Annual Meeting of the Berkeley Linguistics Society.* Berkeley: Berkeley Linguistics Society.

Forthcoming   "Does Knowledge of the Southeast Asian Type Produce Blind Spots? Near-addressee Demonstratives in Hmongic." In *Southeast Asia as a Linguistic Area*, Special Publications in Linguistics no. 2, edited by Eric Schiller. Chicago: University of Chicago.

Rhodes, Richard A. and John M. Lawler
1981   "Athematic Metaphors," *CLS* 17, 318-342.

Ruey Yih-fu
1958   "Terminological Structure of the Miao Kinship System." *BIHP* 29, 613-39.

Ruey Yih-fu and Kuan Tung-kuei
1962   *Chuannan Yaqiao Miao de hun sang lisu* [Marriage and mortuary customs of the Magpie Miao, Southern Szechuan, China]. Academia Sinica, the Institute of History and Philology Monographs Series A, no. 23. Taipei: Academia Sinica. (Unpublished translation of introduction to glossary by Jiang Zixin.)

Schein, Louisa
1986   "The Miao in Contemporary China: A Preliminary Overview." In *The Hmong in Transition,* edited by Glenn L.

263

Hendricks, Bruce T. Downing, and Amos S. Deinard, 73-85. New York: Center for Migration Studies.

Smalley, William A.
1976   "The Problems of Consonants and Tone: Hmong (Meo, Miao)." In *Phonemes and Orthography: Language Planning in Ten Minority Languages of Thailand* (Pacific Linguistics Series C, no. 43), edited by William A. Smalley, 85-123. Canberra: Australian National University.

Solnit, David B.
1985   "Introduction to the Biao Min Yao Language." *Cahiers de Linguistique Asie Orientale* 14:2, 175-91.

Sprigg, R. K.
1975   "The Inefficiency of 'Tone-change' in Sino-Tibetan Descriptive Linguistics." *LTBA* 2:2, 173-81.

Srinuan Duanghom
1976   *Mpi-Thai-English Dictionary.* Bangkok: Indigenous Languages of Thailand Research Project.

Strecker, David
1987   "Some Comments on Benedict's 'Miao-Yao Enigma: The Na-e Language'" and "Some Comments on Benedict's 'Miao-Yao Enigma': Addendum." *LTBA* 10:2, 22-53.

Thurgood, Graham
1981   *Notes on the Origins of the Burmese Creaky Tone.* Institute for the Study of Languages and Cultures of Asia and Africa.

Ts'ao Ts'ui-yün, see Cao Cuiyun.

Vwj Tsawb, Vaj P., Yaj S., T. Vwj, K. Yaj, N. Muas, Z. Xyooj, and Xyooj P. V.
1983   *Phau Qhia Nyeem Ntawv Hmoob Dawb* [White Hmong literacy primer]. Washington D.C.: Center for Applied Linguistics.

Wang Fushi
1957   "The Classifier in the Wei Ning Dialect of the Miao Language in Kweichow." In *Miao and Yao Linguistic Studies: Selected Articles in Chinese, Translated by Chang Yü-hung and Chu Kwo-ray* (Linguistic Series V, Data Paper no. 88, Southeast Asia Program Cornell University), edited

by Herbert C. Purnell, Jr., 111-185. Ithaca: Cornell Southeast Asia Program, 1972. (Originally published in *YYYJ* 2, 75-121 [in Chinese].)

1979   *Miaoyu fangyan sheng yun mu bijiao* [The comparison of initials and finals of Miao fangyan]. Monograph presented at the 12th ICSTLL, Paris, October. (Unpublished translation by Jiang Zixin.)

1983   *"Miaoyu fangyan huafen wenti"* [On the fangyan divisions of the Miao language]. *MZYW* no. 5, 1-22.

1985   (editor) *Miaoyu jianzhi* [A sketch of the Miao language]. Beijing: *Minzu Chubanshe* [Nationalities Press].

1986a   Personal letter to David Strecker, January 10.

1986b   "A Preliminary Investigation of the Genetic Affiliation of the Miao-Yao Languages." Translated by Mark Hansell. Paper presented at the International Symposium on the Minority Nationalities of China, Santa Barbara, January 27-29. (Published in *MZYW* no. 1, 1-18, 79.)

1988   "Miaoyu guyin gouni wenti" [Problems in reconstructing the ancient sounds of proto-Miao]. MZYW no. 2, 1-8.

Wang Fushi and Wang Deguang
1982   *"Guizhou Weining Miaoyu de fangweici"* [The localizers of Miao in Weining, Guizhou Province]. *MZYW* no. 4, 20-34. [Unpublished translation by Jiang Zixin.]

1983   *"Guizhou Weining Miaoyu de Zhuangci"* [Manner words in the Miao dialect of Weining County, Guizhou Province]. *YYYJ* no. 2, 192-211. [Unpublished translation by Jiang Zixin.]

1984   *"Guizhou Weining Miaoyu de sheng diao"* [The Tones of the Miao spoken in Weining, Guizhou Province]. Beijing: Institute of Nationalities (mimeographed).

Wescott, Roger
1973   "Tonal Icons in Bini." *Studies in African Linguistics* 4.

Xiang Rizheng
1983   *"Xiangxi Miaoyu de si zi bing lie jiegou"* [The four-syllable coordinative constructions in the Western Hunan fangyan of Miao]. *MZYW* no. 3, 26-32. (Unpublished translation by Jiang Zixin.)

Xiong Lang, Xiong Joua, and Xiong Nao Leng
1983   *English-Mong-English Dictionary.* Milwaukee: By the authors.

Yaj Txooj Tsawb
1987   *"Piav tus txheej txheem kab tshoob kev kos"* [Outline of Marriage Rites]. Excerpt translated and annotated by David Strecker. In *The Hmong World* 1, edited by Brenda Johns and David Strecker, 99-123. New Haven: Yale Southeast Asia Studies.

Yang Dao
1980   *Dictionnaire Français-Hmong Blanc.* Paris: Comité National d'Entraide et Jacques Lemoine.

Ying Lin
1962   "Chinese Loanwords in Miao." In *Miao and Yao Linguistic Studies: Selected Articles in Chinese, Translated by Chang Yü-hung and Chu Kwo-ray* (Linguistic Series V, Data Paper no. 88, Southeast Asia Program Cornell University), edited by Herbert C. Purnell, Jr., 55-81. Ithaca: Cornell Southeast Asia Program, 1972. (Originally published in *ZGYW* 115, 218-229 [in Chinese].)

INDEX
(of Dialects, Languages, and Language Groupings, excluding White Hmong)

White Miao 7, 21, 36, 62, 63, 68
XIANJIN 16, 21, 33, 41, 63, 64, 95, 106, 107, 108, 109, 111, 123, 133, 134, 135
XISHANJIE 4, 16
XUYONG 33, 63, 101, 103, 106, 107, 108, 109, 111, 123, 128, 129, 130, 131, 133, 134, 135
YANGHAO 16, 21, 41, 100, 101, 103, 104, 108, 134, 135
Yao 16
YAOLU 16
ZHENFENG 100
ZONGDI 4, 17, 21, 108, 134, 135